C000128573

797,885 Books

are available to read at

www.ForgottenBooks.com

Forgotten Books' App
Available for mobile, tablet & eReader

ISBN 978-1-330-14745-0
PIBN 10037552

This book is a reproduction of an important historical work. Forgotten Books uses
state-of-the-art technology to digitally reconstruct the work, preserving the original format
whilst repairing imperfections present in the aged copy. In rare cases, an imperfection in
the original, such as a blemish or missing page, may be replicated in our edition. We do,
however, repair the vast majority of imperfections successfully; any imperfections that
remain are intentionally left to preserve the state of such historical works.

Forgotten Books is a registered trademark of FB &c Ltd.
Copyright © 2015 FB &c Ltd.
FB &c Ltd, Dalton House, 60 Windsor Avenue, London, SW 19 2RR.
Company number 08720141. Registered in England and Wales.

For support please visit www.forgottenbooks.com

1 MONTH OF
FREE
READING

at
www.ForgottenBooks.com

By purchasing this book you are eligible for one month membership to ForgottenBooks.com, giving you unlimited access to our entire collection of over 700,000 titles via our web site and mobile apps.

To claim your free month visit:
www.forgottenbooks.com/free37552

* Offer is valid for 45 days from date of purchase. Terms and conditions apply.

English
Français
Deutsche
Italiano
Español
Português

www.forgottenbooks.com

Mythology Photography **Fiction**
Fishing Christianity **Art** Cooking
Essays Buddhism Freemasonry
Medicine **Biology** Music **Ancient
Egypt** Evolution Carpentry Physics
Dance Geology **Mathematics** Fitness
Shakespeare **Folklore** Yoga Marketing
Confidence Immortality Biographies
Poetry **Psychology** Witchcraft
Electronics Chemistry History **Law**
Accounting **Philosophy** Anthropology
Alchemy Drama Quantum Mechanics
Atheism Sexual Health **Ancient History**
Entrepreneurship Languages Sport
Paleontology Needlework Islam
Metaphysics Investment Archaeology
Parenting Statistics Criminology
Motivational

ARISTOTLE

NICOMACHEAN ETHICS

BOOK SIX

CAMBRIDGE UNIVERSITY PRESS WAREHOUSE,
C. F. CLAY, MANAGER.
London: FETTER LANE, E.C.
Edinburgh: 100, PRINCES STREET.

Berlin: A. ASHER AND CO.
Leipzig: F. A. BROCKHAUS.
New York: G. P. PUTNAM'S SONS.
Bombay and Calcutta: MACMILLAN AND CO., Ltd.

[*All Rights reserved*]

ARISTOTLE
NICOMACHEAN ETHICS

BOOK SIX

WITH ESSAYS, NOTES, AND TRANSLATION

BY

L. H. G. GREENWOOD, M.A.

FELLOW OF KING'S COLLEGE, CAMBRIDGE

CAMBRIDGE :
at the University Press
1909

FRANCISCO AUGUSTO HARE

GRAECARUM LITTERARUM EXIMIO DOCTORI
OLIM DISCIPULUS
INGRATUS NULLO TEMPORE FUTURUS
HAS QUALESCUMQUE PRIMITIAS
D. D. D. AUCTOR

PREFACE

IN spite of the manifest importance of the Sixth Book of
the Nicomachean Ethics, there is probably no book
among the whole ten which has received so little attention
from Aristotelian students. No separate edition of it has
ever been undertaken, and some half-dozen dissertations by
German scholars, together with the miscellaneous notes supplied by editors of the Ethics as a whole, leave much room
for further criticism and explanation. The present volume,
which is a slightly altered and enlarged form of a dissertation
submitted in 1906 to the electors to fellowships at King's
College, Cambridge, is an attempt to supply this deficiency
to some extent. It is introduced by an examination of the
evidence for and against Aristotle's authorship of the Sixth
Book, on the strength of which Aristotle is thereafter referred
to as the author. This is followed by a full discussion of the
doctrine of the Sixth Book, and its relation to the whole treatise.
The Greek text is not identical with any already published, but
is closer to Bywater's than to Susemihl's. It does not rest on
any fresh examination of the manuscripts : and it contains only
one reading (1139 b 28) that lacks the support of all modern
editors of standing. It seemed worth while to append to the
text, not such a critical apparatus as Bekker, Susemihl and
Bywater have already provided, upon which any important

improvement seemed impossible, but rather an account of the readings, in all passages where the reading is really doubtful, of the best manuscripts and of the chief modern editors. The English translation that accompanies the text aims rather at accuracy than at elegance. The two essays, on Dialectic Method and on Formal Accuracy, have a somewhat wider range of application than the Sixth Book itself: at the same time their results are, if sound, of considerable value towards the understanding of the Sixth Book, from which, moreover, the illustrations are all drawn. Finally, a considerable number of Miscellaneous Notes, which are chiefly concerned with interpretation, aim at leaving no difficulty of detail unhandled or unsolved. ἐπιεικὲς τὸ ἔχειν περὶ ἔνια συγγνώμην : and this book contains many obvious faults that can put forward no better claim to be forgiven.

L. H. G. G.

CHRISTCHURCH, NEW ZEALAND,
October, 1908

CONTENTS

INTRODUCTION

SECTION I.

ON THE AUTHORSHIP OF THE SIXTH BOOK.

ANY attempt to throw fresh light on the meaning of the sixth book of the *Nicomachean Ethics* at once brings the inquirer face to face with the problem of the book's authorship. Such problems are not often easy of solution, and this one is amongst the hardest of its class. There is indeed one circumstance that lessens the labour of the search in one direction, though it is at the cost of greatly increased difficulty in reaching a final answer to the whole question. It is not necessary, in order to discover whether this book is really Eudemian or Nicomachean, to know the relative frequency with which the words or phrases or small turns of thought that are found in it are found also in the undoubtedly Eudemian and the undoubtedly Nicomachean books respectively. Statistics on this head, however accurate they might be, would be as likely to mislead as to inform: and whereas their evidence is particularly untrustworthy unless it is presented in great quantity and is of well-marked uniformity, it is undeniable that in the case of the Ethics the evidence is and can be neither. The pupils of Aristotle so closely copied their master's vocabulary, style, and even mannerisms, that they have here left the critic little or no ground to go upon. Not that the critics have not turned this way. Fischer and Fritzsche make a detailed comparison of the wording and style of the disputed books with those of the undoubtedly Eudemian books, on the strength of which alone, were other

G.   T

evidence wanting, they would pronounce the disputed books
Eudemian. If their comparisons are carefully examined it
will be agreed, I think, that they are less weighty than their
authors suppose, especially as similar comparisons of the
disputed books with the Nicomachean books have not been
made. But such detailed comparisons are hardly worth the
trouble of making. When one writer copies the style of
another as closely as Eudemus has admittedly copied the
style of Aristotle, resemblances in points of detail may be
numerous and close without betraying the actual writer.
English scholars have as a rule been reasonable enough to
take this view. Grant indeed has brought forward among
his proofs of Eudemian authorship the 'peculiarly explicit
mode of introducing literary quotations' which he regards as
common to the Eudemian and the disputed books but as
absent from the Nicomachean : and he relies to some extent
on the uses of certain formulae, such as ὅρος and ἁπλῶς
ἀγαθόν, to prove the same point. But he frankly admits that
he is not justified in attaching a great deal of importance to
this kind of evidence. Munro is distinctly of the same
opinion[1]. Stewart appears to agree with them: Burnet merely
takes the line that the evidence is unsound in itself[2]. The
arguments from the form of any Peripatetic work can never
be as strong as the argument from its substance. Some of
the detailed points that have been adduced will be considered
elsewhere: but I have considered myself to be fairly exempted
from any systematic examination along the lines of Fischer
and Fritzsche.

We are further without the toil, and without the corresponding advantage, of weighing one piece of external testimony against another. There was little discussion of the
point, little at any rate of which any record has been preserved,
in ancient times : and that little was by persons who were ill
qualified to get at the truth. There are no opinions of
antiquity that are, in this matter of authorship, of any appre-
ciable use to us.

---

[1] *Journal of Sacred and Classical Philology*, 1855 (pp. 70—81).
[2] See his edition of the *Ethics*, Introduction p. xiii.

Unhelped by external evidence, unhelped by the internal evidence of style, we are forced to depend on the internal evidence of doctrine alone; and all arguments connected with the doctrine of this book are liable to become involved in an embarrassing circle. Here is a discussion, whose meaning is far from plain at first sight, that has some claim to be considered a part of each of two large treatises allowed to be in the main the work of two different authors. Its meaning can be properly determined only by reference to its context, its context—we have just been forced to admit—only by reference to its meaning. Interpretation, moreover, has to concern itself with everything from the main problems to the smallest details. Finally, all other difficulties are greatly increased by our uncertainty as to the original text, and the extent to which it has suffered losses, interpolations and dislocations due to accident, or design, or both.

In maintaining the Eudemian authorship of this book as well as that of V and VII, scholars have relied on the cumulative effect of a number of different lines of argument rather than on any one line in particular. Each has to be examined in itself before the validity of the main conclusion can fairly be judged: but there is one observation, applying about equally to them all, that is of importance to the present discussion. The fate of the sixth book is not bound up with the fate of the others. Some of the characteristics of VI, it is true, are alleged to belong to the other two books as well and not to the undoubtedly Nicomachean books: and in so far as this can be shown true, whatever special reasons there may be for thinking V or VII to be Eudemian will go some way to show VI to be Eudemian also. But as a matter of fact each book is so independent of the others in subject and treatment, and the objections to considering each as a true part of the Nicomachean work are of such a nature, that whatever can be shown true of any one of them is practically no argument that the same is true of either of the others.

This contention can be justified only by examination of the principal arguments that have actually been submitted to the contrary. Fritzsche, in his edition of the *Eudemian*

Ethics, maintaining that NE VI and VII are Eudemian, tries to prove that VI is Eudemian, not only on independent grounds, but on the ground that VI is by the same author as VII is, and that VII is Eudemian. Whether VII is or is not partly or wholly Eudemian is a question that I do not propose to discuss here, because I see no reason to think that VI is necessarily by the same author as VII, and therefore the question is not of practical importance for determining the authorship of VI. But it will be desirable to examine the reasons Fritzsche gives for believing VI and VII to be by the same author. If they are found inadequate, it will readily be admitted that there is no better reason for believing V and VI to be by the same author : so that my contention will be justified, that the authorship of VI in no way determines or is determined by the authorship of V or VII. For Munro's argument—that it is much harder to suppose that certain parts of the disputed books are Eudemian than to suppose that the whole is Eudemian—does not seem to be recommended by anything beyond the weight of so great a man's personal opinion.

Fritzsche's view that VI and VII are by the same author, whoever that author may be, depends on the following contentions :—

(i)   The matter, method, style and vocabulary of VI and VII are alike (res methodus stilus verba eundem auctorem produnt).

(ii)   The questions discussed in VII follow those discussed in VI in a natural and logical order.

(iii)   Definite references are made in VII to the conclusions reached in VI.

(iv)   Other passages in VII plainly assume passages in VI, though they do not definitely refer to them.

(v)   Words are used in VII only intelligible because used in VI, and these could not have occurred if VI had not been written.

These reasons cannot be held strong enough to prove that VI and VII are by the same author, or even, as I think, to raise any strong presumption in favour of that view. (i) What Fritzsche means by saying that the 'res' of the two books is the same I do not quite know. The subjects of the two books are different: and that differences of doctrine between the two are not found where they might possibly occur does not show much, considering how closely Eudemus agrees with Aristotle as a rule where their respective points of view can be compared with certainty. As for the 'method,' Fritzsche argues with small confidence from the frequency of ἀπορίαι and of backward and forward references, which he admits are nearly as common in Aristotle as in Eudemus, in other books nearly as common as in VI and VII: and the other points, such as great subtlety and agreement of authors quoted and so on, are highly disputable. The same may be said of arguments from style and vocabulary, which, as I have already said, cannot well be useful in discussing the authorship of any Aristotelian work, seeing that the whole school express themselves with wonderful uniformity of manner. (ii) Fritzsche's other four reasons may be met by a single observation. Even supposing the facts to be entirely as alleged, it only follows that a book corresponding fairly closely to VI was written by the author of VII—supposing, that is, that the author of VII did not take over VI as it stands and write VII with reference to it—and not that VI is the actual book. The reasons given by Dr Jackson for supposing that Aristotle, if he did not write V VI VII, wrote their equivalents, as against Grant who supposes that Aristotle never wrote their equivalents or at any rate not until after he wrote VIII IX X, show that either VI or its equivalent was in existence when VII was written: so that the passages of VII that imply the conclusions or usages of VI are quite intelligible, no matter who wrote either of the present books VI and VII.

If then Fritzsche fails to prove that VI is necessarily the work of the author of VII, no amount of certainty that Aristotle did not write VII[1] can prove that he did not write VI. There are however other grounds, it is alleged, for believing

[1] It is enough to observe that Professor Burnet, for instance, does not reject the Aristotelian authorship of VII.

that VI is the work not of Aristotle but of Eudemus: and these it is necessary to examine. They are set forth clearly and completely in Grant's essay on the subject, and may be classified as follows, only so much of them being here taken into account as applies to VI either alone or in common with V and VII :—

(*a*) That the passage *Metaphysics* 981 b 25—27, which some think is in favour of Aristotle's authorship of VI, really tells rather against it in favour of Eudemus.

(*b*) That books VIII IX X ignore matters discussed in VI to which it would have seemed natural to refer.

(*c*) That certain references in VI to what has been said already 'correspond more closely with places in the earlier books of the *Eudemian Ethics* than to similar places in the earlier books of the Nicomachean treatise[1].'

To these reasons may be added a number of small points, made not in the Essay but in the notes to VI, which in one way or another are meant to support Eudemus' authorship. These arguments of Grant's must now be considered in detail: many of the same points appear in Fritzsche's prolegomena and notes in his edition of the *Eudemian Ethics*.

(*a*) Grant admits that *Metaphysics* 981 b 25—27 Εἴρηται μὲν οὖν ἐν τοῖς Ἠθικοῖς τίς διαφορὰ τέχνης καὶ ἐπιστήμης καὶ τῶν ἄλλων τῶν ὁμογενῶν must refer either to NE VI or to a similar lost book: but maintains (1) that it would equally well apply to a similar lost book, (2) that Asclepius' record of the tradition of Eudemus' editorship of the *Metaphysics* gives ground for thinking the passage quoted an Eudemian interpolation. To this it may be replied that (1) leaves the question where it is, merely showing that the passage is no argument for or against either view, while (2) is a mere conjecture which Grant himself, it is plain, regards as ingenious rather than plausible.

(*b*) Grant maintains that VI (like the other disputed books) appears in its natural place if read as part of the

---

[1] See Grant's edition of the *Ethics* i·56.

Eudemian Ethics, and that the later books of the *Eudemian Ethics* are in harmony with it, but that the later books of the *Nicomachean Ethics* (VIII IX X) ignore matters discussed in VI to which it would have seemed natural to refer. Now Dr Jackson has shown (Introduction to V, pp. xxix—xxxi) that VIII to X do not ignore altogether the matter discussed in VI; though he does not suppose VI to be Aristotle's work, but assumes an Aristotelian equivalent of VI to have been written. I shall later give reasons for believing that X ignores VI even less than has hitherto been supposed. But even if Grant were right in maintaining that VIII IX X ignore VI, his case would be little the better off for this unless he could show that *Eudemian Ethics* VII VIII ignore NE VI less than NE VIII IX X ignore NE VI. But this he fails to do. The few places[1] in EE VII VIII where he believes NE V VI VII to be recognised all refer, if they refer to NE V VI VII at all, either to V or to VII, but in no case to VI. I shall try later to show that EE VIII as a matter of fact takes considerably less account of NE VI than NE X does. If it be urged that EE VIII is incomplete, and would no doubt if completed have taken more account of NE VI and its doctrine, one can only reply that there is no external or internal evidence of EE VIII's incompleteness: its shortness is nothing to the point, being the natural consequence of the omission of any discussion of Pleasure or of the connection between Ethics and Politics, but for which NE X would hardly be longer than EE VIII is: while to assume EE VIII incomplete simply because the results of NE VI are ignored in it as it stands is of course to beg the question.

(*c*) Grant next gives certain references in the disputed books to what has been said already, which he contends 'correspond more closely with places in the earlier books of the *Eudemian Ethics* than to similar places in the earlier books of the Nicomachean treatise.' Four of these references are from NE VI, and a fifth is added soon afterwards[2]. How far is Grant's contention justified in reference to them?

---

[1] Grant, i 59.   [2] Grant, i 56, 57.

(1) The opening words of NE VI are compared with
EE 1222 a 6—12 Ἐπεὶ δ' ὑπόκειται ἀρετὴ εἶναι ἡ τοιαύτη
ἕξις ἀφ' ἧς πρακτικοὶ τῶν βελτίστων καὶ καθ' ἣν ἄριστα
διάκεινται περὶ τὸ βέλτιστον, βέλτιστον δὲ καὶ ἄριστον τὸ
κατὰ τὸν ὀρθὸν λόγον, τοῦτο δ' ἐστὶ τὸ μέσον ὑπερβολῆς καὶ
ἐλλείψεως τῆς πρὸς ἡμᾶς κτλ. But whereas in NE VI the
μέσον is defined by ὡς ὁ λόγος ὁ ὀρθὸς λέγει, in EE IV τὸ κατὰ
τὸν ὀρθὸν λόγον is defined by τὸ μέσον: so that the reference
is not so satisfactory as the likeness of wording might at first
make it seem probable. And from such passages in the NE
as 1114 b 26 Κοινῇ μὲν οὖν περὶ τῶν ἀρετῶν εἴρηται ἡμῖν τό τε
γένος τύπῳ, ὅτι μεσότητές εἰσιν καὶ ὅτι ἕξεις, ὑφ' ὧν τε
γίνονται, ὅτι τούτων πρακτικαὶ <καὶ> καθ' αὑτάς, καὶ ὅτι
ἐφ' ἡμῖν καὶ ἑκούσιοι, καὶ οὕτως ὡς ἂν ὁ ὀρθὸς λόγος
προστάξῃ: 1103 b 31 τὸ μὲν οὖν κατὰ τὸν ὀρθὸν λόγον
πράττειν κοινὸν καὶ ὑποκείσθω—ῥηθήσεται δ' ὕστερον[1] περὶ
αὐτοῦ, καὶ τί ἐστιν ὁ ὀρθὸς λόγος, καὶ πῶς ἔχει πρὸς τὰς ἄλλας
ἀρετάς: the well-known definition of moral virtue reached at
1106 b 36 Ἔστιν ἄρα ἡ ἀρετὴ ἕξις προαιρετικὴ ἐν μεσότητι
οὖσα τῇ πρὸς ἡμᾶς ὡρισμένῃ λόγῳ καὶ ᾧ ἂν ὁ φρόνιμος ὁρίσειεν:
1115 b 12 (ὁ ἀνδρεῖος) ὡς δεῖ καὶ ὡς ὁ λόγος ὑπομενεῖ τοῦ
καλοῦ ἕνεκα, and so 1115 b 19, 1117 a 8, etc.—from such
passages the statement at the beginning of NE VI follows
as naturally and easily as from the sum of corresponding
passages in the EE. Of course the wording of the beginning
of NE VI does not even make it probable that the reference
is to one special passage rather than to a whole line of
argument worked out in various places.

(2) NE (VI i 3) 1138 b 35 Τὰς δὴ τῆς ψυχῆς ἀρετὰς
διελόμενοι τὰς μὲν εἶναι τοῦ ἤθους ἔφαμεν τὰς δὲ τῆς διανοίας
is compared with EE 1221 b 27 ἐπειδὴ δύο μέρη τῆς ψυχῆς,
καὶ αἱ ἀρεταὶ κατὰ ταῦτα διήρηνται, καὶ αἱ μὲν τοῦ λόγου
ἔχοντος διανοητικαί, ὧν ἔργον ἀλήθεια, ἢ περὶ τοῦ πῶς ἔχει ἢ
περὶ γενέσεως, αἱ δὲ τοῦ ἀλόγου ἔχοντος δ' ὄρεξιν. But simple
inspection shows the references to be as good or better to

---

[1] This passage has been suspected on doctrinal grounds : but (as Professor
Burnet justly indicates by his reference in his note ad locum) it must stand or
fall with 1144 b 27.

NE 1102 a 26—28...τὸ μὲν ἄλογον αὐτῆς εἶναι τὸ δὲ λόγον ἔχον, and the following explanation of this, together with 1103 a 3 διορίζεται δὲ καὶ ἡ ἀρετὴ κατὰ τὴν διαφορὰν ταύτην· λέγομεν γὰρ αὐτῶν τὰς μὲν διανοητικὰς τὰς δὲ ἠθικάς, κτλ.

(3) NE (VI viii 1) 1141 b 23—24 Ἔστι δὲ καὶ ἡ πολιτικὴ καὶ ἡ φρόνησις ἡ αὐτὴ μὲν ἕξις, τὸ μέντοι εἶναι οὐ ταὐτὸν αὐταῖς is compared with EE 1218 b 12 Τοῦτο δ᾽ ἐστὶ τὸ ὑπὸ τὴν κυρίαν πασῶν. αὕτη δ᾽ ἐστὶ πολιτικὴ καὶ οἰκονομικὴ καὶ φρόνησις. διαφέρουσι γὰρ αὗται αἱ ἕξεις πρὸς τὰς ἄλλας τῷ τοιαῦται εἶναι. πρὸς δ᾽ ἀλλήλας εἴ τι διαφέρουσιν, ὕστερον λεκτέον. It is true the three-fold division πολιτικὴ οἰκονομία φρόνησις occurs earlier in the EE, and does not occur in the NE. But NE VI 1141 b 23 does not really *refer* to it at all— there is nothing to show that the division is not being intro- duced here for the first time in the treatise. No doubt the anticipation in EE 1218 b 15 proves that Eudemus wrote, or intended to write, a book like NE VI (supposing NE VI not to be his): but there is no reason to think that Eudemus would depart from the three-fold division of Practical Wisdom if Aristotle had made it already: and the way in which Eudemus anticipates the division rather points to its having been made and recognised already.

(4) NE (VI xii 10) 1144 a 31—36 οἱ γὰρ συλλογισμοὶ τῶν πρακτῶν ἀρχὴν ἔχοντές εἰσιν, ἐπειδὴ τοιόνδε τὸ τέλος καὶ τὸ ἄριστον...τοῦτο δ᾽ εἰ μὴ τῷ ἀγαθῷ οὐ φαίνεται· διαστρέφει γὰρ ἡ μοχθηρία καὶ διαψεύδεσθαι ποιεῖ περὶ τὰς πρακτικὰς ἀρχάς is compared with EE 1227 b 28—32 ὥσπερ γὰρ ταῖς θεωρητικαῖς αἱ ὑποθέσεις ἀρχαί, οὕτω καὶ ταῖς ποιητικαῖς τὸ τέλος ἀρχὴ καὶ ὑπόθεσις· ''Ἐπειδὴ δεῖ τόδε ὑγιαίνειν, ἀνάγκη τοδὶ ὑπάρξαι, εἰ ἔσται ἐκεῖνο,' ὥσπερ ἐκεῖ, 'Εἰ ἔστι τὸ τρίγωνον δύο ὀρθαί, ἀνάγκη τοδὶ εἶναι.' The doctrine of the Practical Syllogism, it is true, is not found in the undoubtedly Nicomachean books: but the above seems to be the only undoubtedly Eudemian passage in which the doctrine occurs: and against this may be placed the passage that Grant himself quotes from the *Psychology* (admittedly Aristotle's own work) 434 a 16 ἐπεὶ δ᾽ ἡ μὲν καθόλου ὑπόληψις καὶ λόγος,

ἡ δὲ τοῦ καθ' ἕκαστα (ἡ μὲν γὰρ λέγει ὅτι δεῖ τὸν τοιοῦτον τὸ τοιόνδε πράττειν, ἡ δὲ ὅτι τόδε τοίνυν τοιόνδε, κἀγὼ δὲ τοιόσδε), ἤδη αὕτη κινεῖ ἡ δόξα, οὐχ ἡ καθόλου. Even if the *Psychology* is a later work than the NE, which is by no means certain, it does not follow that Aristotle only thought of the doctrine of the Practical Syllogism between the time when he wrote the NE and the time when he wrote the *Psychology*, and therefore that no passage in the Ethics where the Practical Syllogism is spoken of can be by him. Nor does the single passage EE 1227 b 28—32 show Eudemus to have been more familiar with that doctrine than Aristotle was, the disputed books apart. It is the author of the *Motions of Animals* who has elaborated the Practical Syllogism most fully[1], and he it is agreed must have lived later than either Aristotle or Eudemus.

(5) The doctrine of NE VI xiii is said to be anticipated by EE 1234 a 28 ἔστι γάρ, ὥσπερ λεχθήσεται ἐν τοῖς ὕστερον, ἑκάστη πως ἀρετὴ καὶ φύσει καὶ ἄλλως μετὰ φρονήσεως. But the answer to (3) applies here too. Eudemus is looking forward in the passage quoted to an exposition, which he may or may not actually have written, on the lines of NE VI. But this passage does not show Eudemus to be the author of NE VI any more than *Metaphysics* 981 b 25—27 (already quoted) would, taken by itself, show Aristotle to be the author of the same book NE VI.

(6) Grant[2] maintains that the psychology of (VI xii 6) 1144 a 6, Ἔτι τὸ ἔργον ἀποτελεῖται κατὰ τὴν φρόνησιν καὶ τὴν ἠθικὴν ἀρετήν· ἡ μὲν γὰρ ἀρετὴ τὸν σκόπον ποιεῖ ὀρθόν, ἡ δὲ φρόνησις τὰ πρὸς τοῦτον, is different from the psychology of Aristotle but identical with that adopted by Eudemus in the earlier books of his Ethics. It is true that Eudemus, in EE II xi, does adopt the same psychology: but Aristotle, in NE X viii, 1178 a 16 συνέζευκται δὲ καὶ ἡ φρόνησις τῇ τοῦ ἤθους ἀρετῇ καὶ αὕτη τῇ φρονήσει, εἴπερ αἱ μὲν τῆς φρονήσεως ἀρχαὶ κατὰ τὰς ἠθικάς εἰσιν ἀρετάς, τὸ δ' ὀρθὸν τῶν ἠθικῶν

---

[1] 701 a 7 seqq. (quoted in Burnet's second appendix to his edition of the *Ethics*).　　　[2] in his note ad locum.

κατὰ τὴν φρόνησιν, makes just the same distinction, whereas Eudemus takes no account of it at all when he discusses καλοκαγαθία in EE VIII iii. It seems to me, though Grant thinks otherwise, that Aristotle in the passage just quoted has the air of having already discussed and justified the position there taken up, as the word εἴπερ (= 'if what we have said is really true, namely') among other things seems to show. It is no fault on Aristotle's part, but rather to his credit, that he does not introduce the distinction in book III, where since intellectual virtue has not yet been treated such a distinction would be unintelligible. Such an early introduction is far more in accord with the less dialectic and more didactic method that characterises Eudemus as compared with Aristotle.

If the above criticisms of Grant's arguments are sound, it must be admitted that he is hardly justified in his conclusion that there is an especially close connection between NE VI and the undisputedly Eudemian books, in so far at least as that conclusion is founded on the arguments already mentioned. In his notes on NE VI he gives a number of further reasons, with reference to particular points, for regarding Eudemus as the author of that book; which it is hard for the most part to bring under any general head, but whose cumulative effect would be considerable if they were sound. Some space must therefore be devoted here to asking whether they are sound or not : and this will conclude my examination of the arguments in favour of Eudemian authorship, since practically all the arguments on this side that have been adduced are contained in the works of either Fritzsche or Grant or both. I shall then bring forward certain positive arguments on the other side, by which I hope to show that at any rate the sixth book not only is not Eudemian but is Nicomachean.

(a) Grant gives, in his notes to VI, a number of references to the EE that are, however, at least as good to the NE where they are not better. Such are :—(i) On VI i 5 πρότερον μὲν οὖν ἐλέχθη κτλ he refers to EE II iv 1[1], but the reference would be as good to NE 1102 a 27 οἷον τὸ μὲν ἄλογον αὐτῆς

εἶναι τὸ δὲ λόγον ἔχον, κτλ. (ii) On VI i 6 (1139 a 13) οὐδεὶς δὲ βουλεύεται περὶ τῶν μὴ ἐνδεχομένων ἄλλως ἔχειν, he refers to EE II x 9[1], but the reference would be as good to NE 1112 a 21 περὶ δὴ τῶν ἀϊδίων οὐδεὶς βουλεύεται...οὐδὲ περὶ τῶν...ἀεὶ κατὰ ταὐτὰ γινομένων εἴτ' ἐξ ἀνάγκης εἴτε καὶ φύσει, κτλ. (iii) On VI ii 2 (1139 a 22) ἡ ἠθικὴ ἀρετὴ ἕξις προαιρετική, Grant refers to EE II x 28[2], but the reference would be as good to 1106. b 36 Ἔστιν ἄρα ἡ ἀρετὴ ἕξις προαιρετική κτλ. (iv) On VI ii 2 (1139 a 23) ἡ προαίρεσις ὄρεξις βουλευτική, Grant refers to EE II x 14[2], but the reference would be as good to NE 1113 a 10 ἡ προαίρεσις ἂν εἴη βουλευτικὴ ὄρεξις τῶν ἐφ' ἡμῖν.

(*b*) Whenever Grant makes an illustratory reference to NE without being able to refer to EE, the argument is in favour of Aristotle's authorship of VI. This is, however, very often the case, e.g.:—(i) NE III ii 13 (1112 a 5) referred to in the note[3] on VI ii 2 (1139 a 24) τόν τε λόγον ἀληθῆ εἶναι, κτλ: (ii) the first section of the NE referred to in the note[4] on VI ii 4—5 (1139 a 31 seqq.) πράξεως μὲν οὖν, κτλ: (iii) NE III iii 7 (1112 a 31) referred to in the note[5] on VI iv 4 (1140 a 13) ὧν ἡ ἀρχή, κτλ: (iv) NE I x 10 (1100 b 12) referred to in the note[6] on VI v 8 (1140 b 28) σημεῖον δ' ὅτι λήθη, κτλ: (v) NE I vi 12 (1096 b 28) referred to in the note[7] on VI xi 6 (1143 b 14) ὄμμα.

(*c*) Grant often argues that changes in usage or developments in doctrine in VI as compared with the undoubtedly Nicomachean books show that VI is not Nicomachean. But Aristotle was quite capable of making such changes or developments himself within the limits of his own treatise[8]. Thus (*a*) with regard to changes in the usage of words

(1) Grant contends that the new use of the word πολιτική (VI viii 3, see Grant, vol. ii p. 168) must be the work of Eudemus—which is not necessary:

---

[1] Vol. ii p. 150.   [2] Vol. ii p. 151.
[3] Vol. ii p. 151 (see also p. 174, note on δόξης δ').
[4] Vol. ii p. 152.   [5] Vol. ii p. 157.
[6] Vol. ii p. 162.   [7] Vol. ii p. 181.
[8] See my essay on 'Formal Accuracy.'

(2) and that the same applies to the use of τέχνη (VI iv 3, see Grant, vol. ii p. 157, note on οὔτε τοιαύτη)—but τέχνη is certainly used, as I have shown elsewhere, in two quite distinct senses within the limits of VI itself.

(β) with regard to developments in doctrine

(1) Grant supposes the section VI ii 6 (1139 b 5) οὐκ ἔστι δὲ προαιρετόν κτλ an addition to Aristotle's list of the marks of προαίρεσις made without special appropriateness here, because Eudemus was vain enough to be 'glad to introduce the above remarks[1].' But I have elsewhere shown that this passage is thoroughly useful to the argument[2], and is not introduced simply to patch a previous gap at the next recurrence of the subject. Even if this latter theory were correct, surely Aristotle might patch his own gap as well as Eudemus for him: and why did Eudemus omit the point in dealing himself with προαίρεσις?

(2) On the discussion of εὐβουλία in chapter ix, Grant, after observing[3] (what really tells against his theory) 'There is a great assumption here of the manner of Aristotle,' remarks 'There is an advance upon Aristotle's account of deliberation (*Eth.* III iii) in two points, (1) the process is illustrated here by the logical formula of the syllogism, (2) there is a mention here of the faculty by which ends are apprehended, which Aristotle had left unnoticed.' To which the answer is (A) there are the same omissions in Eudemus' previous account of βούλευσις, and the supplemental remarks in VI ix bear therefore the same relation to each previous account: (B) it is in any case quite natural that these supplemental remarks should only be made where the context renders them both pertinent and intelligible.

(d) Grant says[4] that σκοπός is a metaphor with Aristotle but has lost its metaphorical associations with Eudemus, and that the disputed books show its use in the Eudemian sense. It is enough to refer to Stewart's demonstration[5] that with

---

[1] Vol. ii p. 153.   [2] 'Miscellaneous Notes' ad locum.
[3] Vol. ii p. 173.   [4] Vol. ii p. 147.
[5] See his 'Notes' Book VI init.

Aristotle also σκοπός is a dead metaphor. The distinction Grant attempts to draw will not hold.

(*e*) Grant points out[1] that the medical illustration of VI i is 'repeated' in EE VIII iii 13. But it is just as reasonable to suppose, with all the evidence that there is of the detailed fashion in which Eudemus copied Aristotle, that Eudemus took his illustration in EE VIII iii 13 from its use here by Aristotle.

(*f*) All the later editors agree that the formula of VI i 2, 1138 b 25, ἔστι δὲ τὸ μὲν εἰπεῖν οὕτως ἀληθὲς μέν, οὐθὲν δὲ σαφές, is not a 'protest against the indefiniteness and relativity of Aristotle's moral theory of 'the mean' and 'the law[1],' as Grant believes.

(*g*) On NE VI ii 5, 1139 a 35, διάνοια δ' αὐτὴ οὐθὲν κινεῖ, ἀλλ' ἡ ἔνεκά του καὶ πρακτική, Grant maintains that Eudemus here is guilty of a confusion that Aristotle had avoided[2]. But the author of VI had just before, in saying that ὄρεξις as well as νοῦς or διάνοια is needed for προαίρεσις, clearly made the distinction that Grant supposes him here to ignore. The confusion that certainly does belong to the form of this statement is thus due merely to formal carelessness and not to any want of perception of the true doctrine. It is just as likely that Aristotle should be guilty of such formal carelessness as that Eudemus should.

(*h*) Grant compares the list of terms given in NE 1139 b 16 (VI iii 1) with that given in the *Posterior Analytics* 89 b 7 (I xxxiii 8), and finds evidence of difference of authorship in the difference of the two lists. The account he gives[3] of the way Eudemus borrowed and altered the list from Aristotle has only to be read through to be seen plainly to be arbitrary and unsupported by evidence. There is nothing to show that Aristotle's list falls into three pairs to be separately discussed. It is not true that the words διάνοια and νοῦς are undistinguished throughout NE VI: there is the clearest distinction between the νοῦς of VI vi (probably the

---

[1] Vol. ii p. 147.   [2] Vol. ii p. 152.   [3] Vol. ii p. 153.

sense in which νοῦς is spoken of in the passage in the *Analytics*) and the νοῦς or διάνοια of VI ii. And though Grant is right in saying that the list of VI iii contains a cross-division, he is wrong in implying that this cross-division ought not to be there, and that no cross-division exists in Aristotle's list in the *Analytics*. The two lists are perfectly consistent, and may well be by the same author: and even if they were not consistent, greater formal inconsistencies than this are often to be found between two passages both undoubtedly by Aristotle.

(*i*) In his note[1] on VI iii 3, 1139 b 27, ἡ μὲν γὰρ δι' ἐπαγωγῆς Grant asserts that Eudemus makes a novel statement in saying that science[2] is sometimes inductive. But the passage 1139 b 27 does not say this, but only what is said at the end of the *Analytics*, that ἐπαγωγή is necessary to provide the materials for science.

(*k*) In his note[3] on VI xi 4, 1143 a 35, καὶ ὁ νοῦς τῶν ἐσχάτων ἐπ' ἀμφότερα Grant says 'now comes in a piece of confusion which is thoroughly Eudemian,' etc. But (A) we often find Aristotle guilty of the kind of confusion Grant alleges to exist here, (B) the confusion does not really exist here—Aristotle is merely pointing out the connection between the two kinds of νοῦς to justify their having a common name.

(*l*) Grant observes that the phrase[4] ἡ ὅλη ἀρετή, used in VI xii 5, 1144 a 5, is never found in the writings of Aristotle, but is frequent in those of Eudemus. But of the five places where the phrase occurs, three are in the disputed books, and only two in the admittedly Eudemian: and the argument is proportionally weakened in consequence. Accident may easily account for the fact, if VI is by Aristotle. Moreover, in EE VIII iii Eudemus calls complete virtue not ὅλη ἀρετή but καλοκαγαθία, and says that he has used the name already. But the word does not occur elsewhere in either of the two treatises. It would thus seem likely that there is a lost Eudemian equivalent of VI, in which what is called ὅλη ἀρετή

---

[1] Vol. ii p. 155.
[2] i.e. ἐπιστήμη.
[3] Vol. ii p. 179.
[4] Vol. ii p. 183.

in VI was called καλοκαγαθία: according to which view VI must be by Aristotle. (Dr Jackson's emendation ἣν καλοῦμεν ἤδη καλοκαγαθίαν[1] is the result of a belief that VI is Eudemian, and cannot be used as an argument in favour of that view.)

Hitherto I have been trying to show that the reasons given for their view by supporters of the Eudemian authorship of VI are inadequate. I have now to bring forward some other facts that appear to tell in favour of the view I support, that VI is, whether V and VII are or are not, a genuine part of the Nicomachean treatise, and not only not the work of Eudemus but actually the work of Aristotle. These facts fall into two main groups:—(1) Those relating to the meaning attached to the word φρόνησις elsewhere in the NE and the EE. (2) The correspondence with NE VI of NE X and EE VIII respectively.

I.   Compare the passages in NE and EE where φρόνησις is mentioned, and it will be seen that the Nicomachean books are, in the meaning that they give to this important word, far more consistent with NE VI than the Eudemian books are.

(a)   In the undoubtedly Eudemian books —:

(i)   In EE 1214 a 30—b 6 φρόνησις is opposed to ἀρετή and ἡδονή, and stands for the τέλος of the intellectual life of speculation as distinguished from the τέλη which are (1) the practical life of public activity and moral virtue, (2) the life of pleasure. This is not inconsistent with the wording of other parts of the undoubtedly Eudemian books; but according to NE VI φρόνησις is inseparable from ἠθική ἀρετή, and it is not φρόνησις but σοφία that belongs to the life of speculation.

(ii)   In EE 1215 a 32—b 6 φρόνησις is in the same way opposed to ἀρετή and ἡδονή, and here its sphere is more clearly defined: it belongs not to the πολιτικός but to the φιλόσοφος, who βούλεται περὶ φρόνησιν εἶναι καὶ τὴν θεωρίαν τὴν περὶ τὴν ἀλήθειαν, and who is also said below (1215 b 12—13) κοινωνεῖν θεωρίας τινὸς θείας. Anaxagoras,

---

[1] 1248 b 10 (for ἐκαλοῦμεν).

whose view of the Good this phrase is meant to describe, is shortly afterwards recorded as saying that the greatest reason for living is θεωρῆσαι τὸν οὐρανὸν καὶ τὴν περὶ τὸν ὅλον κόσμον τάξιν.

(iii)   In EE 1216 a 38, and

(iv)   In EE 1218 b 34, the same use occurs : φρόνησις has the same meaning, and is opposed in the same way to ἀρετή and ἡδονή.

(v)   Though at first sight EE 1220 a 5 ἐπαινοῦμεν οὐ μόνον τοὺς δικαίους ἀλλὰ καὶ τοὺς συνετοὺς καὶ τοὺς σοφοὺς seems to recognise the distinction of NE VI, and though it does not really tell against it, yet the use of συνετούς as a synonym for φρονίμους is plainly inconsistent with the special meaning given to συνετός in NE VI x.

(vi)   If the table of virtues and vices in EE 1220 b 38— 1221 a 12 is not a later interpolation, the inclusion of φρόνησις among moral virtues as a mean between πανουργία and εὐήθεια does not seem to look forward to NE VI : and even the interpolation is hard to explain, as far as φρόνησις is concerned, if NE VI was recognised as forming part of the EE when the interpolation was made.

(b)   In the undoubtedly Nicomachean books, on the other hand, far greater consistency with NE VI is to be found, as regards the use of the word φρόνησις, than in the un- doubtedly Eudemian. Thus—

(i)   NE 1096 b 23 τιμῆς δὲ καὶ φρονήσεως καὶ ἡδονῆς is, owing to the context, quite non-committal on this point : and since the passage is concerned with Platonic metaphysics the word is not unnaturally used in its Platonic sense. The evidence of the passage is thus negatively in favour of my view.

(ii)   NE 1098 b 23 τοῖς μὲν γὰρ ἀρετή, τοῖς δὲ φρόνησις, ἄλλοις δὲ σοφία τις εἶναι δοκεῖ: a careful distinction of φρόνησις from σοφία, and of both from ἠθικὴ ἀρετή, fully consistent with the usage of NE VI.

(iii)   NE 1103 a 6 σοφίαν μὲν καὶ σύνεσιν καὶ φρόνησιν διανοητικάς (sc. ἀρετὰς λέγομεν): a less convincing, but still striking, anticipation of NE VI.

G.   2

(iv) NE X is strictly consistent with NE VI (see 1178 a 16, 1180 a 22, 1180 b 28), except in the Platonic quotation 1172 b 30, where Plato's usage of the word is followed. And it may be remarked that the same consistency is shown in the use of σοφία: see 1177 a 23, 1179 a 30 and 32.

II. Compare the final results of the investigation reached in NE X and in EE VIII respectively with the general tenor and the particular results of NE VI. The final results in question are contained in NE X vi—viii and in EE VIII iii. On the one hand, the final chapter of EE takes practically no account at all of the conclusions of NE VI. The nature of καλοκαγαθία or Perfect Virtue is determined wholly without reference to φρόνησις or any form of intellectual virtue: it is simply a combination of all the moral virtues. Not only is intellectual virtue not put above moral virtue, but it is not even mentioned. And as καλοκαγαθία, a purely moral ἕξις, appears to be considered the ἕξις of the εὐδαίμων, so the ἐνέργεια of the εὐδαίμων is at least more moral than intellectual, τὸν θεὸν θεραπεύειν καὶ θεωρεῖν. This phrase, truly religious in its vague reverence, whatever it may mean, means at any rate something very different from the θεωρία which is the ἐνέργεια of the σοφός in NE VI. The highest of ἐπιστῆμαι is indeed θεολογική according to Aristotle: but θεολογική is not τὸν θεὸν θεραπεύειν καὶ θεωρεῖν. And what becomes, in the Eudemian formula, of μαθηματική and φυσική, recognised in NE VI and elsewhere as true parts of σοφία? On the other hand, NE X vi—viii makes the most satisfactory use of NE VI. The distinction of true and secondary εὐδαιμονία as θεωρία and πρᾶξις expressed in NE X is founded on the carefully elaborated definitions of σοφία and φρόνησις in NE VI, and agrees with the preference accorded to σοφία in NE VI, 1141 a 19 κεφαλὴν ἔχουσα ἐπιστήμη τῶν τιμιωτάτων, 1143 b 34 χείρων τῆς σοφίας οὖσα (sc. ἡ φρόνησις) κυριωτέρα αὐτῆς ἔσται. The statement 1177 a 17 ὅτι δ' ἐστὶ θεωρητική, εἴρηται, which has been thought to show that NE VI is not Aristotle's work, is quite consistent with NE VI if understood to refer to the general doctrine of the book and not to a

particular passage fixing the usage of the single word
θεωρητική[1]. In fact NE X vi—viii is as unintelligible without
NE VI as EE VIII iii is intelligible without it and even
unintelligible with it. This fact does not of course show
that NE VI is the original Nicomachean book on the subject,
but it does show that NE VI either is or closely resembles
the original book, while EE VIII can so well dispense with
any such argument as that contained in NE VI that it seems
doubtful whether the corresponding book for the EE was
ever written, though, as has been admitted, it was no doubt
designed. It is, then, very hard to believe that NE VI is
Eudemian: and there is no further obstacle in the way of
believing that it is Nicomachean, the genuine work of Aristotle
himself.

The importance of the conclusion that I have tried to
establish—that NE VI is really part of the Nicomachean
Ethics, and therefore was written by Aristotle—may easily
be over-rated, but is of course very considerable for anyone
who tries to elucidate the meaning of this book. Though it
is a book detached to a large extent by the nature of its
subject from all others except a part of the later *Great
Ethics*; though it is often as necessary as it is natural to
look no further for the explanation of difficulties than some
other part of the book itself; though it is always dangerous to
interpret a passage in one Aristotelian work by a passage in
another; and though all Peripatetic philosophy hangs so
much together that such interpretation is almost equally safe
or dangerous, no matter who the author is actually found or
supposed to be: yet, as I have said, doctrine must be determined by context as well as context by doctrine, and the
view taken of the authorship of this book can never be a
matter of indifference. I hope, therefore, that I have done
enough to justify my explaining the general bearing of
NE VI as part of the Nicomachean and not as part of the
Eudemian work, and my giving this or that meaning to an

[1] The probability that the words should be so understood is greatly increased
by the fact that the passage 1143 b 14—17 makes just this kind of reference.

otherwise obscure passage because such meaning is consistent with other parts of the Nicomachean treatise, whether consistent with the Eudemian or not. The undoubtedly Nicomachean books will for this purpose have greater authority than the undoubtedly Eudemian. So little use has to be made of NE v in treating of NE vi, and so little even of NE vii, that I have not thought it necessary to multiply my labour three-fold by attempting to handle the question of the authorship of NE v and vii. I am content at present to allow that question to remain open: but throughout my work I have assumed that Aristotle is the author of at any rate the Sixth Book itself. If however it should be thought that this assumption lacks adequate support, I do not think that many of my contentions will be invalidated on that ground alone.

SECTION II.

ARISTOTLE'S DOCTRINE OF INTELLECTUAL GOODNESS.

A. INTRODUCTORY.

TWO reasons are given in VI for the inquiry into the nature of intellectual ἀρετή, and some trouble is caused by the want of any explicit statement of connection between them. The first is the necessity of completing our knowledge of moral ἀρετή. It is not said in so many words that we cannot know what moral ἀρετή is till we know what intellectual ἀρετή is. But it is said that we cannot know what moral ἀρετή is until we know what that ὀρθὸς λόγος is by which the μέσον in any given case is always determined. It is later shown that this ὀρθὸς λόγος is the ἀρετή of the λόγου ἔχον part of the soul, or more properly perhaps of the λόγου ἔχον part of the soul in its good condition, part of whose work, or the work of a part of which, is to determine the moral μέσον as aforesaid. It thus appears, what was not formally apparent at the time, that the discussion of intellectual ἀρετή—the ἀρετή, that is, of the λόγου ἔχου μέρος—was directly useful for the immediate purpose of making more explicit the definition of moral ἀρετή. This object is attained not only by fully describing the function of the ὀρθὸς λόγος in so far as it is concerned with moral ἀρετή, but also, though less directly, by showing that not all ὀρθὸς λόγος has to do with moral ἀρετή, by carefully distinguishing that which has to do with it from that which has not, and by describing in detail not only φρόνησις, which has to do with it, but also σοφία, which has not. Directly or indirectly, the whole of the discussion of VI furthers this first object. But there is a second object, which is stated quite clearly at the outset—as complete a knowledge as possible of what intellectual ἀρετή is, of its various kinds and their relative excellence. The attainment of this object must of course contribute directly to the attainment of the main object of the Ethics, the knowledge of what the greatest good for man is. For that depends on knowing what the best and completest ἀρετή is, which in its turn depends on knowing clearly and in detail what the several ἀρεταί are. In the absence or assumed absence of a priori evidence, moral ἀρετή and intellectual ἀρετή are equally likely to be best and completest, and so the nature of both must be equally clearly understood. The importance of VI is that it completes the discussion of the one and says all that there is to say about the other.

Now it does not follow that the same handling of the subject will forward the above-mentioned two objects to the same extent. If it is desired to find out how far and in what way intellectual ἀρετή has to do with moral ἀρετή, the rational division of intellectual ἀρετή will naturally be into that which is and that which is not concerned with human πρᾶξις or responsible action. But it does not follow that this is the most natural division to make when considering intellectual ἀρετή in and by itself: and when in the second chapter intellectual ἀρετή is so considered, a different division does in fact appear to be made, into that which has to do with μὴ ἐνδεχόμενα and that which has to do with ἐνδεχόμενα ἄλλως ἔχειν. The class ἐνδεχόμενα ἄλλως ἔχειν appears to be a far larger one than the class πρακτά, the class μὴ ἐνδεχόμενα ἄλλως ἔχειν a far smaller one than the class μὴ πρακτά. What is more, there are certain indications in VI that those ἐνδεχόμενα that are not πρακτά are to some extent taken into account.

(1) The name λογιστικόν is given (1139 a 12) to the second part of the λόγον ἔχον, instead of the name βουλευτικόν, for no obvious reason, and in spite of the risk of confusion with the Platonic use of λογιστικόν as meaning λόγον ἔχον.

Probably in order not to exclude ἐνδεχόμενα μὴ πρακτά, which βουλευτικόν would do, since βούλευσις is of πρακτά only.

(2) The sentence τοῦ δ' ἐνδεχομένου ἄλλως ἔχειν ἔστι τι καὶ ποιητὸν καὶ πρακτόν (1140 a 1) suggests by its form that a class of ἐνδεχόμενα is thought of though not mentioned that is neither ποιητόν nor πρακτόν but simply θεωρητόν. Otherwise we should expect τοῦ δ' ἐνδεχομένου ἄλλως ἔχειν τὸ μὲν ποιητόν ἐστι τὸ δὲ πρακτόν.

(3) οὔτε τῶν ἐξ ἀνάγκης ὄντων ἢ γινομένων ἡ τέχνη ἐστὶν οὔτε τῶν κατὰ φύσιν (1140 a 14) marks off τὰ κατὰ φύσιν from τὰ ἐξ ἀνάγκης and so from τὰ μὴ ἐνδεχόμενα ἄλλως ἔχειν. Now τὰ κατὰ φύσιν are the objects of non-practical θεωρία: they form the subject matter of a great part of Aristotle's research. From this passage they appear also to be considered as ἐνδεχόμενα ἄλλως ἔχειν.

(4) The conclusion λείπεται ἄρα...κακά (1140 b 4—6) is not the result of a proof by exhaustion: λείπεται only means 'it must follow that...,' as elsewhere. The validity of the conclusion depends on the fact that φρόνησις has already been shown to be (because βουλευτική) περὶ τῶν πρακτῶν, and not that every other field for intellectual ἀρετή has been mentioned and rejected—νοῦς and σοφία have spheres not yet mentioned at all. This statement does not, then, exclude the taking into account of non-practical θεωρία τῶν ἐνδεχομένων.

(5) 1140 b 26 θατέρου ἂν εἴη ἀρετή (sc. ἡ φρόνησις), τοῦ δοξαστικοῦ· ἥ τε γὰρ δόξα περὶ τὸ ἐνδεχόμενον ἄλλως ἔχειν καὶ ἡ φρόνησις. This suggests strongly that non-practical θεωρία is taken into account as being part of the activity of the λογιστικὸν μέρος. For whereas λογιστικόν included the meaning βουλευτικόν, δοξαστικόν does not, and is not an appropriate name for the part of the soul that deliberates and is concerned with πρακτά. But the giving of the name δοξαστικόν here is plainly significant of something.

This being so, the question is, which of the two divisions is followed in distinguishing—as is done at 1143 b 14— one group of intellectual ἀρεταί under the name σοφία from the other under the name φρόνησις? Is σοφία of μὴ ἐνδεχ-όμενα as opposed to φρόνησις which is of ἐνδεχόμενα? Or is σοφία of μὴ πρακτά as opposed to φρόνησις which is of πρακτά (that is, θεωρητική as opposed to πρακτική)? On the one hand σοφία is said (1177 a 18) to be θεωρητική, and the description, which follows this statement, of its claims to be the best ἀρετή applies as well, a priori at least, to a ἕξις concerned with ἐνδεχόμενα as to one concerned with μὴ ἐνδεχόμενα, whereas it is plain that φρόνησις can neither in VI nor X be considered as non-practical. Moreover φυσική, which must be capable of meaning the science of τὰ κατὰ φύσιν, is recognised both in VI (1142 a 17—18) and elsewhere[1] as being one branch of σοφία, coordinate with metaphysics and mathematics: and according to 1140 a 15 (already quoted) φυσική must be considered as having to do with ἐνδεχόμενα ἄλλως ἔχειν, though the treatise called the *Physics* is pure metaphysics. In this view, then, σοφία may be concerned with ἐνδεχόμενα ἄλλως ἔχειν, such as have nothing to do with πρᾶξις: and in this view σοφία is distinguished from φρόνησις as θεωρητική from πρακτική, and may be the ἀρετή of part of the λογιστικόν μέρος as well as of all the ἐπιστη-μονικόν: so that the distinction of chapter i is followed and not that of chapter ii. But on the other hand σοφία is defined as being νοῦς and ἐπιστήμη (1141 a 19), both of which are expressly said to be of μὴ ἐνδεχόμενα only: and as being ἐπιστήμη τῶν τιμιωτάτων, and necessary truth is more τίμιον than contingent. It must then be conceded that σοφία in the strictest sense is of μὴ ἐνδεχόμενα only, and only in a qualified sense, if at all, of ἐνδεχόμενα[2]. But even ἐνδεχόμενα are only considered with the object of discovering general principles, which are eternally true (and not like the principles of φρόνησις relative to the person and occasion) except for the interference of τὸ αὐτόματον. Now τὸ αὐτόματον can never be the subject of any exercise of intellectual ἀρετή, for

---

[1] *Metaphysics* 1064 b 1 τρία γένη τῶν θεωρητικῶν ἐπιστημῶν ἐστί, φυσικὴ μαθηματικὴ θεολογική, 1025 b 21 οὔτε πρακτικὴ (sc. ἡ φυσικὴ) οὔτε ποιητική, 26 θεωρητική τις ἂν εἴη.

[2] *Metaphysics* 1005 b 1 ἔστι δὲ σοφία τις ἡ φυσικὴ ἀλλ' οὐ πρώτη.

it is quite unknowable by any θεωρία, just as the element of τύχη cannot be estimated in βούλευσις. In this sense it is always the μὴ ἐνδεχόμενον that is the object of θεωρητική and so of σοφία: and on the other hand all the ἐνδεχόμενον that, as such, is the proper object of the exercise of intellectual ἀρετή, is πρακτικόν: for the regular operations of nature are only properly considered in so far as they are μὴ ἐνδεχόμενα, and τὰ τύχῃ and τὰ αὐτόματα are not properly considered at all. By thus reasoning the classes of μὴ ἐνδεχόμενα and ἐνδεχόμενα may be made to coincide, in so far as they are the objects of good intellectual activity, with the classes of θεωρητά and πρακτά respectively. It is probably thus that Aristotle reasoned in his own mind, but as he has openly recognised neither the essential difference between the two classifications nor the steps that must be taken to make the corresponding classes coincide, his reasoning was evidently far from clear. One source of confusion to him was probably the Platonic doctrine on this subject. According to Plato, the ideas are μὴ ἐνδεχόμενα (to use Aristotle's phrase) and the phenomena ἐνδεχόμενα, there is ἐπιστήμη of ideas and δόξα of phenomena: which doctrine the terms ἐπιστημονικόν and δοξαστικόν in VI suggest that Aristotle bears in mind and is not willing wholly to reject. But the division of intellectual ἀρετή into θεωρητική and πρακτική is wholly un-Platonic, and at the same time it is the division essential to Aristotle's ethical theory, as the great conclusions of X vi—viii prove.

The way is now cleared for as careful an examination as can be made of Aristotle's view of intellectual ἀρετή in detail. From what has just been said it follows that intellectual ἀρετή is of two main kinds and two only. For all proper objects of intellectual activity are of two main kinds and of two only: either μὴ ἐνδεχόμενα ἄλλως ἔχειν and at the same time μὴ πρακτά, or else ἐνδεχόμενα ἄλλως ἔχειν and at the same time πρακτά. This distinction must correspond exactly to that between the intellectual activities themselves, the parts or faculties of the soul that possess these activities, and the ἀρεταί or good permanent qualities of the parts of the soul: 1139 a 16 ἡ ἀρετὴ πρὸς τὸ ἔργον τὸ οἰκεῖον. For according to

Aristotle's psychological theory, the thinking soul is potentially the same as the objects of thought, as δεκτικὸν τοῦ εἴδους ἄνευ τῆς ὕλης : therefore whatever distinction exists between the objects of thought must exist also in the thinking soul. The ἀρετή of the one part of the soul Aristotle calls σοφία, of the other part φρόνησις. This nomenclature does not prevent the subdivisions of either σοφία or φρόνησις being quite properly called ἀρεταί themselves: nor does it prevent the ·use of the name φρόνησις in a narrower sense: neither does it indicate a distinction essentially more radical than that made between ποιητική and πρακτικὴ ἀρετή, or than that made between νοῦς and ἐπιστήμη. But it does indicate just the distinction which is óf prime importance as regards the settlement of the great question of the Ethics, What is the greatest good for man? the distinction upon which, for this reason, the whole discussion of VI is founded.

B. Σοφια or Theoretic Wisdom.

Σοφία is defined twice (1141 a 19, 1141 b 2) as νοῦς καὶ ἐπιστήμη and as having for its object τὰ τιμιώτατα τῇ φύσει. Its nature is defined partly by statements made about it as a whole single thing, but chiefly by the description given of its two component parts. It will be convenient first to examine these parts separately, and then to see how they combine into one whole, and what peculiar qualities the whole possesses as distinguished from its parts.

Ἐπιστήμη Aristotle defines as that ἕξις of the soul that gives rise to the attainment and possession of necessary truth by means of syllogistic reasoning. The premisses of the syllogism must be true and necessary, the reasoning must be correct, and the conclusion in consequence true and necessary. Ἐπιστήμη does not, it is afterwards pointed out (1140 b 34), itself lead to the formation of true premisses, except in so far as they are the conclusions of previous syllogisms: but the premisses being given and being correct, it leads to the drawing of true conclusions from them. It would be necessary to describe in detail the syllogizing process, but that this has already been done in another treatise in a different connection. The *Prior Analytics* described the nature of correct syllogizing with great fulness, and the *Posterior Analytics* equally fully described the conditions under which correct syllogizing leads to truth. In determining the ἔργον τῆς ψυχῆς to which the ἀρετή τῆς ψυχῆς called ἐπιστήμη gives rise, it is thus only necessary to refer to the *Analytics*. Since however the *Analytics* have nothing to do with the ethical point of view, it is necessary to insist on the relation of the ἐνέργεια to the ἕξις, for the fact that the ἕξις can only be defined in terms of the ἐνέργεια makes the two liable to be confused with each other. But even in the *Analytics* the relation of the two is noticed: as may be seen from the wording of the passage *Analytics* 99 b 15—19 Περὶ μὲν οὖν συλλογισμοῦ καὶ ἀποδείξεως, τί τε ἑκάτερόν ἐστι καὶ πῶς γίνεται, φανερόν, ἅμα δὲ καὶ περὶ ἐπιστήμης ἀποδεικτικῆς· ταὐτὸν γάρ ἐστιν. (I.e. from the point of view of the *Analytics*. But this separate mention shows that from some other point of view they can be regarded as different.) περὶ δὲ τῶν ἀρχῶν, πῶς τε γίνονται γνώριμοι καὶ τίς ἡ γνωρίζουσα ἕξις, ἐντεῦθέν ἐστι δῆλον προαπορήσασι πρῶτον. All Aristotle does in the chapter on ἐπιστήμη to clear up this point is to declare ἐπιστήμη to be a ἕξις in the defining formula 1139 b 31: otherwise the description is partly of the objects of the ἐνέργεια and partly of the nature of the ἐνέργεια itself, in each case merely though accurately recapitulating the results of either the *Analytics* or the *Metaphysics*. The objects of the activity of ἐπιστήμη are μὴ ἐνδεχόμενα ἄλλως ἔχειν, ἐξ ἀνάγκης ὄντα ἢ γινόμενα (see 1140 a 14 οὔτε γὰρ τῶν ἐξ ἀνάγκης ὄντων ἢ γινομένων ἡ τέχνη ἐστίν), ἀΐδια, ἀγένητα καὶ ἄφθαρτα. The ἐνέργεια itself is κατὰ διδασκαλίαν καὶ μάθησιν, ἐκ προγινωσκομένων, συλλογισμός, ἀποδεικτική, ἐκ γνωριμωτέρων τοῦ συμπεράσματος (see Burnet or Stewart for the references): and the remark καὶ ὅσα ἄλλα προσδιοριζόμεθα ἐν τοῖς ἀναλυτικοῖς refers to such a passage as *Analytics* 71 b 20 ἐξ ἀληθῶν τε...καὶ πρώτων καὶ ἀμέσων...καὶ προτέρων καὶ αἰτίων τοῦ συμπεράσματος with the justification of this definition that follows. The whole of the doctrine of the *Analytics*

is drawn upon and assumed to be known : and there is no
inconsistency with the *Analytics* either in matter or in form :
ἐπιστήμη it is true is here regarded as necessarily ἀποδεικτική,
while in the *Analytics* ἐπιστήμη ἀποδεικτική is distinguished
from ἐπιστήμη ἀναποδεικτική (99 b 16, 71 b 20, 88 b 36, and
specially 72 b 19), but this difference of expression appears
to be openly recognised, and the consequent danger of misunderstanding averted, by the words 1139 b 18 εἰ δεῖ
ἀκριβολογεῖσθαι καὶ μὴ ἀκολουθεῖν ταῖς ὁμοιότησιν, which
suggest that ἐπιστήμη ἀναπόδεικτος is only to be called·
ἐπιστήμη by a ὁμοιότης, and not strictly·

The subject of ἐπιστήμη, then, presented few difficulties
to Aristotle, and need present few to us. The position of
νοῦς is very different, and it is not easy to feel certain of
what Aristotle supposed νοῦς to be. There is no elaborate
description of νοῦς elsewhere to which we can refer to supple-
ment its scanty treatment in VI : the testimony of other
treatises is small in quantity, and moreover highly obscure
and wanting in consistency. Two passages in VI, 1139 b 26—
31 and the sixth chapter, supply certain undoubted facts to
go upon. The premisses in the syllogisms of ἐπιστήμη
cannot, it is said, be themselves reached by syllogism (1139
b 30, 1140 b 35). This is not strictly accurate, for as a
matter of fact the conclusion of one syllogism may become
a premiss in another. But syllogism is in any case only the
immediate and not the ultimate means of forming true
premisses : carry the chain of reasoning far enough back,
and some premiss is certain to be reached which is not the
conclusion of any syllogism that can be made : so that the
validity of all syllogistically reached conclusions depends
entirely on the validity of certain propositions wholly independent of syllogism. They must be as general, as knowable,
as true, in fact as possessed of all the essential qualities of
syllogistic premisses, as any subsequent premisses reached by
syllogism can be. Some intellectual activity must be concerned with the production of these, some intellectual ἀρετή

---

¹ I do not of course mean to imply that the reference is to this particular
ὁμοιότης : *all* loose uses of ἐπιστήμη are excluded by it.

lead to truth about them. The name of this ἀρετή it is not, Aristotle thinks, hard to determine, for νοῦς seems the only name that is dignified enough to serve, except σοφία, which must be held to include ἐπιστήμη and so is too general in meaning. Much the same argument, only omitting the point about σοφία, leads to the selection of the same name for the same thing, *Analytics* 100 b 5—12, where the reason is not as in VI vi disguised under the veil of a proof by exhaustion[1]. The name then is easily determined : but the nature of the ἀρετή is harder to fix : it depends, as has been-said, on that of the ἐνέργεια—what is the ἐνέργεια by which ἄμεσοι προτάσεις are truly stated ? Θεωρία κατ' ἐπαγωγήν, or induction : for there is no other possible. Now the nature of ἐπαγωγή has been set forth in the *Analytics* (99 b 20 foll.) and reference is made to the *Analytics* for fuller information about it. But in spite of the great practical use that Aristotle made of the method of induction, and his theoretical recognition of its value and of Socrates' importance[2] as its introducer, he never worked it out in detail, and the little he did do for it is very far from satisfactory. His conception of it has to be gathered from a number of scattered passages rather than from any single exposition. The simplest and best account of it comes in the *Topics*, where it is said to be one sort of διαλεκτικὸς λόγος, and is opposed to συλλογισμός[3]. This account is equally applicable to scientific ἐπαγωγή, from which Aristotle would probably distinguish it as being (1) less exhaustive, and taking a smaller number of τὰ καθ' ἕκαστα into account, (2) less founded on facts, because the καθ' ἕκαστα need not be really true so long as the opponent is ready to concede their truth. With this view of induction, which is substantially the modern one, all the references to ἐπαγωγή in Aristotle agree, with one exception. A certain fact being given as true in a number of particular instances, the inference is

1 Disguised merely : because the original selection of five names, on the completeness of which the validity of the proof depends, was made on the ground of the dignity and goodness which is in common language associated with these names, and with these alone except for such as have a plainly specialised meaning.

2 *Metaphysics* 987 b 1—4.

3 *Topics* 105 a 13—19 ἐπαγωγὴ ἡ ἀπὸ τῶν...ἄριστος.

made that it is true in all the other particular instances also, and this inference is stated in a general formula applicable to all instances. The single exception to this view is of course the extraordinary chapter in the *Analytics*, 68 b 15—37, where Aristotle tries to express the inductive process in a syllogistic formula, and produces an argument entirely different from that of ordinary induction. The words 68 b 28 ἡ γὰρ ἐπαγωγὴ διὰ πάντων (sc. τῶν καθ᾽ ἕκαστον) cuts at the root of the ordinary inductive theory, the whole point of which is that induction is *not* διὰ πάντων τῶν καθ᾽ ἕκαστον, because it is inconvenient or impossible to examine *all* the καθ᾽ ἕκαστα, but διὰ τινῶν καθ᾽ ἕκαστον. The assumption that what is true of particular instances that have been examined is true of all the other particular instances that have not been examined is very different from the assumption that all the particular instances have been examined. Aristotle fails to see this, and his συλλογισμὸς ἐξ ἐπαγωγῆς is thus merely a formula for turning a proposition referring to a number of particulars separately into a proposition referring in general terms to precisely the same particulars collectively. Fortunately this curious and unsatisfactory passage can be nearly neglected in trying to understand what Aristotle really meant by ἐπαγωγή: it certainly does not express what he means as a rule. This is plain from the continual opposition of ἐπαγωγή to συλλογισμός, as in 1139 b 27 here, *Analytics* 42 a 3, 68 b 30—37, *Topics* 105 a 16, 157 a 18: to ἀπόδειξις, as in *Analytics* 81 a 40, 92 a 35—38, *Physics* 252 a 24 ἢ ἐπαγωγὴν ἢ ἀπόδειξιν φέρειν, *Metaphysics* 992 b 31—33, 1025 b 14 (where a certain kind of ἐπαγωγή is said not to supply ἀπόδειξις) and similarly 1064 a 8: to λόγος, as in *Parts of Animals* 646 a 30, ἐκ τῆς ἐπαγωγῆς being there opposed to κατὰ τὸν λόγον. But neither these passages nor any of the many others where ἐπαγωγή is mentioned show Aristotle to have clearly grasped the essential feature of induction, that it may be from few particulars or from many but is essentially not from all, and that it can never lead to theoretical certainty no matter from how many particulars it may be, but only to a very high degree of probability.

Dialectical inductions he would no doubt admit lead only to probable results, like dialectical deductions. But ἐπαγωγή as the process by which νοῦς provides the ἀρχαί for θεωρία κατ' ἐπιστήμην is held to lead to results that are absolutely certain and not merely certain enough for all practical purposes: for the essence of σοφία is the complete theoretical exactness and certainty of all the conclusions to which it leads, and the ἀρχαί of ἐπιστήμη must be more certain than any of the propositions deduced by ἐπιστήμη from them. That such certainty is unattainable Aristotle would have seen if he had investigated the nature of ἐπαγωγή more fully: as it was he plainly failed to see this. That ἐπαγωγή is the process by which the ἀρχαί of ἐπιστήμη are found through the ἀρετή of νοῦς is stated in two places only, and then not in so many words but only by means of neighbouring statements inconsistent on the surface and only to be reconciled by the supposition mentioned. The passages are of course well known: 1139 b 28—31 together with VI vi, and *Analytics* 100 b 3—5 and 5—17. The conclusion is unavoidable. The precise relation of νοῦς to ἐπαγωγή has indeed been the subject of some misunderstanding: Stewart, while right in rebutting the charge of inconsistency[1] strangely brought by Grant against the above pairs of passages, is hardly right in distinguishing νοῦς, as that which sees what is common in a number of particulars presented, from ἐπαγωγή, as the process in which the particulars are presented[2]: for a mere succession of particular presentations, without any attempt to derive a universal from them, is not an ἐπαγωγή. Ἐπαγωγή implies the statement of the καθόλου conclusion as well as of the καθ' ἕκαστα premisses (so to call them), just as συλλογισμός implies the statement of the συμπέρασμα as well as of the two premisses. Ἐπαγωγή is to νοῦς just what συλλογισμός is to ἐπιστήμη. Just as it is only when συλλογισμός produces a true conclusion that the corresponding ἕξις of the intellect is ἐπιστήμη, so it is only when ἐπαγωγή produces a true conclusion that the corresponding ἕξις of the intellect is

---

[1] i.e. *material* as opposed to *formal* inconsistency.

[2] Stewart 'Notes' ii 51 (on 1141 a 7).

νοῦς. Just as ἐπίστασθαι = ὀρθῶς συλλογίζεσθαι, so νοεῖν (in the sense in which it corresponds to νοῦς here) = ὀρθῶς ἐπαχθῆναι.

But there is a further difficulty. In neither of the two passages in VI already referred to that deal with νοῦς as leading to the knowledge of the ἀρχαὶ ἐπιστήμης, nor in any other place where this νοῦς is mentioned, is the nature of these ἀρχαί made at all clear. The immediate ἀρχαί of a syllogism are undeniably the two premisses, which are propositions: but the three terms (ὅροι) contained in the two premisses may also be considered ἀρχαί, not only of the premisses but of the syllogism itself, and at first sight it seems that these may be the ἀρχαί referred to, and that νοῦς may lead not to the making of καθόλου propositions but only to the conception of καθόλου terms. Some such view as this has been very generally accepted by commentators. It may seem supported by the wording of 1142 a 25 ὁ μὲν γὰρ νοῦς τῶν ὅρων and 1143 a 35 ὁ νοῦς τῶν ἐσχάτων...τῶν πρώτων ὅρων...ὁ μὲν κατὰ τὰς ἀποδείξεις τῶν ἀκινήτων ὅρων καὶ πρώτων: for the normal meaning of ὅρος is not 'definition' or any kind of 'proposition' but simply 'term.' Further in *Analytics* 100 a 15—b 3 the example given of the operation of νοῦς by induction is the formation from such conceptions as Καλλίας of such conceptions as ἄνθρωπος, and from these again of such conceptions as ζῷον: which seems to exclude the view that νοῦς forms propositions. The words καθόλου and καθ' ἔκαστον are of course applicable equally to propositions and to terms. The opening of VI vi certainly implies that νοῦς is not μετὰ λόγου, which Prof Burnet takes to mean that νοῦς apprehends its object directly and not by any sort of reasoning. He refers to *Metaphysics* 1051 b 24. This passage reads thus: ἐστὶ τὸ μὲν ἀληθὲς θιγεῖν καὶ φῶναι (οὐ γὰρ ταὐτὸ κατάφασις καὶ φάσις) τὸ δ' ἀγνοεῖν μὴ θιγγάνειν. ἀπατηθῆναι γὰρ περὶ τὸ τί ἐστιν οὐκ ἔστιν ἀλλ' ἢ κατὰ συμβεβηκός. There is also the passage, which Prof. Burnet does not quote, *Psychology* 430 b 26 ἔστι δ' ἡ μὲν φάσις τι κατά τινος, ὥσπερ ἡ κατάφασις, καὶ ἀληθὴς ἢ ψευδὴς πᾶσα· ὁ δὲ νοῦς οὐ πᾶς, ἀλλ' ὁ τοῦ τί ἐστι κατὰ τὸ τί ἦν εἶναι ἀληθής,

˙* καὶ οὐ τὶ κατά τινος : which refers to the same facts, though with a broader use of the word φάσις. The view thus supported is nevertheless incorrect. It is true that induction of general conception from particular conceptions is not only possible but inevitable, and that the condition of soul in which such induction is well done may be considered an intellectual ἀρετή. It is true that the example of induction given at the close of the *Analytics* (100 a 15 above referred to) may be and probably is an example of this kind of induction. And it may be true that this kind of induction is thought of as at least included in the induction referred to in VI. But the following facts show that the inductive function of νοῦς spoken of in VI is to make propositions and not merely to apprehend terms.

(1) The formation of the propositions that serve as the premisses of the syllogisms of ἐπιστήμη is otherwise not taken into account—surely a serious omission.

(2) νοῦς is described along with the other four ἀρεταί at 1139 b 17 as ᾧ ἀληθεύει ἡ ψυχὴ τῷ καταφάναι ἢ ἀποφάναι, and though φάναι need not imply making a proposition, καταφάναι and ἀποφάναι always must.

(3) In *Analytics* 72 a 7—24 the ἀρχαὶ ἀποδείξεως are described as being propositions ; they are ἀποφάνσεις, ἄμεσοι προτάσεις, whether θέσεις or ἀξιώματα, ὑποθέσεις or ὁρισμοί.

(4) ὅρος is often used to mean ὁρισμός and even πρότασις. See Bonitz sub voce. But even if ὅροι, in the passages quoted above, means 'terms,' the meaning may easily be that νοῦς leads to propositions containing these ὅροι.

(5) The passage quoted *Analytics* 100 a 15—b 3 does not exclude other kinds of induction than the one of which an example is there given. And that example may be of the formation not of ὅροι or terms but of ὁρισμοί or definitions, which are of course propositions.

(6) Prof. Burnet's example of an immediately-apprehended ἀρχή is the principle of contradiction. This is an ἀξίωμα, and an ἀξίωμα is one kind of proposition. But plainly a false ἀξίωμα can be made: the cognition of a proposition,

whether an axiomatic proposition or not, is not θιγεῖν (see Burnet's note, p. 266, ad locum). The passage from the *Metaphysics*[1] distinctly refers to ἀσύνθετα (= ἀδιαίρετα, detached concepts): but an ἀξίωμα, like any other proposition, is σύνθετον. So too the parallel passage quoted, *Psychology* 430 b 26, refers to ἀσύνθετα only.

(7) Practical νοῦς, which is said (1143 b 3) to be τῆς ἑτέρας προτάσεως, and so is plainly considered to lead to propositions of some kind, is there co-ordinated with the νοῦς of σοφία in such a fashion that the latter is evidently considered there as also leading to propositions.

It is then the work of νοῦς to form, from καθ' ἕκαστον propositions, καθόλου propositions by the method of induction.

So much then for ἐπιστήμη and νοῦς considered separately in themselves. And now let the combination of the two, called σοφία by Aristotle, be considered, so far at least as this can profitably be done before dealing with φρόνησις, contrast with which best makes the nature of σοφία clear.

The definition arrived at in 1141 a 19 and b 2 is νοῦς καὶ ἐπιστήμη ὥσπερ κεφαλὴν ἔχουσα ἐπιστήμη τῶν τιμιωτάτων τῇ φύσει. In the argument leading to this it is important to distinguish two different points. (1) The name σοφία in its particular or qualified uses is given to various forms of intellectual ἀρετή on the ground of ἀκρίβεια: the more ἀκριβής a person is at any particular thing, the more σοφός he is as regards that thing. Therefore the name σοφία without qualification will most appropriately be given to the intellectual ἀρετή that possesses most ἀκρίβεια, no matter what that ἀρετή may be, nor what may exactly be meant by ἀκρίβεια. (2) Because ἀκρίβεια has a certain meaning, it is argued that the ἀκριβεστάτη of intellectual ἀρεταί must be a compound of νοῦς and ἐπιστήμη, no matter whether this compound be called σοφία or by some other name. The force of this argument turns on two facts, the meaning of ἀκρίβεια, which is not explicitly declared, and the nature of νοῦς and ἐπιστήμη, which has already been set forth. The word ἀκρίβεια must

[1] 1051 b 24.

then be examined. From its general use, and from the analogy of the sculptor in this passage, it may be said, I think, to include the three notions of accuracy, completeness, and stability. It is the second of these notions that seems to be to the front in the connecting argument δεῖ ἄρα τὸν σοφὸν μὴ μόνον τὰ ἐκ τῶν ἀρχῶν εἰδέναι ἀλλὰ καὶ περὶ τὰς ἀρχὰς ἀληθεύειν. But the first also applies, for unless the premisses of ἐπιστήμη are accurate the conclusions are inaccurate, and ἐπιστήμη without νοῦς cannot secure the accuracy of its premisses: and the third applies, for it is only accurate and complete knowledge that is ἀμετάπειστος· From this argument the conclusion follows that the ἀκριβεστάτη of intellectual ἀρεταί must be the compound of νοῦς and ἐπιστήμη: but it has already been shown that the ἀκριβεστάτη of intellectual ἀρεταί is σοφία: therefore σοφία is the compound of νοῦς and ἐπιστήμη. It must be carefully observed that τῶν τιμιωτάτων is a fresh point, and not part of the conclusion, in spite of the casual way in which it is appended to the formula which really *is* the conclusion of the previous argument. That σοφία is τῶν τιμιωτάτων has to be proved, and is in fact proved in the following passages 1141 a 20—22, a 33—b 2: and it is this point on which stress is laid in the repeated definition of σοφία 1141 b 2—3.

Σοφία then is a ἕξις τῆς ψυχῆς, compounded of two ἕξεις: for ἐπιστήμη has been said to be a ἕξις, and νοῦς can clearly be inferred to be one.

For νοῦς is in VI vi treated as on a level with ἐπιστήμη and φρόνησις, both of which are expressly called ἕξεις. Also compare 1139 b 12—13 καθ' ἃς οὖν μάλιστα ἕξεις ἀληθεύσει ἑκάτερον (sc. μόριον) αὗται ἀρεταὶ ἀμφοῖν, with what follows, 15 ἔστω δὴ οἷς ἀληθεύει, κτλ, where οἷς = καθ' ἃς ἕξεις by implication. The vagueness of οἷς here is parallel to the vagueness of οἷς in VI vi εἰ δὴ οἷς ἀληθεύομεν, κτλ, which is to be similarly explained. Also in 1143 a 26 νοῦς is a ἕξις, and though it is νοῦς πρακτικὸς that is there most thought of, νοῦς θεωρητικὸς is mentioned and regarded as parallel with νοῦς πρακτικός (only in another sphere) and therefore equally with νοῦς πρακτικός a ἕξις.

Like the ἕξεις of which it is composed, the nature of the ἕξις σοφία can best be described by reference to its ἐνέργεια. The method of this ἐνέργεια is already plain from what is known of the methods of the ἐνέργειαι of νοῦς and ἐπιστήμη. The quality of ἀκρίβεια (which may be said to attach to the ἐνέργεια of σοφία as well as to the ἕξις) is peculiar to the compound as distinguished from the ingredients, illustrating the general principle that the qualities of a whole are not necessarily the sum of the qualities of its parts.

So much we already know of σοφία; and this is all true to some extent of every kind of σοφία, even of the inferior kinds less properly called σοφία. But what is the subject-matter of σοφία? what can be said of this subject-matter besides that it is τὰ μὴ ἐνδεχόμενα ἄλλως ἔχειν? (1) It must be τὰ τιμιώτατα τῇ φύσει, for other intellectual ἀρεταί are concerned with man and his interests only, and man and his interests are not the noblest things in the world that are objects of thought. (2) Using the results of the *Physics* and *Metaphysics* we may divide the subject-matter of σοφία into three main parts:

(*a*) χωριστὰ ἀκίνητα, the subject-matter of πρώτη φιλο-σοφία or θεολογική;

(*b*) ἀχώριστα ἀκίνητα, the subject-matter of μαθηματική;

(*c*) ἀχώριστα κινητά, the subject-matter of φυσική[1].

This division is not formally made in VI, not because it is less important than the division of φρόνησις according to subject-matter in VI viii, but because it has been made elsewhere, whereas that of φρόνησις can only be made appro-priately in the *Ethics*: the reason is thus the same as the reason for not discussing ἐπιστήμη and νοῦς more fully in VI. But 1142 a 17 μαθηματικὸς μὲν παῖς γένοιτ' ἂν σοφὸς δ' ἢ φυσικὸς οὔ plainly assumes the division in question to be familiar and understood.

[1] See in particular *Metaphysics* 1026 a 13—23, where θεολογική is said to be, as compared with μαθηματική and φυσική, itself τιμιωτάτη and περὶ τὸ τιμιώτατον γένος.

(It may be noted here that the division of σοφία into νοῦς and ἐπιστήμη corresponds to that of φρόνησις into φρόνησις proper, εὐβουλία, σύνεσις, γνώμη, νοῦς πρακτικός, etc.: while the division of σοφία into θεολογική, μαθηματική, φυσική, corresponds to that of φρόνησις into πολιτική with its sub-divisions, οἰκονομική, φρόνησις περὶ ἕνα καὶ αὐτόν.) Further consideration of the nature of σοφία must be deferred till φρόνησις has also been examined in detail.

C. ΦΡΟΝΗΣΙΣ OR PRACTICAL WISDOM.

a. *In general.*

The word φρόνησις is used in VI in four senses. Common to all is the meaning 'ἀρετή of the intellect leading to the knowledge of truth as far as concerns human action.' The four senses are as follows: (*a*) In the narrowest of the four φρόνησις is merely said to lead to the knowledge by each man of what is good for himself as distinguished from other people (ἡ περὶ αὐτὸν καὶ ἕνα φρόνησις). (*b*) φρόνησις as distinguished from εὐβουλία is the ἀρετή that leads to the comprehending and retaining of practical truth as distinguished from the searching for it and finding it—this will be shown later in my examination of εὐβουλία. (*c*) φρόνησις as distinguished from τέχνη is the ἀρετή that leads to truth about πρακτά as distinguished from ποιητά. (*d*) In the broadest of the four senses φρόνησις is the ἀρετή that leads to truth about all human action whether πρᾶξις or ποίησις. It is in this last and broadest sense that φρόνησις is opposed to σοφία (1143 b 14), as the ἀρετή of the whole of the λογιστικὸν μέρος, and as concerned with all ἐνδεχόμενα ἄλλως ἔχειν that are the proper objects of any intellectual activity at all. It is in this broadest sense that it will here to begin with be examined.

This broadest sense is that which is intended (*a*) in chapter vii where σοφία is opposed to φρόνησις, 1141 a 20—b 22; (β) in chapter viii, 1142 a 11—30; (γ) all through chapters xii and xiii, where all the finer distinctions of intellectual ἀρεταί are completely ignored. It is in this sense also that φρόνησις corresponds to the διάνοια ἡ ἕνεκά του καὶ πρακτική of chapter ii, whose virtue φρόνησις is, and which is there distinctly stated to deal with ποίησις as well as πρᾶξις (1139 b 1 αὕτη γὰρ καὶ τῆς ποιητικῆς ἄρχει· ἕνεκα γάρ του ποιεῖ πᾶς ὁ ποιῶν, κτλ). This broadest sense is, then, the prevailing sense of the book: but the others are not counted less correct in their places, not even the narrowest one founded on a mistaken judgment of fact[1]. It may moreover be allowed from the outset that in discussing this subject the author often finds no occasion to distinguish this broadest sense from the next broadest in which τέχνη is excluded, and that most of his remarks apply equally well to φρόνησις in this rather narrower sense.

To begin with, certain facts concerning the general arrangement of this book may be noticed as having a special interest in their application to the handling of φρόνησις. The method of discussion in the latter part of chapter i and in chapter ii suggests, in the light of what follows, that from the outset φρόνησις and σοφία—as they are afterwards called—are thought of as the two main divisions of intellectual ἀρετή. The whole book appears to have been carefully planned: the author keeps carefully before him his intention to make these two divisions and to give them these names. But on a first reading not only is there no plain indication of the general use of these names until we reach 1143 b 14, but there is not even anything to show that intellectual ἀρετή is going to fall into the two groups which these names denote. The division made in the latter part of chapter i is formally quite independent of the division made in chapter ii, except for a very rough connection given in the few words 1139 b 12 ἀμφοτέρων δὴ τῶν νοητικῶν μορίων ἀλήθεια τὸ ἔργον—καθ' ἃς οὖν μάλιστα ἕξεις ἀληθεύσει ἑκάτερον αὗται ἀρεταὶ ἀμφοῖν, a connection that is in any case not justified by the argument of chapter ii. Chapter iii makes an entirely fresh beginning (a fact indicated by the opening sentence 1139 b 14 Ἀρξάμενοι οὖν ἄνωθεν περὶ αὐτῶν πάλιν λέγωμεν), neglecting the results

---

[1] 1142 a 9, compare 1141 b 30—31.

of the first two chapters as a source of information, though using some of the formulae of those chapters. Only after discussing the various intellectual ἀρεταί in detail, minor as well as major, does Aristotle make a synthesis of them into two main groups: then and then only can the application of the latter part of chapter i and of chapter ii be seen, and not till chapter xiii is the earlier part of chapter i shown to be connected with the rest of the book. As for φρόνησις itself, the ὀρθὸς λόγος of the early part of chapter i is φρόνησις, the ἀρετὴ τοῦ λογιστικοῦ μέρους of the later part of chapter i is φρόνησις, the ἀρετή of the πρακτικὴ διάνοια (giving rise to λόγος ἀληθὴς in harmony with ὄρεξις ὀρθή) of chapter ii is φρόνησις: but it is not seen till much later that either of these three things is φρόνησις, nor that the three are thus identical with each other. Φρόνησις is introduced in chapter v quite independently of all the results of chapters i and ii: the thing is defined, and the name justified as applied to the thing: then varieties of φρόνησις are distinguished as regards both subject-matter and method of activity: then these varieties are all shown to be connected, and the name φρόνησις for the first time plainly conferred on all alike and on the synthesised whole: it is shown that this φρόνησις is the ἀρετὴ τοῦ λογιστικοῦ[1]: finally it is shown that φρόνησις is that λόγος ἀληθής which, according to chapter ii, harmonises with ὀρθὴ ὄρεξις, and the ὀρθὸς λόγος which, according to the earlier part of chapter i, determines the moral mean.

Now though the connection of the latter part of chapter i with chapter ii is not shown at the time, it is possible, and will be useful, to point out at once what that connection is. These two sections of the discussion make two divisions of the intellectual part of the soul, the first metaphysical, the second psychological: or rather both are psychological, but the first alone has a metaphysical basis. Chapter i divides things, by a metaphysical axiom, into necessary and contingent—the exact meaning of this division I have discussed

---

[1] Cf. 1143 b 16 ὅτι ἄλλου τῆς ψυχῆς μορίου ἀρετὴ ἑκατέρα (sc. ἡ σοφία καὶ ἡ φρόνησις) with the division of the διανοητικὸν μέρος into ἐπιστημονικόν and λογιστικόν at 1139 a 11.

elsewhere[1]; and then, on the psychological principle that like
is known by like—the meaning of this also I have explained
in another place—infers a corresponding distinction in the
part of the soul that knows these things and in the ἀρετή of
the soul that leads to such knowledge : to the parts of the
soul are dogmatically assigned the names ἐπιστημονικόν and
λογιστικόν respectively. Chapter ii takes a different line.
Whatever the greatest good for man may be, knowledge of
truth and goodness of action are, it asserts, specifically human
ends. Consider the parts or processes of the soul by which
these ends are attained. It is reasoning (νοῦς or διάνοια) that
leads to truth. Now it is plain from observation that some
reasoning has nothing to do with action, so that its goodness
or badness is independent of the goodness or badness of any
action, while other reasoning has everything to do with action,
so that its goodness or badness is inseparably bound up with
the goodness or badness of the action with which it has to do.
Action, we learn, is caused by προαίρεσις or purpose, which
is, as the *Ethics* has already shown, a combination of
reasoning with ὄρεξις or desire. Therefore the goodness or
badness of action must depend on the goodness or badness of
both reasoning and desire. The reasoning that has to do
with action is, like other reasoning, only a means to an end.
But whereas other reasoning attains its end, which is truth, if
it is good in itself, reasoning that has to do with action does
not necessarily attain its end by being good in itself, but only
by also harmonising with good desire : indeed it cannot in
practice ever be called good in itself, because it is in practice
inseparable from desire, and the goodness of its relation to
that desire is, as it were, an essential part of its own goodness.
Now the nature of this relation it is, Aristotle perceives,
important to define. From the purely psychological (as
distinguished from the ethical) point of view, it must be
noted that the reason and the desire must concern the same
things, or there is no purpose at all : and in corresponding
ways, or there is no purpose either—κατάφασις (attraction of
the reason, affirmation) must coincide with δίωξις (attraction

---

[1] See also Prof. Stewart's 'Notes' ii 9 (on 1138 a 6).

of the desire, appetition) about the same thing, or else ἀπόφασις (repulsion of the reason, negation) must coincide with φυγή (repulsion of the desire, avoidance) about the same thing[1]. From the ethical point of view it must be added, that if there is to be not merely purpose but good purpose, true κατάφασις must coincide with right δίωξις, or true ἀπόφασις with right φυγή: to put it generally, true λόγος (reasoning) must coincide with right ὄρεξις (desire). These two requisites—one for *all* προαίρεσις, the other for good προαίρεσις, must not be confused: Aristotle distinguishes them, though not with formal clearness: the first is indicated by the words 1139 a 25—26 καὶ τὰ αὐτὰ τὸν μὲν φάναι τὴν δὲ διώκειν, the second in 1139 a 24 τόν τε λόγον ἀληθῆ εἶναι καὶ τὴν ὄρεξιν ὀρθήν. The latter is elaborated at the end of the book in the discussion about the relation of φρόνησις (the ἀρετή that produces true λόγος) to ἠθικὴ ἀρετή (the ἀρετή that produces right ὄρεξις).

In considering the nature of action certain distinctions at once present themselves quite independently of any examination either of the way in which προαίρεσις causes action or of the relation of the elements of προαίρεσις to each other. (1) Actions differ in what may be called their sphere, as περὶ πόλιν, περὶ οἰκίαν, περὶ αὐτὸν καὶ ἕνα. This classification will be considered later: here it need only be noted that the intellectual ἀρετή that helps to cause good actions must be correspondingly divisible. (2) Actions also differ in their own nature as being either doing (πρᾶξις) or else making (ποίησις). This latter division, and Aristotle's treatment of it, I proceed to consider at once: noting that the two divisions just spoken of are cross-divisions, and that the corresponding divisions of intellectual ἀρετή are also cross-divisions accordingly.

While πρᾶξις or doing is really different from ποίησις or making, there is (Aristotle holds) a certain relation between them—ποίησις is essentially a means to πρᾶξις. Good πρᾶξις is more directly a means to Happiness, the supreme end, than

---

1 It may be gathered that Aristotle holds προαίρεσις to be *properly* positive, and the combination of ἀπόφασις and φυγή not *really* to constitute προαίρεσις.

good ποίησις is: good ποίησις is only a means to Happiness because it is a means to good πρᾶξις. It is useless to be able to make things well unless one knows how to use them when they are made. (Aristotle does not recognise the existence of anything that is made as a good thing in itself, no matter how beautiful it may be: and he appears in his treatment of τέχνη to be severely utilitarian, if he is to be understood as meaning that nothing made by man is even good for the effect it produces on the mind unless that effect is the means to good subsequent action. This can hardly be his view: he must be thinking here of the productions of craftsmen rather than of artists, of the great majority of things made that are useful rather than of the minority that are delightful or noble or meant for pure contemplation.) The intellectual ἀρετή that leads to good ποίησις is therefore subordinate to that which leads to good πρᾶξις. Just as λόγος in προαίρεσις is not really good unless it is both good in itself and also in harmony with right ὄρεξις, so ποίησις is not really good unless it is both good in itself and also leads to right πρᾶξις. (It follows that, indirectly but really, good ὄρεξις is necessary for good ποίησις.) At the same time there is this genuine distinction between ποίησις and πρᾶξις, that neither is a species of the other—ποίησις is not πρᾶξίς τις. In ποίησις the activity and the result are different, in πρᾶξις they are the same: πρᾶξις and πρακτόν are identical, ποίησις and ποιητόν are different. Hence the ἀρετή that leads to good ποίησις is correspondingly distinct from the ἀρετή that leads to good πρᾶξις. It is convenient to say first what more there is to be said about the ποιητικὴ ἀρετή.

Its name τέχνη is given to it by Aristotle simply in accordance with ordinary usage. Of its nature little more need be said here, nor does Aristotle himself say much: not that there was not much to say on the subject, but that the main purpose of the discussion, which he keeps steadily in view, would not be greatly helped by his saying it. Things are, he maintains, always made as the result of reasoning—the practical syllogism may be ποιητικός (examples of this are to be found in the treatise on the *Motions of Animals* 701 a 16 ποιητέον μοι ἀγαθόν, οἰκία δ᾽ ἀγαθόν, ποιεῖ οἰκίαν εὐθύς, 18 οὗ δέομαι ποιητέον, ἱματίου δέομαι, ἱμάτιον ποιητέον)—and things are well made as the result of good reasoning : the ἀρετή is therefore of the reasoning part, intellectual, μετὰ λόγου ἀληθοῦς. All ποίησις must have to do with ἐνδεχόμενα ἄλλως ἔχειν, and implies the coming into existence of a thing by external agency and not by its own. Therefore τὰ κατὰ φύσιν are not ποιητά, for they grow of themselves : they are indeed not strictly ἐνδεχόμενα, for they are ὡς ἐπὶ τὸ πολύ, invariable except for the interference of chance, τὸ αὐτόματον. Ποίησις is in a way connected with chance, τύχη : the accidental results of human actions are caused by τύχη : and τύχη affects the results of ποίησις even more than it affects the results of πρᾶξις. But whereas in φύσις the *only* variable element is that of chance, ποίησις (like πρᾶξις) is itself variable, as well as subject to the interference of chance the external variant. Aristotle takes no account of the things that are the results of the joint operation of φύσις and τέχνη, such as a crop of corn for example : no doubt because such points, though interesting in themselves, can throw no light on the main inquiry.

Φρόνησις proper, as distinguished from τέχνη, is the intellectual ἀρετή that leads to good πρᾶξις, as distinguished from good ποίησις. The following reasoning will convey a fuller general notion of what this ἀρετή is, and will also justify the giving of the name φρόνησις to it :—Good πρᾶξις, it has been shown, is caused by intellectual ἀρετή in agreement with moral ἀρετή : for good λόγος and good ὄρεξις about the same thing combine to form a good προαίρεσις which gives rise to a good πρᾶξις. Reasoning that leads to πρᾶξις is βούλευσις περὶ τὰ ἀγαθά, or deliberating about and deciding what ought to be done : the good reasoning that leads to good πρᾶξις is good βούλευσις : the ἀρετή that leads to such good reasoning is the ἀρετή whose activity is εὖ βουλεύεσθαι περὶ τὰ ἀγαθά. From this it follows, popular usage being our guide, that φρόνησις is the proper name for this ἀρετή. For according to popular usage the φρόνιμος about a particular end is the man who εὖ βουλεύεται about the good thing to do as means to that particular end, and so the φρόνιμος in general is the man who εὖ βουλεύεται about the good thing to do as means to the general end. So φρόνησις may be defined as the intellectual ἀρετή that leads to knowledge of the good things to do as means to the great end for man, which is εὖ ζῆν or εὐπραξία or εὐδαιμονία[1].

It is plain that to know what the means to any end are it is necessary to know what the end itself is: and so the φρόνιμος must know what Happiness is before he can know what the means to Happiness are. It does not indeed follow that φρόνησις is the ἀρετή that leads among other things to the correct statement of the proposition that Happiness is so-and-so: but such a correct statement must by some means or other be made if φρόνησις is to do its work. When Aristotle says 1141 b 14 οὐδ' ἐστὶν ἡ φρόνησις τοῦ καθόλου μόνον ἀλλὰ δεῖ καὶ τὰ καθ' ἕκαστα γνωρίζειν, he implies that τὸ καθόλου γνωρίζειν is essential, though not the only thing essential, to φρόνησις. How the statement of the καθόλου is made, and in what sense φρόνησις can be said to make or help make it, must be discussed later.

But it may be asked now, What is this proposition? It is of course the great conclusion of the tenth book and of the treatise, which may be thus expressed—ἡ εὐδαιμονία καὶ τὸ τέλος καὶ τὸ ἄριστόν ἐστι θεωρητικὴ ἐνέργεια τῆς ψυχῆς κατὰ σοφίαν, i.e. κατὰ νοῦν καὶ ἐπιστήμην τῶν τιμιωτάτων τῇ φύσει. Upon this general proposition all the reasoning of the truly φρόνιμος must ultimately be founded, though it does not follow that in practice he will always take this most general form of it directly into account. This general proposition is the καθόλου that according to 1141 b 14 it is necessary for the φρόνιμος to know, and the fact that modified forms of it may in practice rightly and usefully be substituted for it does not prevent its being the ultimate basis of all.

But actions are always particular. Unless therefore a man can apply his general principle to each particular action, as occasion for action arises, his knowledge of that general principle will be useless. This Aristotle distinctly recognises,

---

[1] See 1095 a 19 for the synonymous nature of these expressions.

and he plainly draws the conclusion that a knowledge of the nature of particular actions is essential to the φρόνιμος: and further, that it is better to know how to do particular good things and be ignorant of all general principles of good action than to know these general principles but be unable to apply them so as to act well in any particular instance, though to know both is obviously much the best[1]. The relation of the knowledge of the particular to the knowledge of the universal is not, however, a simple one, since all actions do not bear equally directly on the final end, and indeed no particular action appears to bear quite directly on the final end at all. A particular act must be a means to the final end because it is a means to some particular end which is a means to the final end: thus a particular piece of exercise is a means to Happiness because it is a means to health and health is a means to Happiness. Now the physician (who possesses φρόνησις κατὰ μέρος, the kind called ἰατρική) regards a piece of exercise as a means to health and to health merely, but the φρόνιμος ὅλως regards it as a means to Happiness: yet, it would appear, only as an indirect means to Happiness, for he cannot neglect to consider the particular end, health; though he does not consider health *the* end, as the physician *qua* physician does, but only as *an* end in relation to particular pieces of exercise; and in relation to *the* end, Happiness, not as an end at all, but simply as a means. It may be objected that certain acts bear on no particular end but only on the final end directly, such as δίκαια καὶ καλά and the activities according to the moral ἀρεταί generally, with which in particular φρόνησις is said to be concerned: 1143 b 21 ἡ φρόνησίς ἐστιν ἡ περὶ τὰ δίκαια καὶ καλὰ καὶ ἀγαθὰ ἀνθρώπῳ, 1144 a 11 πρακτικωτέρους διὰ τὴν φρόνησιν τῶν καλῶν καὶ δικαίων. This is true, if moral activity be the final end, as for some persons perhaps it must be: but it is not the ideal final end— that is θεωρία κατὰ σοφίαν, to which moral ἀρετή is only a means, co-ordinate, as regards the final end, with health and the like. But in any case it is plain the φρόνιμος ὅλως is not concerned with moral actions only. Πολιτική, which is

[1] 1141 b 21.

φρόνησις or the highest part of φρόνησις (see 1140 b 7—10), is said in the first book to estimate the goodness of all other ἀρεταί and the desirableness or objectionableness of the corresponding activities: 1094 a 28 τίνας γὰρ εἶναι χρεὼν τῶν ἐπιστημῶν ἐν ταῖς πόλεσι, καὶ ποίας ἑκάστους μανθάνειν καὶ μέχρι τίνος, αὕτη (sc. ἡ πολιτική) διατάσσει· ὁρῶμεν δὲ καὶ τὰς ἐντιμοτάτας τῶν δυνάμεων ὑπὸ ταύτην οὔσας, οἷον στρατηγικὴν οἰκονομικὴν ῥητορικήν. The same fact is indicated in VI by the addition at 1143 b 22 of ἀγαθὰ ἀνθρώπῳ to δίκαια καὶ καλά: ἀγαθὰ ἀνθρώπῳ is nearly equivalent to συμφέροντα ἀνθρώπῳ, and these are not for anyone moral activities only[1]. So that altogether it is plain that φρόνησις ὅλως is not of a different class of actions from those with which the φρονήσεις κατὰ μέρος are concerned, but is of all particular actions, all of which are considered as related to the final end, ultimately, though it may be very indirectly and through a long series of intermediate ends. It does not follow that we need to know all the intermediate steps: as regards health, for instance, we do not need to know all the steps to health ourselves—the physician indeed must know them, but for his patient it is enough to be told the particular things to do, and to trust his doctor for their being means to the end, health: 1143 b 32 βουλόμενοι γὰρ ὑγιαίνειν οὐ μανθάνομεν ἰατρικήν. There are however reasons why as regards moral virtue everyone should know all the steps: we cannot be morally good without knowledge in the way we can be healthy without knowledge, and cannot place ourselves, to save trouble, in the hands of a moral physician. This question however will be discussed and explained later.

All the above is either plainly expressed in the text of VI, or can be directly and easily inferred from it. But in considering the doctrine of the final end and of the means thereto, a new question arises, the importance of which does not seem to have been grasped by Aristotle himself; and so it is not easy to tell how he answers or would have answered it. A thing may be a means to an end in either of two

---

[1] See also 1140 a 26 φρονίμου εἶναι τὸ δύνασθαι καλῶς βουλεύεσθαι περὶ τὰ αὑτῷ ἀγαθὰ καὶ συμφέροντα.

senses, as component part of it, or as wholly external to it. To take a trivial example, fire and basin and cloth are means to a pudding in the latter sense, suet and flour and currants in the former. Or again, Happiness being considered as the end, the contemplation of beautiful pictures may be considered rightly or wrongly as a means to this end in the component sense, the going to picture galleries as a means to it in the external sense: the journey may be painful, or unhealthy, or otherwise bad in itself, or at least not good in itself, and yet it may be good as a means to an end that is entirely different from and external to itself. The only place in VI, or perhaps indeed anywhere, where Aristotle appears to feel this distinction is 1144 a 3—6 ἔπειτα καὶ ποιοῦσι μὲν, οὐχ ὡς ἡ ἰατρικὴ δὲ ὑγίειαν, ἀλλ᾽ ὡς ἡ ὑγίεια οὕτως ἡ σοφία εὐδαιμονίαν· μέρος γὰρ οὖσα τῆς ὅλης ἀρετῆς τῷ ἔχεσθαι ποιεῖ καὶ τῷ ἐνεργεῖν εὐδαίμονα (if this reading is right). The usual explanation of this passage, that after ἀλλ᾽ ὡς ἡ ὑγίεια we ought to understand the words ὑγίειαν ποιεῖ, and suppose the ἕξις of ὑγίεια to be opposed to the ἐνέργεια of ὑγίεια, lays too much stress upon, and implies a difficult and unlikely antithesis between, τῷ ἔχεσθαι and τῷ ἐνεργεῖν : it also destroys the point of μέρος γὰρ οὖσα τῆς ὅλης ἀρετῆς. Two other explanations may be given. (1) Understanding ὑγίειαν ποιεῖ after ἀλλ᾽ ὡς ἡ ὑγίεια as above, we may take the meaning to be that the health of any part of the body is a means to the health of the whole body (μέρος οὖσα τῆς ὅλης ὑγιείας). (2) Or, as I think better, understand after ἀλλ᾽ ὡς ἡ ὑγίεια the words εὐδαιμονίαν ποιεῖ, when the argument becomes perfectly simple. ἰατρική, the meaning will then be, is an external means to ὑγίεια but ὑγίεια a component means to εὐδαιμονία, and σοφία and φρόνησις are component means to it in the same way. The next sentence goes on to show that φρόνησις is also an external means : and 1144 a 9—11 τοῦ δὲ τετάρτου μορίου, κτλ, which might be supposed to tell against the above interpretation of a 3—6, merely asserts that ὑγίεια (the ἀρετή of τὸ θρεπτικόν) is not an external means to Happiness : for to be an external means implies πρᾶξις, and τὸ θρεπτικόν is involuntary, and so without πρᾶξις, in all its functions. Here then is a recognition of the distinction between component and external means : it is not recognised as a general principle, but as embodied in certain particular instances, which was as far perhaps as Aristotle ever succeeded in thinking it out. Now as regards the question, In which sense is φρόνησις held by Aristotle to give knowledge of the means to Happiness? different opinions have been held and expressed by previous commentators. Stewart thinks the means are regarded as component[1], and looks on φρόνησις as the virtue by which a man perceives the harmony and adjustment of the various elements in the good character, moral and intellectual, as a whole. But the usual view is the other, that the means are external and independent : the particular act is always, it is thought, considered by Aristotle as a means of the external kind to an end wholly distinct from it. I have attempted to indicate my own view, that the two notions of means are really combined in the sixth book's definition of φρόνησις, or—as it would be truer to say—that they were never properly distinguished from each other, but were both confusedly taken into account, artificially unified by their possession of a common name.

This question is closely connected with another, one of the most fundamental in the whole book, the relation to each other of moral ἀρετή and φρόνησις. Its treatment is much confused by the way in which it is introduced in chapter xii. That chapter opens by asking of what use σοφία and φρόνησις are, how they are means, that is to say, to εὐδαιμονία the end. Two answers are given that apply alike to σοφία and φρόνησις (1144 a 1—3 and 3—6). A third follows, which applies to φρόνησις only : φρόνησις is said to be a means to εὐδαιμονία because of its necessary connection with moral ἀρετή, on the joint operation of which with φρόνησις the proper performance of man's ἔργον depends. This connection, it is said, requires very careful examination[2]: and indeed it is intricate, and it

---

[1] See for instance his note on 1144 b 16 'This clear consciousness of the moral order is the fully formed ἕξις of φρόνησις': also the last section of his note on 1144 a 6 (ii 100), and the middle paragraph on p. (ii) 76, note on 1142 a 28.

[2] 1144 a 22 λεκτέον δ' ἐπιστήσασι σαφέστερον.

later appears¹ that false views have previously been taken of
it. The attack and defence metaphor that is used at the
opening of the question—certain enemies of φρόνησις de-
nouncing it as worthless, the author on the other hand
undertaking to defend it as of great value—tends to obscure
the fact that what is here sought is still precise definition, of
φρόνησις and of ἠθικὴ ἀρετή and of their relations to each
other. And there is the peculiar difficulty, not due to any
defect of treatment, that we are required to define the relation
of two things neither of which can be perfectly defined itself
until the relation between the two has been to some extent
determined.

It has been said that good προαίρεσις or purpose is
two-fold, and this in two senses. It is the combination of
ὀρθὸς λόγος with ὀρθὴ ὄρεξις, and it implies the comprehension
of the end to be attained and also of the means whereby to
attain it. Now some people, such as Socrates, have said that
good λόγος or reasoning is all that is wanted for good
προαίρεσις and πρᾶξις, so that all moral goodness is φρόνησις:
while others say that good ὄρεξις is all that is wanted for
good προαίρεσις, so that φρόνησις is not wanted at all.
The former say that everyone is agreed on what the τέλος is,
and that the whole point is what τὰ πρὸς τὸ τέλος are, and
that people disagree on this, the wise with the foolish. The
latter say that everyone naturally sees what τὰ πρὸς τὸ τέλος
are, and that the whole point is what the τέλος is, and that
people disagree on this point, the virtuous with the vicious.
Both views, Aristotle holds, in their aim at simplifying the
notion of προαίρεσις are wrong : the true view is that προαίρεσις is essentially two-fold, is the result of the activity of the
ἄλογον (ὀρεκτικόν) and of the λόγον ἔχον (λογιστικόν) together,
and that it may be wrong as the result of wrongness in either
λόγος or ὄρεξις. It was one of Aristotle's great services to
science and philosophy that he did much to destroy the
previously accepted assumption of the simplicity of psychological phenomena.

¹ 1144 b 17—30.

G.

4

The reasoning that leads to προαίρεσις is syllogistic. The major premiss in a syllogism of this kind is a statement that such-and-such things ought to be done. It may, it is true, be expressed in the form that so-and-so is the end and ought to be attained. But such a proposition is not fit to be the major premiss of a syllogism whose conclusion is a proposition that a particular action A ought to be done: for it makes the whole syllogism take the following form—

> X is the end,
> but A is the means to X,
> therefore A ought to be done:

which though true is not clear or cogent reasoning, for there is doubt about the precise significance of the major premiss. In fact the above single syllogism is really a combination of two syllogisms—

> 1. X is the end,
> A is the means to X,
>   therefore A is the means to the end.
>
> 2. The means to the end ought to be done,
> A is the means to the end (proved),
>   therefore A ought to be done.

But as a matter of fact the proposition 'X is the end' is equivalent[1] to the proposition 'the means to X ought to be done': they are the same thing stated from different points of view. The general formula for the practical syllogism may therefore be stated both accurately and clearly as follows—

> The means to the end X ought to be done,
> but A is the means[2] to the end X,
> therefore A ought to be done.

The formation of any conclusion such as the above at once causes the particular ὄρεξις of doing the action A, which ὄρεξις, combining into a single though complex state of mind with the aforesaid reasoning, constitutes the προαίρεσις of doing the action A: whereupon the πρᾶξις or doing of the

---

[1] For practical purposes: I do not, of course, mean that the two propositions signify the same thing.

[2] This does not, of course, imply that A is the *only* means to the end X.

action *A* naturally follows in due course. Now this particular ὄρεξις of doing the action *A* cannot arise unless the general ὄρεξις, of doing the class of actions of which *A* is one, is already present. The major premiss of the syllogism is the statement of this general ὄρεξις: if the ὄρεξις is right, the major premiss is true. Right ὄρεξις is the good activity of the ἄλογον, whose good ἕξις is ἠθικὴ ἀρετή. It is then ἠθικὴ ἀρετή that makes the major premiss of the practical syllogism true. This is plainly the doctrine of 1144 a 31—36 οἱ γὰρ συλλογισμοὶ τῶν πρακτῶν...περὶ τὰς πρακτικὰς ἀρχάς: and it is also the doctrine of the passage on σωφροσύνη and φρόνησις, 1140 b 11—20 ἔνθεν καὶ τὴν σωφροσυνήν...ἡ κακία φθαρτικὴ ἀρχῆς.

Φρόνησις is, however, concerned with the formation of the major premiss, in conjunction with moral ἀρετή. Just as theoretic νοῦς by ἐπαγωγή forms universals from particulars to serve as the premisses for theoretic deduction, so practical νοῦς by ἐπαγωγή forms universals from particulars to serve as the premisses for practical deduction: 1143 b 4 ἀρχαὶ γὰρ τοῦ οὗ ἕνεκα αὗται[1]· ἐκ τῶν καθ᾽ ἕκαστα γὰρ τὰ καθόλου· τούτων οὖν ἔχειν δεῖ αἴσθησιν, αὕτη δ᾽ ἐστὶ νοῦς. The intellectual ἐπαγωγή goes along with moral ἐθισμός: the repeatedly doing or wishing to do a thing gets one into the habit of doing or wishing to do it, and repeated particular judgments that the actions *A¹ A² A³*, etc., are good combine into the universal judgment that all actions of the type *A* are good. The moral habituation and the intellectual induction are not indeed separable in practice: but they are separable logically. The statement, then, that moral ἀρετή 'makes the end right' (1144 a 7 ἡ μὲν γὰρ ἀρετὴ τὸν σκοπὸν ποιεῖ ὀρθόν, ἡ δὲ φρόνησις τὰ πρὸς τοῦτον[2]) must be modified to this extent. And since the actual stating of any proposition is an intellectual and not a moral act, the actual stating of the τέλος as the major premiss of the practical syllogism must be the work not of moral ἀρετή but of φρόνησις.

The passage 1140 b 11—20 relating to σωφροσύνη and

---

[1] sc. τὰ ἔσχατα καὶ ἐνδεχόμενα.

[2] Cf. also 1144 a 20, 1145 a 5.

φρόνησις throws some light on the subsequent doctrine that
moral ἀρετή makes the end right. Σωφροσύνη there is said
to do just what moral ἀρετή later is said to do: to preserve,
namely, the correctness of the οὗ ἕνεκα or end in view. There
is a certain danger of confusion in this connection, because
σωφροσύνη is not in general identical with moral ἀρετή, but is
one among others of the many moral ἀρεταί.

It seems possible to state Aristotle's view of the difference
between the respective relations to φρόνησις of σωφροσύνη
and ἠθικὴ ἀρετή somewhat as follows. The various moral
virtues cause men to desire various good activities: and
φρόνησις shows how the good activities are means to the
supreme good activity of happiness. This φρόνησις may or
may not be highly developed: but one thing is necessary in
any case, if it is to have free play—that the soul shall not be
led astray by pleasure or pain. For the desire of pleasure
and the shrinking from pain obtrude themselves as the
supreme end in place of the real supreme end of Happiness;
and so, however flourishing the several moral virtues may be,
or rather the several moral virtuous instincts, there can be no
power of ordering them with a view to the attainment of that
supreme end which is not in view at all so long as the desire
of pleasure or the shrinking from pain takes its place. Thus
σωφροσύνη clears and keeps open the field in which φρόνησις
and the ἠθικαὶ ἀρεταί maintain their mutual relations and act
and re-act upon each other. It is the indispensable preliminary,
and though it cannot be said itself to be quite independent of
intellectual virtue—for like other moral virtues it is a μεσότης
that is ὡρισμένη λόγῳ καὶ ᾧ ἂν ὁ φρόνιμος ὁρίσειεν—yet it is
peculiarly the result of ἐθισμός from earliest youth: 1119 a 25
ἐθισθῆναι ῥᾷον πρὸς αὐτά (sc. the temptations to ἀκολασία),
1103 b 23 οὐ μικρὸν οὖν διαφέρει τὸ οὕτως ἢ οὕτως εὐθὺς ἐκ
νέων ἐθίζεσθαι ἀλλὰ πάμπολυ μᾶλλον δὲ τὸ πᾶν, 1104 b 8
περὶ ἡδονὰς γὰρ καὶ λύπας ἐστὶν ἡ ἠθικὴ ἀρετή· διὰ μὲν γὰρ
τὴν ἡδονὴν τὰ φαῦλα πράττομεν διά τε τῶν λυπῶν τῶν καλῶν
ἀπεχόμεθα· διὸ δεῖ ἦχθαί πως εὐθὺς ἐκ νέων (ὡς ὁ Πλάτων
φησίν) ὥστε χαίρειν τε καὶ λυπεῖσθαι οἷς δεῖ· ἡ γὰρ ὀρθὴ
παίδεια αὕτη ἐστίν.

It is perhaps possible to distinguish two views of σω-φροσύνη in a way that will clear up this question. σωφροσύνη may be regarded as that ἕξις in which a man never allows his moral action to be influenced either by desire of pleasure or by avoidance of pain: or it may be regarded as that ἕξις in which he takes pleasure and pain in the right things, at the right time, to the right amount, and so on. It is when looked at in the former way that σωφροσύνη bears its peculiar relation to φρόνησις, and so to moral virtue generally, including itself as looked at in the latter way: and it is in the former way that it is looked at in this passage, 1140 b 11—20. It is then not a mean but an absolute state: not depending on φρόνησις, but securing room for the activity of φρόνησις. Viewed in the second way, σωφροσύνη simply takes its place along with the other moral virtues, is like the others a mean state, is subject to the determination of the ὀρθὸς λόγος, and refers more especially to the bodily pleasures and pains[1], whereas in the first view it seems to refer to *all* pleasures and pains. In the same way ἀκολασία has the double meaning of 'consistent pleasure-seeking' (the absolute vice, opposed to the absolute virtue which is σωφροσύνη in the former sense, that which prevents the activity of φρόνησις and destroys all conception of the true end) and 'bodily intemperance' (one of the extremes corresponding to the μέσον which is σωφροσύνη in the latter sense).

If we now return to the distinction that I have drawn between 'external' and 'component' means to an end, it will appear that φρόνησις is with equal propriety said to lead to the knowledge of the means to the great end for man, in whichever sense 'means' is understood. With regard to external means this is particularly obvious: but it is also true of component means: what I take to be Professor Stewart's view has truth in it, as well as the opposing view that is maintained, as it seems, by the majority of critics. Suppose θεωρία κατὰ σοφίαν to be admitted to be the great end for man. External means to this end will be such as

---

1 1118 a 1 περὶ δὲ τὰς σωματικὰς (ἡδονὰς) εἴη ἂν ἡ σωφροσύνη...a 24 ὧν καὶ τὰ λοιπὰ ζῷα κοινωνεῖ.

reading a certain book or talking to certain people : it is evidently φρόνησις that will give rise to the knowledge of these means. Component means will be particular acts of θεωρία κατὰ σοφίαν such as the apprehension of a geometrical proposition or demonstration. These particular acts may be performed when the mind is on the whole, as far as they are concerned, in the stage of induction and habituation, and so without reference to any universal principle stating that θεωρία κατὰ σοφίαν is the greatest good, for no such principle is as yet accepted. But the same sort of acts may be performed when the mind is in a developed state, when moral ἀρετή and φρόνησις have acted upon and completed each other, when the main universal principle of action has been formed along with such other less universal principles as may be convenient in practice to save perpetual conscious reference to the main principle, and when practical propositions are stated as the conclusions of deduction by applying the universal principle (in its ultimate or in some derived form) to particular circumstances. In the latter cases it is φρόνησις, and φρόνησις alone, that causes the knowledge that a particular act is one of a good class of actions and so a component means to the end which is (in some sense) the aggregate of such actions. The particular form of the practical syllogism that is suitable to reasoning about component means may be stated thus—

> The end is an aggregate of actions of the class A (i.e. every action of the class A is a component means to the end, and therefore ought to be done),
> but A is an action of the class A,
> therefore A ought to be done.

An instance of the syllogism of the component means is indicated 1147 a 31, ὅταν οὖν ἡ μὲν καθόλου ἐνῇ κωλύουσα γενέσθαι…ἡ μὲν οὖν λέγει φεύγειν τοῦτο. The second syllogism there mentioned, and the phenomenon of ἀκρασία, are not to the point now : but incidentally this passage exhibits the scheme of a good practical syllogism of the component means. The major premiss is not stated properly, but is equivalent to δεῖ μὴ γενέσθαι τῶν μὴ ὑγιεινῶν: the minor premiss is ἀλλὰ τοῦτο οὐχ ὑγιεινόν ἐστιν: the conclusion is δεῖ μὴ γενέσθαι τούτου, or δεῖ φεύγειν τούτου[1]. Here it is clear that the means to the end is component: for it is the avoidance of a particular unwholesome thing that is regarded as the means to the avoidance of unwholesome things in general which is the end. The perception that a particular thing is an instance of a class is obviously a purely intellectual act: such perception when right is obviously due to intellectual not to moral ἀρετή.

In chapters xii and xiii the relation to each other of φρόνησις and ἠθικὴ ἀρετή is explained by the introduction of two new conceptions, δεινότης and φυσικὴ ἀρετή. The difficulties raised thereby are less than is commonly supposed. In a note on terminology I have pointed out that the circular argument summarised in 1144 b 30—32 δῆλον οὖν ἐκ τῶν εἰρημένων ὅτι οὐχ οἷόν τε ἀγαθὸν εἶναι κυρίως ἄνευ φρονήσεως, οὐδὲ φρόνιμον ἄνευ τῆς ἠθικῆς ἀρετῆς is verbally circular, and only verbally. But the substance of the doctrine of δεινότης and φυσικὴ ἀρετή must be examined rather more closely. The nature of Aristotle's views on this subject may be best stated in the following formal fashion:

Human life involves the repeated occurrence of προαίρεσις, whether good or bad προαίρεσις. Though reasoning about practical matters may occur without desire, and desire may occur without practical reasoning, yet as a rule they combine to form προαίρεσις; and it is only in so far as they do so combine that they are ethically important and are properly said to be good or bad. But they are logically separable, and their qualities are logically separable, even when considered as in practice combined. Λόγος or reasoning may be considered in itself as good or bad: ὄρεξις or desire may be considered in itself as good or bad. Λόγος when combined with ὄρεξις remains the same in itself, it may be said, neither better nor worse than before: and the same may be said of

---

[1] The major premiss here does not of course state the great end for man: it is a καθόλου proposition, but less καθόλου than the main universal principle of action from which it is or may be syllogistically derived.

ὄρεξις when combined with λόγος. But observation shows how often it happens that (*a*) λόγος good in itself combined with ὄρεξις bad in itself produces a worse whole (the προαίρεσις) than is produced by λόγος bad in itself combined with the same ὄρεξις bad in itself, and also (*b*) ὄρεξις good in itself combined with λόγος bad in itself produces a worse whole (the προαίρεσις) than is produced by ὄρεξις bad in itself combined with the same λόγος bad in itself. In the former case the result is effectual villainy, which is worse than ineffectual villainy: in the latter case the result is (for instance) effectual fanaticism, which is worse than ineffectual fanaticism. Now it appears that the goodness or badness of λόγος and ὄρεξις in themselves cannot be their real goodness or badness: (i) on the general ground that λόγος and ὄρεξις are really only means to the end προαίρεσις (the immediate cause of πρᾶξις) and that the character of the end must determine the real character of the means: (ii) because it seems absurd that, other means being constant, a means that leads to a bad end should really be a better thing in itself than a means that leads to a good end or less bad end. It therefore follows that the real goodness or badness of λόγος and ὄρεξις is determined in part by the character of the end to which they lead : and as the character of the end is determined by the character in itself of one of the means combined with the character in itself of the other means, it follows that the character of the λόγος in itself determines the real character of the ὄρεξις and the character of the ὄρεξις in itself determines the real character of the λόγος. Now the goodness of the λόγος in itself Aristotle calls δεινότης, and the goodness of the ὄρεξις in itself he calls φυσικὴ ἀρετή (sc. ἠθική). Suppose then the λόγος and the ὄρεξις both good in themselves, then δεινότης and φυσικὴ (ἠθική) ἀρετή are present: combination with φυσικὴ (ἠθική) ἀρετή makes δεινότης into φρόνησις, and combination with δεινότης makes φυσικὴ (ἠθική) ἀρετή into κυρία (ἠθική) ἀρετή. This is simply the above truth stated in a special terminology, and with reference to the ἕξεις rather than to the activities. A certain notice is taken of the perverted προαιρέσεις and the corresponding perverted ἕξεις, which may be fully and symmetrically stated thus—

1. Combination with φυσικὴ ἠθικὴ κακία makes δεινότης into πανουργία (an intellectual vice),

2. Combination with δεινότης makes φυσικὴ ἠθικὴ κακία into κυρία ἠθικὴ κακία,

3. Combination with φυσικὴ ἠθικὴ ἀρετή makes stupidity into intellectual fanaticism or the like,

4. Combination with stupidity makes φυσικὴ ἠθικὴ ἀρετή into moral fanaticism or the like.

It only remains, as regards this question, to decide whether Aristotle regards δεινότης and φυσικὴ ἠθικὴ ἀρετή as ἕξεις or as merely δυνάμεις, a point that is obviously of some importance when we attempt to decide the relations of δεινότης to the ἕξις φρόνησις and of φυσικὴ ἀρετή to the ἕξις κυρία ἀρετή. On the one hand δεινότης is introduced as a δύναμις 1144 a 23, and in a 29 φρόνησις is said to be the corresponding ἕξις. But φυσικὴ ἠθικὴ ἀρετή is apparently a ἕξις (1144 b 9) as is further suggested by b 13 ἡ δ' ἕξις ὁμοία οὖσα τότ' ἔσται κυρίως ἀρετή. Now there seems no reason why, if δεινότης is not an intellectual ἕξις, φυσικὴ ἠθικὴ ἀρετή should be regarded as a moral ἕξις: nor conversely why, if φυσικὴ ἠθικὴ ἀρετή is a moral ἕξις, δεινότης should not be regarded as an intellectual ἕξις. It also appears that the uses of ἕξις and δύναμις are not always carefully distinguished, cf. 1143 a 25 Εἰσὶ δὲ πᾶσαι αἱ ἕξεις εὐλόγως εἰς ταὐτὸ τείνουσαι with a 28 (referring to the same things) πᾶσαι γὰρ αἱ δυνάμεις αὗται· Probably Aristotle was dimly aware of what the truth seems to be, that regarded in themselves both δεινότης and φυσικὴ ἠθικὴ ἀρετή are ἕξεις, for their qualities in themselves are fixed : but regarded with reference to each other and with reference to the end to which they are means, they are δυνάμεις, capable of having further given qualities good or bad according to the quality of what they are combined with. To take a simple illustration of my meaning—a dress may have some qualities that are or resemble ἕξεις, such as whiteness or beauty, and others that are δυνάμεις, such as comfort or utility—for it is only useful, for example, if there is someone (and that the right sort of person) to wear it. In the same way δεινότης and φυσικὴ ἠθικὴ ἀρετή have certain absolute qualities which are ἕξεις and certain relative qualities that are δυνάμεις[1].

At the end of VI Aristotle finds himself in a position to answer the question propounded at the beginning of the book, What is the ὀρθὸς λόγος that determines the μέσον that constitutes moral ἀρετή? His answer can at this point be satisfactorily discussed, though nothing has yet been said of his treatment of the subdivisions and minor forms of φρόνησις: for the latter subject has no direct bearing upon the point now to be examined.

First it must be noticed that the function of λόγος in determining the moral μέσον is a narrower one than that of φρόνησις with regard to action generally. This would be true even if activity in accordance with moral ἀρετή were the greatest good for man. For there are many external means to that end which it would be the duty of φρόνησις to determine, the determining of which is not the same function as the determining of the moral mean itself: this latter is rather the determining of the *component* means. But as a matter of fact activity in accordance with moral ἀρετή is, we learn from the tenth book, not the final end, but a means to the final end, which is θεωρία κατὰ σοφίαν. There are means to this final end, other than good moral activity, which it is the work of φρόνησις to discover and know: and in so far as φρόνησις has this other work to do, it is not the determinant of the moral μέσον, nor of any μέσον at all. So that when it is said 1144 b 27 ὀρθὸς δὲ λόγος περὶ τῶν τοιούτων ἡ φρόνησίς ἐστιν, the meaning is not that φρόνησις is nothing else but ὀρθὸς λόγος περὶ τῶν τοιούτων, but that it is this, as well as being something else besides.

With this safeguard it may now be asked how φρόνησις is held to determine the moral μέσον. Now the final end θεωρία κατὰ σοφίαν is something quite different from good moral

---

[1] Not of course that absoluteness and relativity are per se the distinguishing marks of ἕξις and δύναμις respectively.

action, and good moral actions are therefore not component but external and independent means to the end. The good-ness of such actions depends on the extent to which they are means to the end : those moral actions that best lead to the end are ipso facto best in themselves. Therefore in describing a good moral state and good moral action as being μεσότης and μέσον between extremes of excess and defect, it is implied that the quality of μεσότης or mean-ness attaching to a moral state or action is the same thing as the quality of being the best means to the end. In fact 'being a μεσότης' and 'being the ἕξις that best leads to the final end θεωρία κατὰ σοφίαν' are practically equivalent expressions and are both accurate descriptions of moral ἀρετή. But whereas the latter is signi-ficant in itself, the former is a mere abstract formula, so that the latter explains the former and not the former the latter. The full explanation is not of course given in VI, because VI only finishes the provision of materials for the conclusion in which the final end is defined, and it is only in X that the conclusion is actually drawn and justified. But except for this the question at the beginning of VI is fully answered in this book. To the question τίς ἐστιν ὁ ὀρθὸς λόγος; the answer is φρόνησις. The σκοπός on which the φρόνιμος keeps his eye, the ὅρος whereby he ὁρίζει, have yet to be found : but whatever the σκοπός and ὅρος may be, it is now known what the vague metaphors expressed by these terms really signify. To keep one's eye on the σκοπός, to measure by means of the ὅρος, signifies to consider precisely what the final end is, and to fix the μέσον accordingly between excess and defect signifies to decide what moral states or moral actions are the best means towards the attainment of that final end. VI gives an explanation fully but implicitly that X makes explicit and perfectly clear.

β. *The varieties of Practical Wisdom.*

Aristotle's account of practical intellectual ἀρετή as a whole having now been adequately examined for the present, I proceed to consider the distinctions that he draws between

various sorts of this ἀρετή : for he devotes a large part of VI
to drawing these distinctions, and this part of his teaching
contains several obscurities that must be removed if possible.

The book makes in all three different divisions of φρόνησις.
(1) That into φρόνησις proper (πρακτική) and τέχνη (ποιητική)
has already been discussed. (2) The second division has to
do with the sphere of action rather than with the kind of
action : that namely into πολιτική, οἰκονομία, φρόνησις περὶ
αὐτὸν καὶ ἕνα—practical intellectual ἀρετή as it concerns the
whole country, a single household, the individual thinker himself. These two are plainly cross-divisions, though Aristotle
does not point the fact out : the differences described in the
second division are not however affected by those described
in the first—e.g. πολιτικὴ ποίησις is different from οἰκονομικὴ
ποίησις precisely as πολιτικὴ πρᾶξις is different from οἰκονομικὴ
πρᾶξις—so that the fact of the cross-division raises no difficulties. (3) The third division is more obscure than the
second, and it is in a sense, at least for the purposes of the
Ethics, more important. It is founded on differences of
intellectual activity itself rather than on differences in the
nature or sphere of the actions to which the activity leads.
(Here again is a cross-division, crossing the other two : and
again, though for clearness' sake it is worth while to point the
fact out, the fact is not important enough to make Aristotle
wish to mention it. Both the second and the third divisions
are of φρόνησις in the broadest sense of the word, that namely
in which it ἄρχει τῆς ποιήσεως and so includes τέχνη.) The
third division includes the heads εὐβουλία, εὐστοχία, ἀγχίνοια,
σύνεσις, γνώμη, νοῦς πρακτικός : with a suggestion of φρόνησις
in a narrow sense as opposed to all of these.—The second
division will here be handled first.

Aristotle appears to have had two reasons for making
in VI the division of φρόνησις into πολιτικὴ οἰκονομία and
φρόνησις περὶ αὐτόν. (1) He has used, and will use, the
terms φρόνησις and πολιτική in very different senses from
those in which they are usually understood. This involves
the danger of confusion in his hearers' and readers' minds ; a
danger that is best prevented by clearly stating what the

popular uses of the two words are; which statement, again, is best made by the classification of the divisions of φρόνησις on the principle here adopted: for it is shown that the names φρόνησις and πολιτική when used in their popular senses properly belong to certain species of φρόνησις that are by this classification brought to light. At the same time Aristotle's own uses of those two words are justified, because it is shown that the popular uses are based on a misconception of facts, and though it is safe and even desirable to retain those popular uses so long as the facts are not misconceived, yet it is not only allowable but desirable to introduce new uses based upon the actual facts. (2) Aristotle naturally wishes to describe as explicitly as he can the nature of practical intellectual ἀρετή, just as he has been anxious in the preceding four books to describe as explicitly as he can the nature of moral ἀρετή. Now from the particular point of view that is here taken, that of the spheres of action belonging to different kinds of practical intellectual ἀρετή, he finds himself saved the trouble of being very explicit in this place: for the *Politics* will have to deal in detail with both οἰκονομία and πολιτική, while φρόνησις περὶ αὑτόν is not only (1) less important than the other two (for man is essentially a πολιτικὸν ζῷον), and closely bound up with the other two (for 1142 a 10 οὐκ ἔστι τὸ αὑτοῦ εὖ ἄνευ οἰκονομίας οὐδ' ἄνευ πολιτείας), but (2) it is actually dealt with more than the others in books II to V and VII to IX of the *Ethics*. What is, however, really wanted in this book is some indication of the connection of the *Politics* with the *Ethics* as regards this question, and this want is supplied by simply making the division here considered, which the *Politics* will afterwards explain in detail. The case is parallel with that of ἐπιστήμη, in which, as I have shown, explicit description, though formally necessary to the completeness of the argument, can practically be dispensed with, because the *Analytics* and the *Metaphysics* between them have explicitly described ἐπιστήμη already, so that all that is wanted is the ethical connection, which is given accordingly.

Chapter viii begins the division by stating the relation of πολιτική and φρόνησις, both words being used in Aristotle's own broad sense. From what immediately follows, as well as from VI as a whole and indeed from the *Ethics* as a whole, it appears that πολιτική is one kind of φρόνησις. The statement might have been put in the clearer form adopted for the distinction of ζητεῖν and βουλεύεσθαι in 1142 a 31, so as to read ἡ δὲ πολιτικὴ καὶ ἡ φρόνησις διαφέρουσιν· ἡ γὰρ πολιτικὴ φρόνησίς τίς ἐστιν: for this is the doctrine meant to be conveyed. Πολιτική is identical with ἡ περὶ πόλιν φρόνησις of the next sentence, as etymology is supposed to show without further explanation: φρόνησις comprehends πολιτική along with οἰκονομία and φρόνησις περὶ αὐτόν. Πολιτική is the only one of the three divisions of φρόνησις that is, for the present purpose, found to need further subdivision. It has two main sub-divisions, the 'architectonic' νομοθετική and the 'cheirotechnic' πολιτική—for the name πολιτική, which properly applies to the architectonic as well as the cheirotechnic φρόνησις περὶ πόλιν, is popularly restricted to the cheirotechnic. This narrower cheirotechnic πολιτική is further subdivisible into βουλευτική (in the very narrow sense of 'parliamentary' wisdom) and δικαστική. Such is the division of φρόνησις according to spheres of action.

In making this division it is found necessary to explain the meaning of the distinction between νομοθετική as architectonic and πολιτική (in the narrow sense) as cheirotechnic. The epithets imply the metaphor that best explains the difference between the two. The ἀρχιτέκτων gives commands, the χειροτέχνης carries them out in practice. The commands of the ἀρχιτέκτων are general (καθόλου), the χειροτέχνης has to consider the special circumstances (καθ᾽ ἕκαστα), and apply the general to the special to form the conclusion, which is itself special, the proposition that a particular thing (ἔσχατον) ought to be done. In politics the ἀρχιτέκτων is the legislator (νομοθέτης), whose commands are laws (νόμοι), which are καθόλου, taking no account (as the *Politics* repeatedly[1] points out) of καθ᾽ ἕκαστα or special circumstances. The administration of the laws is in the hands of the political χειροτέχναι, the practical politicians (πολιτικοί or πολιτευόμενοι) who apply

[1] See for instance 1286 a 9.

the καθόλου principle of the νόμος to the special circumstances and form a particular conclusion as to what ought to be done, which is embodied in a ψήφισμα. The ψήφισμα is καθ' ἕκαστον or ἔσχατον: it is not the thing to be done, but the legal proposition stating what the thing to be done is. It is therefore not accurately described in 1141 b 27 as πρακτόν: but probably there was at this point confusion in Aristotle's mind between the two notions τὸ γὰρ ψήφισμα περὶ τοῦ πρακτοῦ and τὸ γὰρ ψηφισθὲν πρακτόν, or he may simply be using the word πρακτόν carelessly for πρακτικόν. Τὸ ψηφισθέν, a particular action, is ἔσχατον in two senses (1) it is the ἔσχατος ὅρος of the practical syllogism, (2) it is the *last* thing arrived at in the analysis of practical deliberation.

It has been said that misconception of fact is at the bottom, and recognised by Aristotle to be at the bottom, of the narrow popular uses of φρόνησις and πολιτική. The wrong belief that has led to the narrow use of φρόνησις is that it is really better to look after one's own private interests than to take part in the government of the country. The wrong belief that has led to the narrow use of πολιτική is that the practical executor of a design really deserves more credit for it than the designer does[1]. Of these two wrong beliefs the first is definitely corrected 1142 a 9—10 καίτοι ἴσως οὐκ ἔστι τὸ αὑτοῦ εὖ ἄνευ οἰκονομίας οὐδ' ἄνευ πολιτείας. The second it is not thought worth while to correct explicitly: the way it is referred to implies that the error is obvious, 1141 b 26 ἡ ὡς τὰ καθ' ἕκαστα τὸ κοινὸν ἔχει ὄνομα, πολιτική ...πολιτεύεσθαι τούτους μόνους λέγουσιν.

It is just worth while in conclusion to point out that τὸ κοινὸν ὄνομα does not mean the same thing at 1141 b 26 and at 1141 b 31, for owing to the form in which the first statement of the chapter is made there is a slight danger that πολιτική and φρόνησις should be taken to be co-extensive and only differing in point of view (like concave and convex in the same curve). At b 26 the ὄνομα πολιτική is κοινόν to all practical intellectual ἀρετή that is περὶ πόλιν: at b 31

[1] See my article in the *C. R.* Feb. 1905, p. 17 § 8.

the ὄνομα φρόνησις is common to all practical intellectual ἀρετή whatsoever.

The third classification of φρόνησις into the varieties εὐβουλία, σύνεσις, etc., is made, and is treated with considerable fulness, also for two reasons. (1) It is desirable to make the meaning of φρόνησις explicit in this direction too, discussing it from every point of view that will help its real nature to be understood. Now in treating of the varieties in the intellectual activities themselves rather than in the spheres of those activities, practically no help can be derived from any other treatise, except here and there as in the case of ἀγχίνοια. It is therefore not enough to give the bare heads of this classification and assume that they will be or have been elsewhere explained in detail: but as with the moral ἀρεταί, so with these practical intellectual ἀρεταί, as full an explanation as is needed must be given, and given here. Hence the comparatively full treatment that this class of intellectual ἀρεταί receives. (2) Certain words in current use, either by people in general or by philosophers, seem to be names for practical intellectual ἀρετή, or for parts of it. To prevent confusion the proper meaning of these words must be fixed. If they, or any of them, are synonyms of φρόνησις, the fact should be noted: if not, their meanings must be distinguished. As it happens, there are—Aristotle finds—real distinctions between different kinds of practical intellectual activity, and between the corresponding ἀρεταί, to which these names properly belong. The regular usage of these words is a guide to the real distinctions they denote, and at the same time is the justification of the usage by which those distinctions are denoted by the names in question. Aristotle has all the ordinary Greek thinker's reverence for language as a divine creation and a guide to reality.

(a) Εὐβουλία. Since εὐβουλία is described by Aristotle in chapter ix in terms that apply, almost without exception, quite well to φρόνησις, there is some difficulty for us about determining the difference he makes between them. Εὐβουλία, it is perfectly clear, is the ἀρετή that corresponds to the good activity εὖ βουλεύεσθαι, and this is said to be the peculiar activity of the φρόνιμος: 1140 a 25 δοκεῖ δὴ φρονίμου εἶναι τὸ δύνασθαι καλῶς βουλεύσασθαι κτλ, 1141 b 9 τοῦ γὰρ φρονίμου μάλιστα τοῦτ᾽ ἔργον. εἶναί φαμεν, τὸ εὖ βουλεύεσθαι. All that distinguishes εὐβουλία from ἐπιστήμη, εὐστοχία, ἀγχίνοια, δόξα, ὀρθότης δόξης, distinguishes φρόνησις from the same things. The threefold character of εὐβουλία—οὗ δεῖ, ὥς, ὅτε —belongs to φρόνησις also, it seems: and the distinction of ἁπλῶς and πρός τι certainly applies to both alike. They are only distinguished formally in one place, the last sentence of chapter ix: and this passage, vague enough otherwise, is made obscurer still by the impossibility of feeling sure whether οὗ refers to συμφέρον or τέλος. All the editors except Professor Burnet seem to agree in referring οὗ to τὸ τέλος, and try to explain away in various fashions the apparent contradiction of the sentence, so understood, with the later statement that φρόνησις is τῶν πρὸς τὸ τέλος. The objection to this is not so much that the contradiction is unexplainable as that it is in fact unexplained by Aristotle himself. There is no gram-matical reason why συμφέρον should not be the antecedent of οὗ. If it is so, and the sentence states that εὐβουλία is ὀρθότης ἡ κατὰ τὸ συμφέρον πρὸς τὸ τέλος while φρόνησις is ἀληθὴς ὑπόληψις τοῦ συμφέροντος πρὸς τὸ τέλος, it is plain that very little help can be got from the wording of this sentence towards understanding the difference between εὐβουλία and φρόνησις: and as has been said, the rest of the chapter describes εὐβουλία for the most part in terms that apply equally well to φρόνησις, as far as can be gathered from the accounts of φρόνησις given elsewhere in the book. Certain hints may be gathered from stray passages in the chapter, but it does not seem possible to state with any confidence the real nature of the difference conceived by Aristotle to exist between φρόνησις and εὐβουλία.

In the first place, εὐβουλία is not called a ἕξις: and though this of itself does not prove that it is not considered by Aristotle to be one, yet there are indications that whereas a ἕξις is a permanent quality, εὐβουλία is thought of as a quality sometimes present and sometimes absent. A careful distinc-tion is drawn between the activity of the mind as searching and inquiring into the truth of something, and the activity of the mind as having finished the search and being in possession of the truth as the result, or at any rate of some conclusion believed to be the truth: and it is inferred that the corresponding qualities of the mind are similarly distinguishable. The same point is made in the three statements (1142 b 11—14)

(1) δόξης δ' ὀρθότης ἀλήθεια,

(2) ὥρισται ἤδη πᾶν οὗ δόξα ἐστίν,

(3) καὶ γὰρ ἡ δόξα οὐ ζήτησις ἀλλὰ φάσις τις ἤδη:

with which contrast the statements about εὐβουλία,

(1) οὐδ' ἄνευ λόγου ἡ εὐβουλία,

(2) διανοίας ἄρα λείπεται (τὴν εὐβουλίαν ὀρθότητα εἶναι),

(3) ὁ βουλευόμενος ζητεῖ τι καὶ λογίζεται· ἀλλ' ὀρθότης τίς ἐστιν ἡ εὐβουλία βουλῆς.

Emphasis is laid on the time to be taken over the deliberative process corresponding to εὐβουλία: a certain amount of time must be taken, δεῖ γὰρ βουλεύεσθαι βραδέως (1142 b 5), but not too much (b 26—28). Εὐβουλία thus seems to be regarded as a quality of the searching, unsatisfied, inquiring mind. But the mind is not always engaged in the activity of searching: and when it is not, the quality of εὐβουλία does not seem to be considered to attach to it: the quality comes and goes with the activity. But φρόνησις is a quality of the satisfied as well as of the inquiring mind. It is the part of the φρόνιμος to possess and to reflect upon and to be stating to himself those φάσεις, ὀρθαὶ δόξαι about τὸ συμφέρον πρὸς τὸ τέλος, to which previous deliberation has led him. This is implied by saying (1142 b 33) that φρόνησις is the ἀληθὴς ὑπόληψις of the συμφέρον: ὑπόληψις implies φάσις (i.e. κατάφασις or ἀπόφασις), whether that φάσις is the result of knowledge or of mere opinion, and is true or untrue. This is also suggested by 1140 b 26 δυοῖν δ' ὄντοιν μεροῖν τῆς ψυχῆς τῶν λόγον ἐχόντων, θατέρου ἂν εἴη ἀρετή (sc. ἡ φρόνησις), τοῦ δοξαστικοῦ· ἥ τε γὰρ δόξα περὶ τὸ ἐνδεχόμενον ἄλλως ἔχειν καὶ ἡ φρόνησις. On the other hand the notion of φρόνησις clearly includes that of εὐβουλία just stated: for the activity εὖ βουλεύεσθαι περὶ τοῦ ἀγαθοῦ is more plainly and oftener attributed to the φρόνιμος than the activity ὀρθῶς δοξάζειν περὶ τοῦ ἀγαθοῦ. So that εὐβουλία must, it seems, be dis- tinguished from φρόνησις as part from whole: in fact it might be said ἡ εὐβουλία καὶ ἡ φρόνησις διαφέρουσιν· ἡ γὰρ εὐβουλία φρόνησίς τίς ἐστιν—not however of course φρόνησις κατὰ μέρος, but a part or aspect of φρόνησις ἁπλῶς. The very close connection of εὐβουλία with φρόνησις that this view involves helps to account for the formal carelessness in the omission of εὐβουλία from the list of ἕξεις εἰς ταὐτὸ τείνουσαι (1143 a 25): for whatever is true in that connection of φρόνησις is a fortiori true of εὐβουλία.

(β) Σύνεσις. The main point about σύνεσις is contained in the words 1143 a 8 ἡ μὲν γὰρ φρόνησις ἐπιτακτική ἐστιν· τί γὰρ δεῖ πράττειν ἢ μὴ τὸ τέλος αὐτῆς ἐστίν· ἡ δὲ σύνεσις κριτικὴ μόνον: and in the words ἄλλου λέγοντος (1143 a 15). Σύνεσις is quite detached from ὄρεξις and so from προαίρεσις: that this is implied by κριτική appears tolerably plain, if the evidence of a later work can be accepted as testifying to an earlier usage, from *Animal Motion*, 700 b 18—24, where τὰ κινοῦντα τὸ ζῷον are enumerated, διάνοια φαντασία προαίρεσις βούλησις ἐπιθυμία: ταῦτα δὲ πάντα, it is said, ἀνάγεται εἰς νοῦν καὶ ὄρεξιν. καὶ γὰρ ἡ φαντασία καὶ ἡ αἴσθησις τὴν αὐτὴν τῷ νῷ χώραν ἔχουσιν· κριτικὰ γὰρ πάντα...βούλησις δὲ καὶ θυμὸς καὶ ἐπιθυμία πάντα ὄρεξις, ἡ δὲ προαίρεσις κοινὸν διανοίας καὶ ὀρέξεως. Φρόνησις on the other hand, as has been fully shown already, though not composed of ὄρεξις, depends for its peculiar character on its relation with ὄρεξις: the man who never makes a προαίρεσις cannot be φρόνιμος, but he may (theoretically speaking) be συνετός. The connection of the notion of κριτική with that of ἄλλου λέγοντος is made in the *Parts of Animals* 639 a 4 πεπαιδευμένου γάρ ἐστι κατὰ τρόπον τὸ δύνασθαι κρῖναι εὐστόχως τί καλῶς ἢ μὴ καλῶς ἀποδίδωσιν ὁ λέγων...πλὴν τοῦτον μὲν περὶ πάντων ὡς εἰπεῖν κριτικόν τινα νομίζομεν εἶναι ἕνα τὸν ἀριθμὸν ὄντα, τὸν δὲ περὶ τινος φύσεως ἀφωρισμένης. The last words throw some light on the special sense of περὶ τὰ πρακτά in which σύνεσις is said in VI to be περὶ τὰ πρακτά. It is admitted (1143 a 12—13, 16—18) that σύνεσις may be

5—2

concerned with the objects of ἐπιστήμη (in the strict sense of the word ἐπιστήμη), that is, with μὴ ἐνδεχόμενα ἄλλως ἔχειν, which are μὴ πρακτά. But Aristotle sees reason to reject such a usage of the word σύνεσις, or at least to recognise as particularly definite and appropriate the usage introduced here, that namely of σύνεσις as πρακτική. He does not justify this by saying that ordinary usage regards σύνεσις as πρακτική: on the contrary, he says that the usage of σύνεσις as μὴ πρακτική is the original one and is still common (a 16 ἐντεῦθεν κτλ, a 17 λέγομεν γὰρ τὸ μανθάνειν συνιέναι πολλάκις): his proceeding is therefore purely arbitrary as far as can be seen, but probably, though he does not say so, the usage of σύνεσις as πρακτική had by his time become the more common in ordinary speech.

The συνετός, it appears, does not himself deliberate. He listens to the reasoning set forth by others who have deliberated: he comprehends the meaning of their syllogisms, and he forms at the end an opinion that they are right, or that they are wrong, as the case may be. But he does not, qua συνετός, go beyond this—he does not use what he has heard from others, or the opinion at which he himself arrived, to construct a practical syllogism with a conclusion that is ἐπιτακτικόν, stating something that he ought to do. The man who does go on to do this is not, in so far as he does so, συνετός but φρόνιμος. The object of the συνετός, the end of his peculiar activity, is in the words of chapter ii ἀλήθεια only and not ἀλήθεια ὁμολόγως ἔχουσα τῇ ὀρέξει τῇ ὀρθῇ, though it is ἀλήθεια περὶ τῶν πρακτῶν. There are then two distinguishing marks of σύνεσις: (1) its activity consists in judging the results of the deliberation of others, (2) its activity does not end in an ἐπιτακτικόν conclusion of the form ' I must do this.' Its relation to φρόνησις is only vaguely indicated by the words 1143 a 6 διὸ περὶ τὰ αὐτὰ μὲν τῇ φρονήσει ἐστίν, οὐκ ἔστι δὲ τὸ αὐτὸ σύνεσις καὶ φρόνησις. This would be quite consistent with holding σύνεσις to be a kind or part of φρόνησις according to the formula of 1142 a 31 already quoted several times. And this it may be allowed to be, and to be considered by Aristotle to be, if one considers, as no doubt Aristotle did to some extent, that to judge the deliberations of others one must in a way go through all the steps of their deliberations in one's own mind, and also that, since the advice of others may and in practice often does guide people in the forming of their conclusions as to what ought to be done, the critical activity of the συνετός may lead ultimately to ἐπίταξις though immediately only to κρίσις.

(γ) Γνώμη. The whole passage dealing with this subject is so badly stated that it is hard to believe Aristotle had his meaning at all clear in his own mind. The *Great Ethics* has a very clear section[1] dealing with ἐπιείκεια, and with γνώμη or rather εὐγνωμοσύνη, which are related as moral ἀρετή and intellectual ἀρετή, and are in fact a special case of moral ἀρετή and φρόνησις as treated in chapters xii and xiii of VI: but it is not possible to read the clearness of that passage into the confusion of this one. It may be noticed that γνώμη is κριτική, like σύνεσις: it is therefore distinguished from φρόνησις (which is ἐπιτακτική) in the same way. It is not however said to be distinguished from φρόνησις as being ἄλλου λέγοντος κρίσις, whether this distinction is intended or not. On the other hand it is distinguished from φρόνησις in a way in which σύνεσις is not, for while the πρακτά with which σύνεσις has to do are the whole class of πρακτά and so are coextensive with the objects of the activity of φρόνησις, the πρακτά with which γνώμη is concerned are only a part of the whole. Any sort of πρᾶξις that is πρὸς ἄλλον may give an opening for ἐπιείκεια (1143 a 31 τὰ γὰρ ἐπιεικῆ κοινὰ τῶν ἀγαθῶν ἁπάντων ἐστὶν ἐν τῷ πρὸς ἄλλον), but it must be πρὸς ἄλλον, and not every πρᾶξις that is πρὸς ἄλλον *necessarily* gives an opening for ἐπιείκεια. The result of this is that γνώμη also may fairly be considered a kind or part of φρόνησις: different from it, but as the part is different from the whole.

(δ) Νοῦς πρακτικός. The word νοῦς is, up to chapter xi, used to mean either of two different things: (1) the whole διανοητικὸν μέρος of the soul, or the activity of that μέρος; (2) the ἀρετή of the ἐπιστημονικὸν μέρος of the διανοητικὸν μέρος, which leads to the statement of universal invariable

---

[1] 1198 b 24—1199 a 3.

undemonstrable truths by correct induction from appropriate
particular true propositions. A third use is considered in
chapter xi co-ordinate with the second, and related to the first
as the second is related to the first. An example of this use
is given by the phrase νοῦν ἔχειν, which means 'to be sensible,'
'to have good sense about some practical matter of conduct.'
For practical deductive reasoning, as for unpractical, premisses
are required that cannot ultimately be deduced from previous
propositions of a more general kind. The ultimate major
premiss of practical reasoning is the statement of the οὗ ἕνεκα
or the final end of action. Analogy would lead us to suppose
that this καθόλου proposition is formed by induction from
καθ' ἕκαστον propositions, just as the καθόλου propositions
that relate to μὴ ἐνδεχόμενα ἄλλως ἔχειν are formed by
induction from καθ' ἕκαστον propositions. This does in fact
appear to be the case; the phenomena of ἐθισμός or habituation
are well-known, and habituation is not only a kind of moral
induction itself but is accompanied by an intellectual process
that is inductive in the strict sense. By doing particular good
things a man acquires the habit of doing such things as a rule
—this is a moral induction: by believing particular things to be
good he acquires the general belief that all such things are
good—this is an intellectual induction. This is precisely
expressed by the two lines 1143 b 4—5 ἀρχαὶ γάρ...αὕτη δ᾽
ἐστὶ νοῦς. Νοῦς πρακτικός is the intellectual ἀρετή that leads
to particular true judgments about practical matters—of the
type 'this action A is good'—being generalised by induction
into universal true judgments and finally into the grand
universal judgment of the nature of the final end. The
particular true judgments must be made directly, just like
sensations : it may in fact be said that the making of them is
αἴσθησις of them (1143 b 5 τούτων οὖν ἔχειν δεῖ αἴσθησιν).
The details of the inductive process are not discussed here
any more than in chapter vi : it is not said whether only such
particular judgments are made as are useful for the induction
to the universal, or whether of all that are made a certain
number are selected as useful for the induction, or whether
the induction is the result of all particular judgments ever

made. This omission is of course only one instance of Aristotle's failure to work out the theory of induction.

The account of νοῦς in the previous lines 1143 a 35—b 3 is obscure enough. The words καὶ γὰρ τῶν πρώτων ὅρων καὶ τῶν ἐσχάτων νοῦς ἐστί go awkwardly with the preceding words ὁ νοῦς τῶν ἐσχάτων ἐπ' ἀμφότερα: for they imply that νοῦς is in one sense τῶν ἐσχάτων in being τῶν πρώτων ὅρων, and in the other sense τῶν ἐσχάτων in being τῶν ἐσχάτων. The word ἔσχατα can hardly mean different things in the two sentences; the formal awkwardness involved in supposing a change would be as great as the material difficulty in the argument otherwise. The best way out of the trouble is to suppose that in the words a 36 τῶν πρώτων ὅρων νοῦς ἐστί, which refer to non-practical induction, the results, the universal propositions, which are ἀκίνητοι πρῶτοι ὅροι, are mentioned, and the materials of the induction, the particular propositions, ἔσχατα, are not mentioned : while in the following words, a 36 καὶ τῶν ἐσχάτων νοῦς ἐστί, the universal propositions, the statements of the οὗ ἕνεκα, are not mentioned, and the materials of the induction, the particular propositions, are mentioned : whereas in b 35 ὁ νοῦς τῶν ἐσχάτων ἐπ' ἀμφότερα, it is the particular propositions that are the materials for the inductions which are mentioned as applying to both sorts of induction.

The second difficulty is raised by the words καὶ τῆς ἑτέρας προτάσεως. Ἡ ἑτέρα πρότασις it is hard to take as meaning anything but the minor premiss of the practical syllogism. But the stating of this minor premiss lies entirely outside the process of induction. In itself it is the intellectual expression of an action of direct perception or sensation (cf. 1142 a 26—30), and it is made as an element of deductive and not inductive practical reasoning. It does not involve a moral judgment at all. The major premiss *is* a moral judgment—'Such-and-such actions ought to be done' or 'Such-and-such is the end': but the minor premiss is not—'The action *A* is such an action' or 'The action *A* is the best means to that end.' Yet the following words (1143 b 4—5), as I have already pointed out, clearly refer to the major premiss and to the particular judgments from which by induction the major premiss is derived. It is perhaps best to suppose that stress is laid on the feature common to the propositions that form minor premisses and those that are the materials for induction—namely, that they are not universal but particular propositions: both the ἕτεραι προτάσεις and the ἀρχαὶ τοῦ οὗ ἕνεκα are ἔσχατα. This is at any rate the fact required to be shown for the purpose of the argument, which is to show that νοῦς is τῶν ἐσχάτων ἐπ' ἀμφότερα. Practical νοῦς has to do with particular contingent (ἐνδεχόμενα) propositions, as distinguished from theoretic νοῦς which has to do with particular invariable (ἀκίνητα) propositions; the common property of both kinds of νοῦς is that they have to do with particular propositions. The use of these particular propositions as material for induction is not exactly common to both: for while θεωρητικὸς νοῦς always so uses them, πρακτικὸς νοῦς so uses them only sometimes, in forming the practical universals that are major premisses of practical syllogisms, and at other times uses them in deductions as minor premisses. The words καὶ τῆς ἑτέρας προτάσεως· ἀρχαὶ γὰρ τοῦ οὗ ἕνεκα αὗται may be paraphrased—'Such propositions are used as minor premisses in practical syllogisms and also as materials for forming the statements of the end of action that are used as major premisses in practical syllogisms.' The same explanation must be given of the difficult passage 1142 a 25—30, where φρόνησις, in so far as it is αἰσθητικὴ τοῦ ἐσχάτου, is said to correspond to νοῦς θεωρητικός, and is evidently identical with νοῦς πρακτικός of 1143 b 2. This identification is made easier by the fact that the guiding principle of the whole passage 1143 a 25—b 5 is the general sameness of φρόνησις and νοῦς and other such qualities.

Practical νοῦς, then, is the intellectual ἀρετή that leads to the making of true particular propositions suitable for, and as means to, good practical induction or deduction. Thus it is also φρόνησίς τις, one kind or part of the whole intellectual ἀρετή that leads to truth about practical matters.

(ε) Εὐστοχία and Ἀγχίνοια. These two good qualities are briefly spoken of in connection with εὐβουλία. They are like εὐβουλία (according to the explanation of εὐβουλία already given) in being qualities that belong to the mind as trying to reach truth and not as having reached it. The general characteristic of εὐστοχία is that it leads to rapid arriving at some truth without any consciousness of intermediate steps of reasoning. Ἀγχίνοια[1] is the particular kind of εὐστοχία that leads to the rapid discovery of the reason for something without any consciousness of intermediate steps of reasoning. Such qualities can of course be exercised in theoretic as well as in practical thinking, and if they are considered in chapter ix as practical, it is because they are there being contrasted with εὐβουλία which is necessarily practical. They are probably mentioned partly to help to define εὐβουλία, partly to prevent the loose use of either word as a synonym for φρόνησις, partly to throw light on a distinct though not very important variety of intellectual ἀρετή. In so far as they are concerned with πρᾶξις they come, like εὐβουλία, under the general head of φρόνησις.

D. THE RELATION OF INTELLECTUAL GOODNESS TO HAPPINESS.

The main question of the *Ethics*, What is the greatest good for man? is directly handled only in a comparatively small part of the whole work. Before the end of the first book it is found to depend on a number of other questions that must first be answered, and it is not till the middle of the last book that it is taken up again. Only here and there in the intervening books are there signs of its being borne in mind. Some such signs occur in VI, but not many: and there are more references backward to the subject of VI in X vi—viii —those important chapters in which the nature of Happiness is fully and finally explained—than anticipations in VI of the coming discussion in X. So that when it is asked, What has intellectual goodness to do with happiness? and how does the knowledge of what intellectual goodness is help to the knowledge of what happiness is? it is X rather than VI that

[1] See *Analytics* 89 b 10.

supplies the answer. It will therefore be desirable, after noticing one or two signs in VI that the main question is not forgotten there, to consider the extent to which X vi—viii refers to, agrees with, and depends upon the statements of VI. By this means it will become clear how far these two discussions may be taken together as presenting a consistent view of the relation of intellectual goodness to happiness, and it will be easier to see what that relation is.

The chief indications in VI that the main question of the *Ethics* is remembered are as follows:—(1) VI i opens with a reminder that the final end for man has yet to be found. Since moral goodness is relative to that final end and not absolute, and since nothing that is relative to another thing can be fully known until the other thing is known, the nature of moral goodness cannot be fully known until the nature of the final end is known. Not only the ὀρθὸς λόγος has to be discovered, but also the σκοπός to which it refers, the ὅρος τῶν μεσοτήτων. This σκοπός or ὅρος is of course Happiness, the final end. (2) In opening the subject of intellectual goodness Aristotle does not indeed refer to the obvious reason for doing so, that in order to answer the main question we must know what the best and completest goodness is and that therefore the nature of intellectual as well as moral goodness must be understood. But ἡ ἀρετὴ πρὸς τὸ ἔργον τὸ οἰκεῖον (1139 a 16), and ἀμφοτέρων δὴ τῶν νοητικῶν μορίων ἀλήθεια τὸ ἔργον (1139 b 12), are statements that recognise the principle of I vii, where it is said that the way to learn what εὐδαιμονία is will be to see what τὸ ἔργον τοῦ ἀνθρώπου is (1097 b 24). VI ii is an argument in exact accord with this principle, for its object is to fix generally the ἔργον of each part of the intellect. Ἀλήθεια, it declares, is this ἔργον: and the final words, 1139 b 12 καθ' ἃς οὖν μάλιστα ἕξεις ἀληθεύσει ἑκάτερον (sc. νοητικὸν μόριον) αὗται ἀρεταὶ ἀμφοῖν, are simply a special application of the general statement of 1097 b 26 ἐν τῷ ἔργῳ δοκεῖ τἀγαθὸν εἶναι καὶ τὸ εὖ. (3) Φρόνησις is according to VI περὶ τὰ ἀγαθὰ καὶ κακὰ ἀνθρώπῳ. This implies that φρόνησις leads to knowledge of the best thing of all for man, and indeed in one place the use of the

superlative expresses this doctrine openly: 1141 b 12 ὁ δ'
ἁπλῶς εὔβουλος ὁ τοῦ ἀρίστου ἀνθρώπῳ τῶν πρακτῶν στοχαστικὸς κατὰ τὸν λογισμόν. (4) The conception of εὐδαιμονία
as the end is introduced quite definitely in chapters xii and
xiii: 1143 b 19 ἡ σοφία οὐδὲν θεωρήσει ἐξ ὧν ἔσται εὐδαίμων
ἄνθρωπος, 1144 a 3—5 οὕτως ἡ σοφία (sc. ποιεῖ) εὐδαιμονίαν...
6 ποιεῖ καὶ τῷ ἐνεργεῖν εὐδαίμονα: and the major premiss of
the practical syllogism is said to be a statement of the final
end: 1144 a 31 οἱ γὰρ συλλογισμοὶ τῶν πρακτῶν ἀρχὴν
ἔχοντές εἰσιν, ἐπειδὴ τοιόνδε τὸ τέλος καὶ τὸ ἄριστον.—The
above special passages show that in VI the scheme of inquiry
laid down in I is consciously adhered to, and the final discussion of X anticipated. It is not hard to see that the general
tenor of VI is consistent with the main purpose of the *Ethics*.

The main question, What is Happiness? is taken up
in X vi in the following way. Certain results of I are recapitulated: that εὐδαιμονία is not a ἕξις but an ἐνέργεια,
that it must be good in itself and not a means to anything
else. In the light of the examination of ἀρετή that has
occupied a large part of the *Ethics*, it is pronounced that αἱ
κατ' ἀρετὴν πράξεις satisfy the above two conditions. The
suggestion that certain kinds of παιδία or amusement also
satisfy those conditions is examined carefully and rejected:
παιδίαι may be good as means, but not as ends: whereas αἱ
κατ' ἀρετὴν πράξεις are good as ends. Chapter vii carries
the argument further. The next step is again one that has
been taken already in I: it was there shown that if there are
more ἀρεταί than one, εὐδαιμονία must be ἐνέργεια according
to the best and completest ἀρετή: this conclusion is simply
repeated in X vii, 1177 a 12 εὔλογον κατὰ τὴν κρατίστην (sc.
ἀρετὴν εἶναι τὴν εὐδαιμονίαν ἐνέργειαν): only it is now known,
what was not known before, that there are in fact more ἀρεταί
than one. The step after this, αὕτη δ' ἂν εἴη τοῦ ἀρίστου, is a
new one: neither in I nor elsewhere has it been said that the
goodness of an ἀρετή is proportional to the goodness of that
of which it is the ἀρετή. This principle is however, if not
openly expressed, at least tacitly assumed in VI[1]. The objects

---

1 Whether or not the principle is sound need not be discussed here.

of the activity of σοφία are shown to be better in themselves than the objects of the activity of φρόνησις: σοφία therefore better than φρόνησις (1141 a 20, 1143 b 34): the part of the soul whose ἀρετή is σοφία therefore better than the part whose ἀρετή is φρόνησις (1145 a 6 ἀλλὰ μὴν οὐδὲ κυρία γ' ἐστὶ (sc. ἡ φρόνησις) τῆς σοφίας οὐδὲ τοῦ βελτίονος μορίου). The nature of τὸ ἄριστον μέρος τῆς ψυχῆς is the next thing described in X vii, in terms that evidently refer to the results of a discussion of intellectual ἀρετή, which can be nothing else than VI if that book—as I have elsewhere tried to show—is Aristotle's work and a genuine part of the Ethics. The ἄριστον μέρος is said (1177 a 13) to be either νοῦς or ἄλλο τι ὃ δὴ κατὰ φύσιν δοκεῖ ἄρχειν καὶ ἡγεῖσθαι καὶ ἔννοιαν ἔχειν περὶ καλῶν καὶ θείων, εἴτε θεῖον ὂν καὶ αὐτὸ εἴτε τῶν ἐν ἡμῖν τὸ θειότατον. The vagueness of this reference to the results of VI is corrected in an external sort of fashion by the next sentence: ὅτι δ' ἐστὶ θεωρητική, εἴρηται. It has been maintained indeed that the ἐνέργεια of the best part of the soul has not, in spite of the assertion here, been said to be θεωρητική: and it may be said that νοῦς is not in VI the name of the part of the soul whose ἀρετή is σοφία and which is said to be the best part of the soul. I shall now try to remove these objections, to show that the θεωρητικὴ ἐνέργεια τοῦ ἀρίστου μέρους τῆς ψυχῆς κατὰ τὴν οἰκείαν ἀρετήν is θεωρία κατὰ σοφίαν according to the definition of σοφία in VI, and generally that X vi—viii is consistent with, and uses, the results obtained in VI.

(a) It is actually implied, and that unmistakably, in X vi—viii, that εὐδαιμονία is intellectual activity κατὰ σοφίαν. Thus at 1177 a 23, arguing that the definition of εὐδαιμονία just given satisfies the requirement that the happy life should be a pleasurable one, Aristotle says ἡδίστη δὲ τῶν κατ' ἀρετὴν ἐνεργειῶν ἡ κατὰ τὴν σοφίαν ὁμολογουμένως ἐστίν· δοκεῖ γοῦν ἡ φιλοσοφία θαυμαστὰς ἡδονὰς ἔχειν: here the use of φιλοσοφία as a synonym of σοφία proves that σοφία means here what it means in VI, for σοφία in VI and φιλοσοφία in the Metaphysics have the same three divisions θεολογική (σοφία in the narrow sense 1142 a 17) μαθηματική φυσική

(*Ethics* 1142 a 17—18, *Metaphysics* 1026 a 18—19), and so are plainly the same thing. Again, at 1177 a 30—34, the δίκαιος, the σώφρων, the ἀνδρεῖος, and the exponents of practical ἀρετή generally, are contrasted with the σοφός. The term σοφός is also used of the θεωρητικός twice at the end of chapter viii : 1179 a 29 πάντα ταῦτα τῷ σοφῷ μάλιστ' ὑπάρχει, a 32 ὁ σοφὸς μάλιστ' εὐδαίμων. As it is only in VI that σοφός and σοφία are marked off as theoretic, it is plain that X vi—viii makes use of the results there obtained.

(*b*) It is true that nowhere in VI is θεωρία κατὰ σοφίαν in so many words said to be θεωρητική. But there is nothing to show that Aristotle is laying stress on the actual use of the term θεωρητικός when he says ὅτι δ' ἐστὶ θεωρητικὴ εἴρηται. He may just as well mean that the activity of the best part of the soul has been shown to possess certain qualities which are (he now implies) expressed by the epithet θεωρητικός. The θεωρητικὸς βίος was opposed in I (1095 b 19, 1096 a 4) to the πολιτικὸς βίος, and as VI shows (indeed states) that the πολιτικὴ ἀρετή is φρόνησις, it must imply that the θεωρητικὴ ἀρετή is σοφία. Again, 1139 a 27 calls the non-practical intellect θεωρητική, opposing it to the πρακτική : and the inference that the activities of these two parts of the intellect may be given the same epithets is not a difficult one.

(*c*) It is true that in VI the best part of the soul, whose ἀρετή is σοφία, is not called νοῦς. It is called τὸ ἐπιστημονικόν in VI, or τὸ βελτίον μόριον, whereas νοῦς in VI is the name of the intellect as a whole, or of one ἀρετή or one part of the ἀρετή of the ἐπιστημονικόν, or in one passage (1143 a 25— b 5) of one ἀρετή of the λογιστικόν, or (as at 1144 b 12 ἐὰν δὲ λάβῃ νοῦν) of the ἀρετή of the λογιστικόν as a whole : but νοῦς never in VI is used to mean τὸ ἐπιστημονικόν. But this need cause no trouble. Νοῦς in X vii is probably used (in much the same sense as in VI ii) to mean the intellect in general, and is distinguished from the inferior part of the soul, whose ἐνέργεια is πρακτική, in the same way as, in VI ii, διάνοια αὐτή is distinguished from διάνοια conjoined with ὄρεξις. And in any case the words (1177 a 14) εἴτε ἄλλο τι show that Aristotle attaches no importance to the question of terminology, and is ready to employ a term of traditional dignity where a term of dignity is wanted, even at the sacrifice of consistent usage.

(*d*) A number of details in x vi—viii show agreement with or dependence upon the doctrine of vi and the form in which it is there expressed. (i) 1177 a 15 ἔννοιαν ἔχειν περὶ καλῶν καὶ θείων agrees with the description in vi of the objects of σοφία as τὰ τιμιώτατα (1141 a 20), τὰ θειότατα τὴν φύσιν (implied by 1141 b 1), θαυμαστὰ χαλεπὰ δαιμόνια (1141 b 6). (ii) The opposition of οἱ εἰδότες (1177 a 26) to οἱ ζητοῦντες accords with vi, where σοφία is not said to lead to good searching into truth, but to the contemplation of it when known, which is regarded as a better thing : whereas the goodness of φρόνησις is essentially productive of good βούλευσις (a form of ζήτησις, as is said at 1142 a 31). (iii) The relation between φρόνησις (which has in x the precise meaning of practical intellectual ἀρετή given it in vi) and ἠθικὴ ἀρετή, determined with great care in vi xii—xiii, is accurately recapitulated 1178 a 16—19, the previous discussion of it obviously assumed. (iv) Just as at the end of vi φρόνησις is said to be a means to the production of σοφία (1145 a 8 ὁρᾷ ὅπως γένηται), so the πολιτικὸς βίος is said to be a means to the production of εὐδαιμονία (1177 b 12—15), which is only another way of stating the same fact.

If the facts given above are enough to show what they are intended to show, that vi and x vi—viii are in the main thoroughly consistent with each other, the way is clear for considering how intellectual ἀρετή (the subject of vi) is related to εὐδαιμονία (the subject of x vi—viii) : for it is from these two portions of the *Ethics* that most or all of the available information about the relation in question will naturally be obtained. The nature of intellectual ἀρετή in itself, the proper subject of vi, I have examined already. The relation of intellectual ἀρετή to εὐδαιμονία is now to be considered, and for this purpose it will be necessary to look carefully at certain of the arguments and conclusions of x vi—viii, where the nature of εὐδαιμονία is set forth.

It must be observed that these chapters are taken up not

so much with describing the particular activity, θεωρία κατὰ σοφίαν, which according to them is εὐδαιμονία, as in making good its claim to be εὐδαιμονία and disputing the claim of other activities to share the distinction with it. What θεωρία κατὰ σοφίαν is has been described in VI, for in describing the ἀρετή that book described the ἐνέργεια κατὰ τὴν ἀρετήν: and VI in its turn, as has been remarked elsewhere, really only applies the information set forth not there but in the Logical, Metaphysical and Physical treatises. In the same way θεωρία κατὰ τὴν ἄλλην ἀρετήν, which together with πρᾶξις κατὰ τὴν ἄλλην ἀρετήν makes, we are told, an inferior kind of εὐδαιμονία, is not in the same three chapters described in itself at any length, for it has been described in II—VI, and VII—IX and the early part of X have all helped to throw light on it : what the three chapters X vi—viii have to do is to apply the results of those books to show how far it is, and how far it is not, a part of εὐδαιμονία the greatest good for man.

The nature of ideal εὐδαιμονία, as set forth in X vi—viii, is not hard to see. It is, as the general definition of εὐδαιμονία in I required that it should be found to be, a pure ψυχῆς ἐνέργεια. It has not, properly speaking, anything to do with any ἐνέργεια of the body or any other ἐνέργεια of the soul— that is, it is independent of all πρᾶξις and of all other kinds of θεωρία : these are only connected with it as servants with their master. It is, according to the doctrine that the best part of a man constitutes his real self, truly human : for it is the activity of the best part of the soul, the theoretic intellect. If human beings were so constituted, and placed in such conditions, that this best part of them could exercise its activity equally well no matter what happened to all the rest of them, there would be no need to carry the inquiry further : no activity of mind or body, except the contemplation of eternal truth, would be necessary either as an ingredient part of happiness or as an external means to its production.

But it is in truth only in a rather mystical and unreal sense that a man can be said to be the best part of himself and that only : the very words in which the statement is made show how inconsistent it is with the plain facts. Man is a composite being, composite of better and worse, and whatever his happiness might be under ideal conditions, under actual conditions it cannot be attained by cultivating one part of himself, even though that be the best, to the neglect of the other parts, even though these be in themselves inferior. His soul is like a household made up of master and servants: the master is the best part of the household, but the happiness of the household will not be secured by neglecting the well-being of the servants. The goodness of the inferior parts of the soul, and their activity according to that goodness, are necessary to the happiness of man, simply because he is a composite being, the divine and the animal intermixed. The question is whether the goodness and good activity of the inferior parts should be considered actual ingredients of the happiness of the composite man, or merely external means to that happiness, made necessary by the fact that man is composite. It will be easier to answer this question after seeing as far as possible what Aristotle takes the goodness and good activity of the inferior parts to be.

The goodness consists in a combination of moral goodness with a certain kind of intellectual goodness, and its nature has been accurately and fully described in the last two chapters of VI. The consequent activity is good προαίρεσις or purpose—the intention of doing certain good things that is the result of the intellectual perception that they ought to be done and the desire to do them. In a sense the making of this kind of προαίρεσις is the whole good activity, and in a sense it is incomplete. Aristotle recognises the difficulty of deciding whether it is the purpose or the fulfilment of the purpose that is really important and that determines the happiness of man in so far as happiness depends on this part of the soul: 1178 a 34 ἀμφισβητεῖταί τε πότερον κυριώτερον τῆς ἀρετῆς ἡ προαίρεσις ἢ αἱ πράξεις, ὡς ἐν ἀμφοῖν οὔσης. He returns answer, with more confidence than he gives grounds for, τὸ δὴ τέλειον δῆλον ὡς ἐν ἀμφοῖν ἂν εἴη. This happiness, then, is not a mere activity of the soul—it depends on the activity of the body as well, if it is to be 'complete.' It does not, therefore, fulfil the requirement of the definition in I that happiness should be an ἐνέργεια τῆς ψυχῆς, for that definition implies that it should not be the ἐνέργεια of anything but the soul, even in part: this inferior happiness does not, in short, deserve the name of happiness as much as the superior kind deserves it. This conclusion is indeed regarded as sound not so much because of its abstract and logical consistency with the definition reached in I as because it is confirmed by a comparison of the qualities found to attach to the two sorts of good activity in practice. The life of θεωρία κατὰ σοφίαν, being set side by side with the life of θεωρία καὶ πρᾶξις κατὰ τὴν ἄλλην ἀρετήν, is found to be superior to it in every point. It is pleasanter: it is more unbroken: it is nobler in itself, as being the activity of the noblest part of the soul: it is more independent of circumstances: it is more final, that is, more desired for itself as an end and not as a means to something else: it is more like what the life of God must be conceived to be: it is more in accordance with the divine will, if a divine will exists. All these advantages are connected with the cardinal difference between it and its rival, that it is pure activity of soul, its rival the joint activity of soul and body.

To return now to the question, How far is the βίος κατὰ τὴν ἄλλην ἀρετήν an end in itself? Is the happiness of the servants in the household necessary because that happiness is a necessary external means to the happiness of the master, who is so situated that he must be a part of a household and cannot dispense with the offices of his servants? Or is the happiness of the servants necessary because they are an integral part of the household, the happiness of which as a whole, and not the happiness of the master only, is the final end to be obtained, and because this happiness of the whole household is really the sum of the happiness of its parts? The fact is that Aristotle does not appear to have asked himself this question, or to have clearly grasped the distinction that it involves. He was indeed dimly conscious of both points of view at different times. Thus in VI he speaks of φρόνησις and σοφία as being valuable in themselves as integral parts of ἡ ὅλη ἀρετή and so of that happiness which is (it is obviously assumed) the activity naturally resulting from ἡ ὅλη ἀρετή (1144 a 3—6): thus putting σοφία on a level with φρόνησις as a mere constituent part of a whole that is different from and superior to either, and consequently putting the βίος κατὰ σοφίαν on a level with the βίος κατὰ φρόνησιν, requiring both to be combined, for the composite human being, to produce that βίος κατ᾽ εὐδαιμονίαν which is better than either separately. On the other hand at the end of VI the inferiority of φρόνησις to σοφία, and the consequently implied inferiority of the βίος κατὰ φρόνησιν to the βίος κατὰ σοφίαν, we find stated in strong terms; this truth being upheld in face of the fact that in actual life the φρόνιμος gives directions to the σοφός, or the practical part of a man to the theoretic part of him, and not vice versa. The wording of X vi—viii is everywhere vague where this question comes up. Thus 1177 b 27 οὐ γὰρ ᾗ ἄνθρωπός ἐστιν οὕτω βιώσεται ἀλλ᾽ ᾗ θεῖόν τι ἐν αὐτῷ ὑπάρχει does not settle the question as to how far a man should live οὕτως and how far ᾗ ἄνθρωπός ἐστιν. Nor does the practical dogma χρὴ ἐφ᾽ ὅσον ἐνδέχεται ἀθανατίζειν (1177 b 31) settle the question as it appears to do at first sight: for it gives no principle by which the question πόσον ἐνδέχεται; can be answered. It tells no more than the equally vague 1178 b 5 ᾗ ἄνθρωπός ἐστι καὶ πλείοσι συζῇ, αἱρεῖται τὰ κατὰ τὴν ἀρετὴν πράττειν. The question still remains, How far should a man in practice ἀθανατίζειν and how far ἀνθρωπεύεσθαι (1177 b 31, 1178 b 7)? Casuistry could present countless cases in which a conflict of duties would arise, where ἀνθρωπεύεσθαι could hinder ἀθανατίζειν and ἀθανατίζειν would hinder ἀνθρωπεύεσθαι. But Aristotle takes no account of the possibility of this. In the same way he refuses to analyse the intellectual standpoint of those persons who choose the πολιτικὸς βίος without any reference to the θεωρητικὸς βίος. Actions are good, according to Aristotle, in proportion as they lead to the θεωρητικὸς βίος as the end. For the man who does not consider this to be the end, and does not in any way aim at it as the end, what standard remains to make any action better or worse than any other? Aristotle evidently cannot make out that there is any standard. He would probably say that the πολιτικός (in the sense of the man who rejects the ideal of the θεωρητικὸς βίος) is a man who does not order his conduct on scientific principles, and must take his rules of conduct, in so far as he has any, from those who do recognise the true standard, and by reference to it know what actions are good and what are bad. The irrational life led by such a man is not that of the true πολιτικός or φρόνιμος, who ὁρᾷ ὅπως ἡ σοφία γένηται, who knows what is really good for man (i.e. what happiness is), and who determines the moral mean by reference to that happiness. Pericles knew what true happiness was : he did not realise it by his own life, as Anaxagoras did, but he knew, better than Anaxagoras, the external means to it : he could ἀνθρωπεύεσθαι better, though he could not ἀθανατίζειν so well. It is only in complete isolation from the ideal of the θεωρητικὸς βίος that the πολιτικὸς βίος becomes irrational. Such seems to be the logical outcome of Aristotle's doctrine, and there is nothing in X vi—viii to contradict this view; but at the same time there is no sufficient evidence in those chapters to show that Aristotle had clearly worked it out. He probably followed to some extent the feelings of the ordinary man in attributing to moral actions an independent goodness of their own, and would allow the πολιτικὸς βίος to possess a certain rationality and value even though it should ignore or contemn the θεωρητικὸς βίος altogether.

The above arguments have attempted to define the rela-tion of intellectual goodness to happiness conceived by Aristotle so far as to show (1) that σοφία is the intellectual ἀρετή which leads, under ideal conditions, to real happiness of the best kind : (2) that since man is a composite being, the conditions are not ideal, so that the possession of σοφία is not in itself enough to ensure him happiness : (3) that φρό-νησις is the intellectual ἀρετή that combines with moral ἀρετή (from which it is in practice inseparable) to form an inferior kind of goodness that gives rise to an inferior kind of good activity : (4) that this inferior goodness and good activity cannot rationally be desired, nor indeed their nature be understood, except as a means to the superior, though in practice they are often irrationally desired and attained for their own sake : (5) that it is uncertain whether this inferior goodness and good activity, when considered in their proper light as means to the higher, should be considered purely external means to a happiness of which they are themselves no part, or rather themselves component parts of a happiness which, as belonging to a being composite of better and worse, must itself be composite of better and worse.

Expressed in less technical language, these conclusions are more or less the following : (1) that the best way any man can pass his life, circumstances permitting him, is in the intelligent study of physics, mathematics and metaphysics : (2) that the circumstances of human life will not allow any man to pass his time in this way uninterruptedly : (3) that the right practical conduct of life is, under the circumstances, a necessity for every man : (4) that the rightness of practical conduct really consists, though people do not always see this, in the extent to which it favours the purely intellectual life : (5) that it is uncertain how far such right practical conduct is good in itself and a part of man's happiness, and how far it is merely a means to that intellectual life which alone is worth having for its own sake.

It thus appears that the relation of σοφία to εὐδαιμονία is far more direct than the relation of φρόνησις to εὐδαιμονία. For whereas the activity that arises from σοφία is either εὐδαιμονία itself or the best and most important part of εὐδαιμονία, the activity that arises from φρόνησις is only one element in that complex activity (ὀρθὴ προαίρεσις) which itself must be combined with πρᾶξις to make a still more complex activity (θεωρία καὶ πρᾶξις κατὰ τὴν ἄλλην ἀρετήν) which is either not εὐδαιμονία at all or is at best an inferior and less important part of εὐδαιμονία. Again to make use of less technical language, this may be stated as follows : Philosophic wisdom gives rise to happiness far more directly than practical wisdom. For the intelligent study of physics mathematics and metaphysics is either the only thing a man can do that is good in itself, or at least the best of the things that are good in themselves. But practical wisdom is only useful because it combines with moral goodness to make people wish to do right actions in practical life; and such a wish is only useful because it leads to the doing of those right actions; and those right actions are either useless in themselves, and only good because they lead to the intellectual life, or else, at best, are less good in themselves than the intellectual life.

ΗΘΙΚΩΝ ΝΙΚΟΜΑΧΕΙΩΝ
Ζ

I

18 ἐπεὶ δὲ τυγχάνομεν πρότερον εἰρηκότες ὅτι δεῖ τὸ
μέσον αἱρεῖσθαι, μὴ τὴν ὑπερβολὴν μηδὲ τὴν ἔλλειψιν,
20 τὸ δὲ μέσον ἐστὶν ὡς ὁ λόγος ὁ ὀρθὸς λέγει, τοῦτο διέλω-
μεν. ἐν πάσαις γὰρ ταῖς εἰρημέναις ἕξεσιν, καθάπερ καὶ
ἐπὶ τῶν ἄλλων, ἔστι τις σκοπὸς πρὸς ὃν ἀποβλέπων ὁ
τὸν λόγον ἔχων ἐπιτείνει καὶ ἀνίησιν, καί τις ἔστιν ὅρος
τῶν μεσοτήτων, ἃς μεταξύ φαμεν εἶναι τῆς ὑπερβολῆς καὶ
25 τῆς ἐλλείψεως, οὔσας κατὰ τὸν ὀρθὸν λόγον. ἔστι δὲ
τὸ μὲν εἰπεῖν οὕτως ἀληθὲς μέν, οὐθὲν δὲ σαφές. καὶ
γὰρ ἐν ταῖς ἄλλαις ἐπιμελείαις, περὶ ὅσας ἐστὶν ἐπιστήμη,
τοῦτ' ἀληθὲς μὲν εἰπεῖν, ὅτι οὔτε πλείω οὔτε ἐλάττω δεῖ
πονεῖν οὐδὲ ῥαθυμεῖν, ἀλλὰ τὰ μέσα καὶ ὡς ὁ ὀρθὸς
30 λόγος· τοῦτο δὲ μόνον ἔχων ἄν τις οὐδὲν ἂν εἰδείη πλέον,
οἷον ποῖα δεῖ προσφέρεσθαι πρὸς τὸ σῶμα, εἴ τις εἴπειεν
ὅτι ὅσα ἡ ἰατρικὴ κελεύει καὶ ὡς ὁ ταύτην ἔχων. διὸ δεῖ
καὶ περὶ τὰς τῆς ψυχῆς ἕξεις μὴ μόνον ἀληθῶς εἶναι
34 τοῦτο εἰρημένον, ἀλλὰ καὶ διωρισμένον τίς ἐστιν ὁ ὀρθὸς
λόγος καὶ τούτου τίς ὅρος.

K = Laurentianus L = Parisiensis O = Riccardianus
M = Marcianus 213 Γ = vetus versio Bek = Bekker 1831
Byw = Bywater 1894 Sus = Susemihl 1880 (ed. altera curavit Apelt 1903)

(The readings of Fritzsche (1851) Grant (1874) and Ramsauer (1878) are the
same as Bekker's unless otherwise stated : and those of Burnet (1900) the same as
Bywater's unless otherwise stated.)

1138 b 19 μὴ K Byw : καὶ μὴ L M Bek Sus
33 ἀληθῶς K Sus Byw.: ἀληθὲς L M Bek
34 τίς ἐστιν K Byw : τίς τ' ἐστιν L M Bek Sus

I

We have said already that it is necessary to choose the 18 mean, and not the excess nor the defect : and since the mean is fixed by Right Reason, let us examine this notion[1]   With 20 all the qualities[2] that have been discussed—and indeed with all other qualities[2] too—there exists some mark, as it were, to be hit, upon which the possessor of Reason keeps his eyes, and bends his bow more or less strongly accordingly : and there is a standard for determining those mean states which, we say, lie between excess and defect, and are fixed by Right 25 Reason.

Now such a statement is true, but not at all instructive· Not only here, but in all other affairs that are regulated by system, it is a true statement that we must not exert ourselves, nor yet take our ease, either too much or too little, but to a middle extent, and as much as Right Reason bids.   But if a man possesses only this-information he cannot thereby be any 30 wiser than before : he cannot know what sort of medicines, for instance, he ought to apply to his body, if he is simply told ' Whatever the medical art prescribes, and according to the directions of the man who understands that art.'   In the same way, with regard to the qualities of the mind, it is necessary not only to make such a true statement as the foregoing, but also to define exactly what Right Reason is, 34 and what the standard is to which this Right Reason refers.

[1] sc. of Right Reason.   [2] sc. good qualities, ἀρεταί.

9 a   τὰς δὴ τῆς ψυχῆς ἀρετὰς διελόμενοι τὰς μὲν εἶναι τοῦ
ἤθους ἔφαμεν τὰς δὲ τῆς διανοίας. περὶ μὲν οὖν τῶν
ἠθικῶν διεληλύθαμεν, περὶ δὲ τῶν λοιπῶν, περὶ ψυχῆς
πρῶτον εἰπόντες, λέγωμεν οὕτως. πρότερον μὲν οὖν
5 ἐλέχθη δύ᾽ εἶναι μέρη τῆς ψυχῆς, τό τε λόγον ἔχον καὶ
τὸ ἄλογον· νῦν δὲ περὶ τοῦ λόγον ἔχοντος τὸν αὐτὸν
τρόπον διαιρετέον, καὶ ὑποκείσθω δύο τὰ λόγον ἔχοντα,
ἓν μὲν ᾧ θεωροῦμεν τὰ τοιαῦτα τῶν ὄντων ὅσων αἱ ἀρχαὶ
μὴ ἐνδέχονται ἄλλως ἔχειν, ἓν δὲ ᾧ τὰ ἐνδεχόμενα· πρὸς
γὰρ τὰ τῷ γένει ἕτερα καὶ τῶν τῆς ψυχῆς μορίων ἕτερον
10 τῷ γένει τὸ πρὸς ἑκάτερον πεφυκός, εἴπερ καθ᾽ ὁμοιότητά
τινα καὶ οἰκειότητα ἡ γνῶσις ὑπάρχει αὐτοῖς. λεγέσθω
δὲ τούτων τὸ μὲν ἐπιστημονικὸν τὸ δὲ λογιστικόν· τὸ
γὰρ βουλεύεσθαι καὶ λογίζεσθαι ταὐτόν, οὐδεὶς δὲ βουλεύεται περὶ τῶν μὴ ἐνδεχομένων ἄλλως ἔχειν· ὥστε τὸ
15 λογιστικόν ἐστιν ἕν τι μέρος τοῦ λόγον ἔχοντος. ληπτέον
ἄρα ἑκατέρου τούτων τίς ἡ βελτίστη ἕξις· αὕτη γὰρ
ἀρετὴ ἑκατέρου. ἡ δ᾽ ἀρετὴ πρὸς τὸ ἔργον τὸ οἰκεῖον.

II

τρία δή ἐστιν ἐν τῇ ψυχῇ τὰ κύρια πράξεως καὶ
ἀληθείας, αἴσθησις νοῦς ὄρεξις. τούτων δ᾽ ἡ αἴσθησις
20 οὐδεμιᾶς ἀρχὴ πράξεως· δῆλον δὲ τῷ τὰ θηρία αἴσθησιν
μὲν ἔχειν, πράξεως δὲ μὴ κοινωνεῖν. ἔστι δ᾽ ὅπερ ἐν διανοίᾳ
κατάφασις καὶ ἀπόφασις, τοῦτο ἐν ὀρέξει δίωξις καὶ φυγή·
ὥστ᾽ ἐπειδὴ ἡ ἠθικὴ ἀρετὴ ἕξις προαιρετική, ἡ δὲ προαίρεσις ὄρεξις βουλευτική, δεῖ διὰ ταῦτα μὲν τόν τε λόγον
25 ἀληθῆ εἶναι καὶ τὴν ὄρεξιν ὀρθήν, εἴπερ ἡ προαίρεσις
σπουδαία, καὶ τὰ αὐτὰ τὸν μὲν φάναι τὴν δὲ διώκειν.
αὕτη μὲν οὖν ἡ διάνοια καὶ ἡ ἀλήθεια πρακτική· τῆς δὲ

1139 a 17   τρία δή Byw : τρία δ᾽ codd. Bek Sus
24   ταῦτα μὲν Κ Byw : ταῦτα Bek Sus : μὲν ταῦτα L O : ταὐτὰ coni. Apelt

Now in classifying the excellences of the mind we said that some were of the moral character[1] and others of the 11 intellect. Moral excellences we have discussed at length; let us now discuss the others.

We must introduce the discussion with some psychology. It was stated before that there are two parts of the mind, that which has reason and that which has not: and now a similar 5 division must be made of the part which has reason. It may be taken as an accepted fact that there are two divisions of the soul that have reason, one with which we consider all those existing things whose elements[2] are invariable, and one with which we consider the things that are variable: for the parts of the soul that are adapted for perceiving generically 10 different things are themselves generically different: since the power which they possess of perceiving those things is due to some kind of resemblance to and kinship with them. Of these parts, the one may be called the scientific; and the other may be called the calculative, for deliberation is the same thing as calculation, and no one deliberates about things that are invariable, so that one division of the part of the soul that possesses reason may be called the calculative. 15

We must, then, discover what the best permanent condition of each of these parts of the mind is: for this best permanent condition is its excellence in each case.

The excellence of each part of the mind must depend upon the special work which that part performs.

II

Now there are in the mind three faculties whose work it is to cause responsible action and knowledge of truth[3]: sense-perception, intellect, and desire. Of these, sense-perception can never[4] cause responsible action: this is shown by the fact that the lower animals possess sense-perception, but are devoid 20 of the power of responsible action.

Assent and denial in intellect correspond to pursuit and avoidance in desire. Since moral excellence is a permanent condition of the mind as concerned with the purposing of actions, and purpose is desire based upon deliberation: it follows that if purpose is to be good, the intellect must be truthful[5], and the desire must be right, and the intellect must 25 assent to the same things as those which the desire pursues. This kind of intellect, and this kind of truth, are concerned

---

[1] i.e. of that part of the mind which has to do with the moral sphere.
[2] or 'fundamental principles.'   [3] i.e. either or both of these in each case.
[4] i.e. directly (it may be the basis of νοῦς or ὄρεξις).   [5] i.e. must *attain* truth.

θεωρητικῆς διανοίας καὶ μὴ πρακτικῆς μηδὲ ποιητικῆς τὸ
εὖ καὶ κακῶς τἀληθές ἐστι καὶ ψεῦδος—τοῦτο γάρ ἐστι
30 παντὸς διανοητικοῦ ἔργον· τοῦ δὲ πρακτικοῦ καὶ διανοητικοῦ ἀλήθεια ὁμολόγως ἔχουσα τῇ ὀρέξει τῇ ὀρθῇ.
πράξεως μὲν οὖν ἀρχὴ προαίρεσις—ὅθεν ἡ κίνησις ἀλλ᾽
οὐχ οὗ ἕνεκα—προαιρέσεως δὲ ὄρεξις καὶ λόγος ὁ ἕνεκά
τινος· διὸ οὔτ᾽ ἄνευ νοῦ καὶ διανοίας οὔτ᾽ ἄνευ ἠθικῆς
35 ἐστὶν ἔξεως ἡ προαίρεσις· [εὐπραξία γὰρ καὶ τὸ ἐναντίον
ἐν πράξει ἄνευ διανοίας καὶ ἤθους οὐκ ἔστιν.] διάνοια
δ᾽ αὐτὴ οὐθὲν κινεῖ, ἀλλ᾽ ἡ ἕνεκά του καὶ πρακτική.
9 b αὕτη γὰρ καὶ τῆς ποιητικῆς ἄρχει· ἕνεκα γάρ του ποιεῖ
πᾶς ὁ ποιῶν, καὶ οὐ τέλος ἁπλῶς (ἀλλὰ πρός τι καί τινος)
τὸ ποιητόν, ἀλλὰ τὸ πρακτόν· ἡ γὰρ εὐπραξία τέλος, ἡ δ᾽
5 ὄρεξις τούτου. διὸ ἢ ὀρεκτικὸς νοῦς ἡ προαίρεσις ἢ
ὄρεξις διανοητική, καὶ ἡ τοιαύτη ἀρχὴ ἄνθρωπος. οὐκ
ἔστι δὲ προαιρετὸν οὐδὲν γεγονός, οἷον οὐδεὶς προαιρεῖται
Ἴλιον πεπορθηκέναι· οὐδὲ γὰρ βουλεύεται περὶ τοῦ γεγο-
νότος ἀλλὰ περὶ τοῦ ἐσομένου καὶ ἐνδεχομένου, τὸ δὲ
γεγονὸς οὐκ ἐνδέχεται μὴ γενέσθαι· διὸ ὀρθῶς Ἀγάθων

10   μόνου γὰρ αὐτοῦ καὶ θεὸς στερίσκεται,
              ἀγένητα ποιεῖν ἅσσ᾽ ἂν ᾖ πεπραγμένα.

ἀμφοτέρων δὴ τῶν νοητικῶν μορίων ἀλήθεια τὸ ἔργον.
καθ᾽ ἃς οὖν μάλιστα ἕξεις ἀληθεύσει ἑκάτερον, αὗται
ἀρεταὶ ἀμφοῖν.

III

ἀρξάμενοι οὖν ἄνωθεν περὶ αὐτῶν πάλιν λέγωμεν.
15 ἔστω δὴ οἷς ἀληθεύει ἡ ψυχὴ τῷ καταφάναι ἢ ἀποφάναι,
πέντε τὸν ἀριθμόν· ταῦτα δ᾽ ἐστὶ τέχνη ἐπιστήμη φρόνη-

1139 a 30 ἀλήθεια K O Byw : ἡ ἀλήθεια L M Bek Sus
     34 εὐπραξία γὰρ...35 οὐκ ἔστιν seclusi

with action. The speculative kind of intellect, which is not concerned with action nor with production, does its work well and ill in reaching truth and falsehood respectively. This reaching of truth, indeed, is the work of every part of the intellect. But the part of the intellect that is 30 concerned with action does its work well when it reaches truth that is in agreement with right desire.

The cause of responsible action (the efficient, not the final cause) is purpose : and the cause of purpose is desire together with intellect referred to some end. So that purpose cannot exist without both intellect (νοῦς or διάνοια) and a moral condition of the mind[1] : for in the sphere of action good action and the reverse cannot exist without intellect and moral character. 35

But intellect by itself excites no action : it is only intellect referred to some end, and concerned with action, that does so. This kind of intellect concerned with action controls as well 11 the intellect concerned with production. For every man who produces a thing produces it with some further end in view : the thing which is made is not an absolute end, but has reference to, and belongs to, something else : whereas the thing done *is* an absolute end, for good activity is an absolute end, and it is this at which desire of action aims.

Purpose, therefore, may be called either intellect based upon desire or desire based upon intellect : and purpose as a 5 cause makes a human being[2]. Nothing that has taken place is purposed : nobody, for instance, purposes to have sacked Troy : for no one even deliberates about what has taken place, but only about what is in the future and may or may not happen, whereas it is not possible that what has taken place should not have taken place, so that Agathon rightly says

> For even God lacks this one thing alone 10
> To make a deed that has been done undone.

The reaching of truth, then, is the proper work of both the intellectual parts of the mind. Therefore the excellence of each part will be the quality that causes it to reach truth.

III

Let us, then, make a fresh beginning, and consider these excellences in a new way. Now it may be taken for granted 15 that there are five conditions of mind that cause it to reach truth in what it affirms or denies : and these are called

---

[1] i.e. the moral part of the mind, active, and in some condition or other.

[2] i.e. it is the peculiar property of human beings (as distinguished from gods and from beasts) to have purpose as the cause of their actions.

σις σοφία νοῦς· ὑπολήψει γὰρ καὶ δόξῃ ἐνδέχεται διαψεύδεσθαι.

ἐπιστήμη μὲν οὖν τί ἐστιν, ἐντεῦθεν φανερόν, εἰ δεῖ
ἀκριβολογεῖσθαι καὶ μὴ ἀκολουθεῖν ταῖς ὁμοιότησιν.
20 πάντες γὰρ ὑπολαμβάνομεν, ὃ ἐπιστάμεθα, μὴ ἐνδέχεσθαι
ἄλλως ἔχειν· τὰ δὲ ἐνδεχόμενα ἄλλως, ὅταν ἔξω τοῦ
θεωρεῖν γένηται, λανθάνει εἰ ἔστιν ἢ μή. ἐξ ἀνάγκης
ἄρα ἐστὶ τὸ ἐπιστητόν. ἀίδιον ἄρα· τὰ γὰρ ἐξ ἀνάγκης
ὄντα ἁπλῶς πάντα ἀίδια. τὰ δὲ ἀίδια ἀγένητα καὶ ἄφθαρτα.
25 ἔτι διδακτὴ πᾶσα ἐπιστήμη δοκεῖ εἶναι, καὶ τὸ ἐπιστητὸν
μαθητόν. ἐκ προγινωσκομένων δὲ πᾶσα διδασκαλία,
ὥσπερ καὶ ἐν τοῖς ἀναλυτικοῖς λέγομεν· ἢ μὲν γὰρ δι᾽
ἐπαγωγῆς, ἢ δὲ συλλογισμῷ. ἡ μὲν δὴ ἐπαγωγὴ ἀρχῆς
ἐστὶ καὶ τοῦ καθόλου, ὁ δὲ συλλογισμὸς ἐκ τῶν καθόλου.
30 εἰσὶν ἄρα ἀρχαὶ ἐξ ὧν ὁ συλλογισμός, ὧν οὐκ ἔστι
συλλογισμός· ἐπαγωγὴ ἄρα. ἡ μὲν ἄρα ἐπιστήμη ἐστὶν
ἕξις ἀποδεικτική, καὶ ὅσα ἄλλα προσδιοριζόμεθα ἐν τοῖς
ἀναλυτικοῖς· ὅταν γάρ πως πιστεύῃ καὶ γνώριμοι αὐτῷ
ὦσιν αἱ ἀρχαί, ἐπίσταται· εἰ γὰρ μὴ μᾶλλον τοῦ συμ-
35 περάσματος, κατὰ συμβεβηκὸς ἕξει τὴν ἐπιστήμην. περὶ
μὲν οὖν ἐπιστήμης διωρίσθω τὸν τρόπον τοῦτον.

IV

0 a   τοῦ δ᾽ ἐνδεχομένου ἄλλως ἔχειν ἔστι τι καὶ ποιητὸν
καὶ πρακτόν. ἕτερον δ᾽ ἐστὶν ποίησις καὶ πρᾶξις (πιστεύομεν δὲ περὶ αὐτῶν καὶ τοῖς ἐξωτερικοῖς λόγοις)· ὥστε
καὶ ἡ μετὰ λόγου ἕξις πρακτικὴ ἕτερόν ἐστι τῆς μετὰ
5 λόγου ποιητικῆς ἕξεως. διὸ οὐδὲ περιέχεται ὑπ᾽ ἀλλήλων·
οὔτε γὰρ ἡ πρᾶξις ποίησις οὔτε ἡ ποίησις πρᾶξίς ἐστιν.

1139 b 20   μὴ L M Bek Sus Burnet : μηδ᾽ K Byw
     25   ἄπασα Byw : ἡ ἄπασα K M : πᾶσα L Bek Sus Burnet
     28   ἀρχῆς cum L scripsi : ἀρχή K M edd.
1140 a 5   περιέχεται K L Ramsauer Sus Byw : περιέχονται M Bek

art¹, scientific knowledge, practical wisdom, philosophic wisdom, and inductive reason: for supposition and opinion may fail to reach truth.

What scientific knowledge is will be clear from the following considerations. (We must use the word in its strict sense, and not be led astray by its analogous uses.) We all hold 20 that what we scientifically know cannot vary: but when what can vary is outside the range of our observation, we cannot tell whether it exists or not. What is scientifically known therefore exists of necessity. It is therefore everlasting: for all things are everlasting that exist of absolute necessity. And everlasting things cannot come into existence or perish. It is held, moreover, that all scientific knowledge must be 25 taught, and that what is scientifically known must be learnt. Now all teaching is based upon facts previously known, as we also observe in the Analytics. It is done partly by induction, partly by deduction. Induction leads to fundamental propositions², which are universals: deduction works *from* universals. There are therefore fundamental propositions, from 30 which deduction works, which cannot be reached by deduction: it is therefore induction that leads to them.

Scientific knowledge, then, is the quality of deductive ability ; and it is all the additional things besides which in the Analytics we define it as being: when a person reaches conviction in a certain way³, and the fundamental propositions⁴ are known to him, then it is that he scientifically knows. But⁵ unless he is surer of his fundamental propositions than of his conclusion, he will only have scientific knowledge in a 35 loose sense of the term⁶. This may be accepted as our definition of scientific knowledge.

IV

The class of variable things includes what is made as well 114 as what is done. Making and doing are two different things —we are safe in believing ordinary people's views on this subject: and therefore also the intellectual quality that is concerned with making is different from the intellectual quality concerned with doing. So different, indeed, that neither is 5 even a part of the other: for doing is not making, and making is not doing.

---

¹ more exactly ' artistic ability.'   ² reading ἀρχῆς
³ viz. as defined in the Analytics.   ⁴ sc. upon which this conviction is based.
⁵ lit. 'for ' (sc. 'and then only, for ').
⁶ i.e. he will have the form without the substance.

ἐπεὶ δ' ἡ οἰκοδομικὴ τέχνη τίς ἐστι καὶ ὅπερ ἕξις τις
μετὰ λόγου ποιητική, καὶ οὐδεμία οὔτε τέχνη ἐστὶν ἥτις
οὐ μετὰ λόγου ποιητικὴ ἕξις ἐστίν, οὔτε τοιαύτη ἣ οὐ
10 τέχνη, τὸ αὐτὸ ἂν εἴη τέχνη καὶ ἕξις μετὰ λόγου ἀληθοῦς
ποιητική. ἔστι δὲ τέχνη πᾶσα περὶ γένεσιν καὶ τὸ
τεχνάζειν καὶ θεωρεῖν ὅπως ἂν γένηταί τι τῶν ἐνδεχομένων καὶ εἶναι καὶ μὴ εἶναι, καὶ ὧν ἡ ἀρχὴ ἐν τῷ
ποιοῦντι ἀλλὰ μὴ ἐν τῷ ποιουμένῳ· οὔτε γὰρ τῶν ἐξ
15 ἀνάγκης ὄντων ἢ γινομένων ἡ τέχνη ἐστίν, οὔτε τῶν
κατὰ φύσιν· ἐν αὑτοῖς γὰρ ἔχουσι ταῦτα τὴν ἀρχήν.
ἐπεὶ δὲ ποίησις καὶ πρᾶξις ἕτερον, ἀνάγκη τὴν τέχνην
ποιήσεως ἀλλ' οὐ πράξεως εἶναι. καὶ τρόπον τινὰ περὶ
τὰ αὐτά ἐστιν ἡ τύχη καὶ ἡ τέχνη, καθάπερ καὶ Ἀγάθων
φησὶ
20 τέχνη τύχην ἔστερξε καὶ τύχη τέχνην.

ἡ μὲν οὖν τέχνη, ὥσπερ εἴρηται, ἕξις τις μετὰ λόγου
ἀληθοῦς ποιητική ἐστιν, ἡ δ' ἀτεχνία τοὐναντίον μετὰ
λόγου ψευδοῦς ποιητικὴ ἕξις, περὶ τὸ ἐνδεχόμενον ἄλλως
ἔχειν.

V

περὶ δὲ φρονήσεως οὕτως ἂν λάβοιμεν, θεωρήσαντες
25 τίνας λέγομεν τοὺς φρονίμους. δοκεῖ δὴ φρονίμου εἶναι
τὸ δύνασθαι καλῶς βουλεύσασθαι περὶ τὰ αὑτῷ ἀγαθὰ
καὶ συμφέροντα, οὐ κατὰ μέρος, οἷον ποῖα πρὸς ὑγίειαν ἢ
πρὸς ἰσχύν, ἀλλὰ ποῖα πρὸς τὸ εὖ ζῆν ὅλως. σημεῖον
δ' ὅτι καὶ τοὺς περί τι φρονίμους λέγομεν, ὅταν πρὸς τέλος
30 τι σπουδαῖον εὖ λογίσωνται, ὧν μὴ ἔστιν τέχνη. ὥστε

1140 a 11 καὶ θεωρεῖν codd. Bek Sus Byw : [καὶ] θεωρεῖν Muretus Coraes
Fritzsche Ramsauer
27 πρὸς ὑγίειαν, πρὸς ἰσχύν K L Byw : πρὸς ὑγίειαν ἢ πρὸς ἰσχύν M O
Sus : πρὸς ὑγίειαν ἢ ἰσχύν Bek
28 ζῆν ὅλως L M Sus Byw :. ζῆν K Bek

Now ability to build houses can be truly defined as an
intellectual quality concerned with making, and it is a kind
of art. And since there is no single art which is not an
intellectual quality concerned with making, and no such
quality which is not an art, the terms ' art ' and ' truth-reaching 10
intellectual quality concerned with making ' must be identical
in meaning.

All art is concerned with coming into existence, [1]and with
contrivance, and with[1] the consideration of how something
may come into existence which is capable of existing or not
existing, and the cause of whose existence is in the maker
and not in the thing made. For art is not concerned with
things that exist of necessity or come into existence of 15
necessity, nor yet with things that come into existence by
nature : for these latter contain the cause of their existence in
themselves.

Since making and doing are distinct, [2]and art is concerned
with making, it cannot therefore[2] be concerned with doing.

Chance and art are in a way concerned with the same
things. As Agathon says

> Art is beloved of Chance, and Chance of Art.   20

Art, then, as has been said, is [3]a truth-attaining intellectual
quality[3], concerned with making. Its opposite, want of art, is
an intellectual quality, concerned with making, that fails to
attain truth. Both are concerned with the variable.

V

We shall get at the truth about practical wisdom by
considering what sort of persons we call practically wise.
Now it is held to be the mark of the practically wise man to 25
be able to deliberate well about the things that are good and
useful for himself: not what is useful for some special purpose,
not, for instance, what is good for his health or his strength :
but what is useful to him for a good life as a whole. This
usage is supported by the fact that when people calculate
well with a view to some particular good end, with which art
is not concerned, we call them practically wise about that 30
thing.

[1] or [καὶ] 'and artistic contrivance is.'
[2] lit. ' art must be concerned with making, and cannot.'
[3] lit. ' a quality with true reason.'

G.

καὶ ὅλως ἂν εἴη φρόνιμος ὁ βουλευτικός. βουλεύεται δ'
οὐθεὶς περὶ τῶν ἀδυνάτων ἄλλως ἔχειν, οὐδὲ τῶν μὴ ἐνδεχομένων αὐτῷ πρᾶξαι. ὥστ᾽ εἴπερ ἐπιστήμη μὲν μετὰ
ἀποδείξεως, ὧν δ᾽ αἱ ἀρχαὶ ἐνδέχονται ἄλλως ἔχειν, τούτων
35 μὴ ἔστιν ἀπόδειξις (πάντα γὰρ ἐνδέχεται καὶ ἄλλως ἔχειν),
ο b καὶ οὐκ ἔστι βουλεύσασθαι περὶ τῶν ἐξ ἀνάγκης ὄντων,
οὐκ ἂν εἴη ἡ φρόνησις ἐπιστήμη οὐδὲ τέχνη, ἐπιστήμη
μὲν ὅτι ἐνδέχεται τὸ πρακτὸν ἄλλως ἔχειν, τέχνη δ᾽ ὅτι
ἄλλο τὸ γένος πράξεως καὶ ποιήσεως. λείπεται ἄρα αὐτὴν
5 εἶναι ἕξιν ἀληθῆ μετὰ λόγου πρακτικὴν περὶ τὰ ἀνθρώπῳ
ἀγαθὰ καὶ κακά. τῆς μὲν γὰρ ποιήσεως ἕτερον τὸ τέλος,
τῆς δὲ πράξεως οὐκ ἂν εἴη· ἔστιν γὰρ αὐτὴ ἡ εὐπραξία
τέλος. διὰ τοῦτο Περικλέα καὶ τοὺς τοιούτους φρονίμους οἰόμεθα εἶναι, ὅτι τὰ αὑτοῖς ἀγαθὰ καὶ τὰ τοῖς
10 ἀνθρώποις δύνανται θεωρεῖν· εἶναι δὲ τοιούτους ἡγούμεθα τοὺς οἰκονομικοὺς καὶ τοὺς πολιτικούς. ἔνθεν καὶ
τὴν σωφροσύνην τούτῳ προσαγορεύομεν τῷ ὀνόματι, ὡς
σῴζουσαν τὴν φρόνησιν. σῴζει δὲ τὴν τοιαύτην ὑπόληψιν. οὐ γὰρ ἅπασαν ὑπόληψιν διαφθείρει οὐδὲ δια-
15 στρέφει τὸ ἡδὺ καὶ λυπηρόν, οἷον ὅτι τὸ τρίγωνον δύο
ὀρθὰς ἔχει ἢ οὐκ ἔχει, ἀλλὰ τὰς περὶ τὸ πρακτόν. αἱ
μὲν γὰρ ἀρχαὶ τῶν πρακτῶν τὸ οὗ ἕνεκα τὰ πρακτά·
τῷ δὲ διεφθαρμένῳ δι᾽ ἡδονὴν ἢ λύπην εὐθὺς οὐ φαίνεται
ἀρχή, οὐδὲ δεῖν τούτου ἕνεκεν οὐδὲ διὰ τοῦτο αἱρεῖσθαι
20 πάντα καὶ πράττειν. ἔστι γὰρ ἡ κακία φθαρτικὴ ἀρχῆς.
ὥστ᾽ ἀνάγκη τὴν φρόνησιν ἕξιν εἶναι μετὰ λόγου ἀληθῆ
περὶ τὰ ἀνθρώπινα ἀγαθὰ πρακτικήν. ἀλλὰ μὴν τέχνης

1140 a 35 (πάντα γὰρ...ἄλλως ἔχειν), καὶ...ὄντων Michelet Fritzsche Bywater :
(πάντα γὰρ...ἄλλως ἔχειν, καὶ...ὄντων) Bekker Ramsauer Grant
Stewart
1140 b 5 ἀληθῆ codd. Bek Byw : ἀληθοῦς Alexander in Metaph. 981 b 25,
Susemihl
14 καὶ λυπηρόν K M Byw : καὶ τὸ λυπηρόν L Bek Sus
15 δύο ὀρθὰς ἔχει Byw : δύο ὀρθὰς ἴσας ἔχει pr. K : δυσὶν ὀρθαῖς ἴσας
ἔχει L M Bek Sus
18 ἀρχή K M Byw : ἡ ἀρχή L Bek Sus

The man who is good at deliberating in general is therefore the man who may be called practically wise in general.

Now nobody deliberates about things which cannot vary, or about things which it is not in his power to do.

Since, then, scientific knowledge is deductive ; and since deduction cannot lead to truth about those things whose fundamental principles can vary—for everything about such things can vary ; and since it is impossible to deliberate about things that exist of necessity :—practical wisdom cannot be the same as scientific knowledge. Nor can it be the same as art. It cannot be the same as scientific knowledge, because what is done can vary : nor the same as art, because there is a generic difference between doing and making.

It therefore follows that it is a truth-attaining intellectual quality concerned with doing and with things that are good and bad for human beings[1].

For in making the end is other than the making itself : but the end of doing cannot be other than the doing itself : for doing well is itself the end[1]

We call Pericles, therefore, and persons like him, practically wise, since they can discern the things that are good for themselves and for human beings ; we hold that those persons can do this who know how to manage households and communities.

(This is why we give self-control its name of σωφροσύνη, that is, preserver of (σώζουσα) practical wisdom (φρόνησις). The kind of opinion that self-control preserves is [2]that which relates to the sphere of practical wisdom[2]. For it is not every kind of opinion that the pleasant and the painful destroy or pervert : not, for instance, the opinion that the triangle contains two right angles, nor the opinion that it does not : but only opinions concerning what is done. For the initial causes[3] of things done are the ends to which the things done are means : and as soon as a man is ruined by pleasure or pain, he can see no such end, nor can he see that he ought to choose and do everything for the sake of that end and on account of that end. For wickedness destroys the knowledge of such causes.)

It must be true, then, that practical wisdom is a truth-attaining intellectual quality concerned with doing and with the things that are good for human beings.

---

[1] these two sentences clearly ought to be transposed.

[2] more literally ' such as has been mentioned.'

[3] sc. initial ' final ' causes.

μὲν ἔστιν ἀρετή, φρονήσεως δ' οὐκ ἔστιν· καὶ ἐν μὲν
τέχνῃ ὁ ἑκὼν ἁμαρτάνων αἱρετώτερος, περὶ δὲ φρόνησιν
ἧττον, ὥσπερ καὶ περὶ τὰς ἀρετάς. δῆλον οὖν ὅτι ἀρετή
25 τίς ἐστι καὶ οὐ τέχνη. δυοῖν δ' ὄντοιν μεροῖν τῆς ψυχῆς
τῶν λόγον ἐχόντων, θατέρου ἂν εἴη ἀρετή, τοῦ δοξαστικοῦ·
ἥ τε γὰρ δόξα περὶ τὸ ἐνδεχόμενον ἄλλως ἔχειν καὶ ἡ
φρόνησις. ἀλλὰ μὴν οὐδ' ἕξις μετὰ λόγου μόνον· σημεῖον
δ' ὅτι λήθη μὲν τῆς τοιαύτης ἕξεως ἔστιν, φρονήσεως
30 δ' οὐκ ἔστιν.

VI

ἐπεὶ δὲ ἡ ἐπιστήμη περὶ τῶν καθόλου ἐστὶν ὑπόληψις
καὶ τῶν ἐξ ἀνάγκης ὄντων, εἰσὶ δ' ἀρχαὶ τῶν ἀποδεικτῶν
καὶ πάσης ἐπιστήμης (μετὰ λόγου γὰρ ἡ ἐπιστήμη), τῆς
ἀρχῆς τοῦ ἐπιστητοῦ οὔτ' ἂν ἐπιστήμη εἴη οὔτε τέχνη
35 οὔτε φρόνησις· τὸ μὲν γὰρ ἐπιστητὸν ἀποδεικτόν, αἱ δὲ
1a τυγχάνουσιν οὖσαι περὶ τὰ ἐνδεχόμενα ἄλλως ἔχειν.
οὐδὲ δὴ σοφία τούτων ἔστιν· τοῦ γὰρ σοφοῦ περὶ ἐνίων
ἔχειν ἀπόδειξίν ἐστιν. εἰ δὴ οἷς ἀληθεύομεν καὶ μηδέποτε διαψευδόμεθα περὶ τὰ μὴ ἐνδεχόμενα ἢ καὶ ἐνδε-
5 χόμενα ἄλλως ἔχειν, ἐπιστήμη καὶ φρόνησίς ἐστι καὶ
σοφία καὶ νοῦς, τούτων δὲ τῶν τριῶν μηδὲν ἐνδέχεται
εἶναι (λέγω δὲ τρία φρόνησιν ἐπιστήμην σοφίαν), λείπεται
νοῦν εἶναι τῶν ἀρχῶν.

1140 b 21 ἀληθῆ Κ L Bek Byw : ἀληθοῦς Μ Γ Alexander Sus
29 μὲν τῆς codd. Byw : τῆς μὲν Γ Bek Sus

Moreover, one may speak of an excellence of art, but not of an excellence of practical wisdom : and in art the man who goes wrong intentionally is better than the man who goes wrong unintentionally, but in the sphere of practical wisdom he is worse, just as he is worse in the sphere of moral goodness. It is therefore plain that practical wisdom is an excellence which is not art.   25

Of the two parts of the mind that possess reason, practical wisdom is the excellence of one, namely, of the opinionative part : ¹for opinion is concerned with what is variable, and so is practical wisdom.

But yet practical wisdom is not a purely intellectual quality. And a proof of this is the fact that a purely intellectual quality may be said to be 'forgotten,' while practical wisdom cannot be said to be forgotten.   30

VI

Scientific knowledge is a way of conceiving which is concerned with universals and with things that exist of necessity; and there must be fundamental principles for what is reached by deduction, and for all scientific knowledge (since scientific knowledge involves reasoning). Now these fundamental principles of what is scientifically known cannot be reached either by scientific knowledge or by art or by practical wisdom: for what is scientifically known must be 35 reached by deduction, while art and practical wisdom are 114 certainly concerned only with what is variable. Moreover, these fundamental principles cannot be reached by philosophic wisdom : for the philosophically wise man must prove certain things by deduction.

Now if it is true that there are four conditions of mind which enable us to reach truth, and never to fail to reach truth, either about invariable or about variable things—scientific 5 knowledge, practical wisdom, philosophic wisdom, inductive reason: and if out of these four it cannot be any one of three by which we reach the fundamental principles in question (the three being practical wisdom, scientific knowledge, philosophic wisdom): it follows that it must be inductive reason by which we reach those fundamental principles.

---

¹ sc. 'and this name *opinionative* is the right one to give to this part of the mind here.'

VII

τὴν δὲ σοφίαν ἔν τε ταῖς τέχναις τοῖς ἀκριβεστάτοις
10 τὰς τέχνας ἀποδίδομεν, οἷον Φειδίαν λιθουργὸν σοφὸν καὶ
Πολύκλειτον ἀνδριαντοποιόν, ἐνταῦθα μὲν οὖν οὐθὲν ἄλλο
σημαίνοντες τὴν σοφίαν ἢ ὅτι ἀρετὴ τέχνης ἐστίν· εἶναι
δέ τινας σοφοὺς οἰόμεθα ὅλως οὐ κατὰ μέρος οὐδ᾽ ἄλλο τι
σοφούς, ὥσπερ Ὅμηρός φησιν ἐν τῷ Μαργίτῃ

15   τὸν δ᾽ οὔτ᾽ ἄρ σκαπτῆρα θεοὶ θέσαν οὔτ᾽ ἀροτῆρα
οὔτ᾽ ἄλλως τι σοφόν.

ὥστε δῆλον ὅτι ἀκριβεστάτη ἂν τῶν ἐπιστημῶν εἴη ἡ
σοφία. δεῖ ἄρα τὸν σοφὸν μὴ μόνον τὰ ἐκ τῶν ἀρχῶν
εἰδέναι, ἀλλὰ καὶ περὶ τὰς ἀρχὰς ἀληθεύειν. ὥστε εἴη
ἂν ἡ σοφία νοῦς καὶ ἐπιστήμη, ὥσπερ κεφαλὴν ἔχουσα
20 ἐπιστήμη τῶν τιμιωτάτων. ἄτοπον γὰρ εἴ τις τὴν πολιτικὴν ἢ τὴν φρόνησιν σπουδαιοτάτην οἴεται εἶναι, εἰ μὴ
τὸ ἄριστον τῶν ἐν τῷ κόσμῳ ἄνθρωπός ἐστιν. εἰ δὴ
ὑγιεινὸν μὲν καὶ ἀγαθὸν ἕτερον ἀνθρώποις καὶ ἰχθύσιν,
τὸ δὲ λευκὸν καὶ εὐθὺ ταὐτὸν ἀεί, καὶ τὸ σοφὸν ταὐτὸ
25 πάντες ἂν εἴποιεν, φρόνιμον δὲ ἕτερον· τὰ γὰρ περὶ αὑτὸ
ἕκαστα τὸ εὖ θεωροῦν φησὶν εἶναι φρόνιμον, καὶ τούτῳ
ἐπιτρέψει αὐτά. διὸ καὶ τῶν θηρίων ἔνια φρόνιμά φασιν
εἶναι, ὅσα περὶ τὸν αὑτῶν βίον ἔχοντα φαίνεται δύναμιν
προνοητικήν. φανερὸν δὲ καὶ ὅτι οὐκ ἂν εἴη ἡ σοφία
30 καὶ ἡ πολιτικὴ ἡ αὐτή· εἰ γὰρ τὴν περὶ τὰ ὠφέλιμα τὰ
αὑτοῖς ἐροῦσι σοφίαν, πολλαὶ ἔσονται σοφίαι· οὐ γὰρ
μία περὶ τὸ ἁπάντων ἀγαθὸν τῶν ζῴων, ἀλλ᾽ ἑτέρα περὶ

1141 a 17   ἀκριβεστάτη Κ Μ Byw : ἡ ἀκριβεστάτη L Bek Sus
25   τὰ γὰρ περὶ αὑτὸ Byw : τὸ γὰρ περὶ αὑτὸ codd. Bek Rassow : τὸ γὰρ
περὶ [αὑτὸ] Burnet : τὰ γὰρ περὶ αὑτὸν Coraes Susemihl
τὸ εὖ K L Sus Byw : εὖ M Bek Rassow
26   φησὶν Κ Byw : φαίεν L M : φαῖεν ἂν Bek Rassow Sus Burnet :
φασὶν Busse (Hermes xviii 137)
ἐπιτρέψει Κ Sus Byw : ἐπιτρέψειεν L O : ἐπιτρέψειαν M Bek
Rassow : ἐπιτρέψειαν ἂν Burnet
αὐτά K L Bek Sus Byw : ἑαυτούς M Rassow

VII

The word σοφία (philosophic wisdom) we apply, in the sphere of the arts, to the character of those who are most perfect[1] in their arts. Thus we call Pheidias σοφός as a sculptor, and Polycleitus σοφός as a statuary. Here, then, we mean nothing more by the word σοφία than excellence in art.

But we hold that certain people are σοφοί in general, not about some particular thing: not as Homer says in the Margites 'wise in anything else'—

> 'Him had the gods not made a wise digger, nor yet a wise ploughman,
> Nor wise in anything else.'

It is plain, therefore, that σοφία (philosophic wisdom) must be the most perfect of the means of knowledge. Hence the philosophically wise man must not only know deductions from his fundamental principles, but also reach truth about those principles. Therefore philosophic wisdom must be a combination of inductive reason and scientific knowledge, what may be called the perfected knowledge of the loftiest subjects. [2] For it is absurd for anyone to suppose that political wisdom or practical wisdom is the noblest kind of knowledge, since a human being is not the finest thing in the world.

Now if it is true that the wholesome and the good are one thing for human beings and another thing for fish, while the white and the straight are the same thing for all: all must agree that the philosophically wise also is the same thing for all, but the practically wise one thing for one and another thing for another. For men give the name of 'practically wise' to what can discern properly the various affairs that concern itself, and it is to such a creature that they are ready to entrust the conduct of those affairs. Therefore people even say that some of the lower animals are practically wise; such namely as plainly have the power of foresight about their own lives.

And it is clear too that philosophic wisdom and political wisdom cannot be the same thing: for if people are going to give the name 'philosophic wisdom' to the wisdom that is concerned with what is good for themselves, there will be a number of kinds of philosophic wisdom. For there cannot be a single such wisdom, concerned with the good of all living beings as a whole: there must be a separate wisdom con-

---

[1] ἀκριβής seems to include the notions of 'exact,' 'complete,' and 'stable.'
[2] sc. The loftiest subjects, I say : for....

ἕκαστον, εἰ μὴ καὶ ἰατρικὴ μία περὶ πάντων τῶν ὄντων.

εἰ δ᾽ ὅτι βέλτιστον ἄνθρωπος τῶν ἄλλων ζῴων, οὐδὲν
1b διαφέρει· καὶ γὰρ ἀνθρώπου ἄλλα πολὺ θειότερα τὴν
φύσιν, οἷον φανερώτατά γε ἐξ ὧν ὁ κόσμος συνέστηκεν.
ἐκ δὴ τῶν εἰρημένων δῆλον ὅτι ἡ σοφία ἐστὶ καὶ ἐπιστήμη
καὶ νοῦς τῶν τιμιωτάτων τῇ φύσει. διὸ Ἀναξαγόραν
5 καὶ Θαλῆν καὶ τοὺς τοιούτους σοφοὺς μὲν φρονίμους δ᾽
οὔ φασιν εἶναι, ὅταν ἴδωσιν ἀγνοοῦντας τὰ συμφέροντα
ἑαυτοῖς, καὶ περιττὰ μὲν καὶ θαυμαστὰ καὶ χαλεπὰ καὶ
8 δαιμόνια εἰδέναι αὐτούς φασιν, ἄχρηστα δ᾽, ὅτι οὐ τὰ
ἀνθρώπινα ἀγαθὰ ζητοῦσιν.

ἡ δὲ φρόνησις περὶ τὰ ἀνθρώπινα καὶ περὶ ὧν ἔστι
10 βουλεύσασθαι· τοῦ γὰρ φρονίμου μάλιστα τοῦτο ἔργον
εἶναί φαμεν, τὸ εὖ βουλεύεσθαι, βουλεύεται δὲ οὐδεὶς
περὶ τῶν ἀδυνάτων ἄλλως ἔχειν, οὐδ᾽ ὅσων μὴ τέλος τι
ἔστιν, καὶ τοῦτο πρακτὸν ἀγαθόν. ὁ δ᾽ ἁπλῶς εὔβουλος
ὁ τοῦ ἀρίστου ἀνθρώπῳ τῶν πρακτῶν στοχαστικὸς κατὰ
15 τὸν λογισμόν. οὐδ᾽ ἐστὶν ἡ φρόνησις τῶν καθόλου μόνον,
ἀλλὰ δεῖ καὶ τὰ καθ᾽ ἕκαστα γνωρίζειν· πρακτικὴ γάρ, ἡ
δὲ πρᾶξις περὶ τὰ καθ᾽ ἕκαστα. διὸ καὶ ἔνιοι οὐκ εἰδότες
ἑτέρων εἰδότων πρακτικώτεροι, καὶ ἐν τοῖς ἄλλοις οἱ
ἔμπειροι· εἰ γὰρ εἰδείη ὅτι τὰ κοῦφα εὔπεπτα κρέα καὶ
20 ὑγιεινά, ποῖα δὲ κοῦφα ἀγνοεῖ, οὐ ποιήσει ὑγίειαν, ἀλλ᾽
ὁ εἰδὼς ὅτι τὰ ὀρνίθεια [κοῦφα καὶ] ὑγιεινὰ ποιήσει
μᾶλλον. ἡ δὲ φρόνησις πρακτική· ὥστε δεῖ ἄμφω

1141 b 19 ἀγνοοῖ K Bek Sus Byw : ἀγνοεῖ L M Michelet Ramsauer
20 [κοῦφα καὶ] Trendelenburg Ramsauer Susemihl Stewart Bywater :
κοῦφα καὶ Bekker Burnet : κρέα καὶ conj. Rassow

cerned with each[1]: unless there is also[2] a single science of healing for all existing things.

Our argument[3] is not affected by the objection that a human being is the highest of all animals. The fact is that there are other beings whose nature is far more divine than the nature of human beings: for example, to mention those most fully revealed to us, the bodies of which the universe is 114 harmoniously composed.

From what has been said, therefore, it is plain that philosophic wisdom is the combination of scientific knowledge with inductive reason, and that it concerns those things whose nature is most exalted. Consequently we call Anaxagoras and Thales and such persons philosophically wise, but say 5 that they are not practically wise, whenever we find them ignorant of what is good for themselves: and we say that the knowledge which they have is rare, and wonderful, and hard to attain, and divinely splendid, but at the same time useless, because they do not seek to know the things that are good for human beings.

But practical wisdom is concerned with the affairs of human beings, and only with such things as can be the objects of deliberation. For we consider that good delibera- 10 tion is pre-eminently the work of the practically wise man: and no one deliberates about things that cannot vary, nor about things that are not the means to some end, and that end a good that can be achieved: and the good deliberator in general is the man who can in his calculation reach the best of achievable goods for man.

Practical wisdom does not lead to the knowledge of 15 general principles only: it is necessary to know particular facts also[4]: for practical wisdom is concerned with action, and action depends upon particular facts. Hence some men without knowledge[5] can act more effectively than others with knowledge[5], especially those who have experience. If a man knows that light meat is digestible and wholesome, but does not know what kind of meats are light, he will not 20 restore one's health; it is the man who knows that poultry is digestible who is more likely to do this. But practical wisdom is concerned with action: we ought therefore[6], if we

---

[1] i.e. with the good of each kind of living being.
[2] sc. (which obviously there is not).
[3] sc. the argument that philosophic wisdom is more lofty than practical or political wisdom.
[4] sc. in order to be practically wise.
[5] i.e. the knowledge of universals.
[6] sc. in order to be practically wise.

ἔχειν, ἢ ταύτην μᾶλλον. εἴη δ᾽ ἄν τις καὶ ἐνταῦθα ἀρχιτεκτονική.

VIII

ἔστιν δὲ καὶ ἡ πολιτικὴ καὶ ἡ φρόνησις ἡ αὐτὴ μὲν
25 ἕξις, τὸ μέντοι εἶναι οὐ ταὐτὸν αὐταῖς. τῆς δὲ περὶ πόλιν
ἡ μὲν ὡς ἀρχιτεκτονικὴ φρόνησις νομοθετική, ἡ δὲ ὡς τὰ
καθ᾽ ἕκαστα τὸ κοινὸν ἔχει ὄνομα, πολιτική· αὕτη δὲ
πρακτικὴ καὶ βουλευτική· τὸ γὰρ ψήφισμα πρακτὸν ὡς τὸ
ἔσχατον. διὸ πολιτεύεσθαι τούτους μόνον λέγουσιν· μόνοι
30 γὰρ πράττουσιν οὗτοι ὥσπερ οἱ χειροτέχναι. δοκεῖ δὲ καὶ
φρόνησις μάλιστ᾽ εἶναι ἡ περὶ αὐτὸν καὶ ἕνα. καὶ ἔχει
αὕτη τὸ κοινὸν ὄνομα, φρόνησις· ἐκείνων δὲ ἡ μὲν οἰκονομία ἡ δὲ νομοθεσία ἡ δὲ πολιτική, καὶ ταύτης ἡ μὲν
βουλευτικὴ ἡ δὲ δικαστική. εἶδος μὲν οὖν τι ἂν εἴη
γνώσεως τὸ αὑτῷ εἰδέναι· ἀλλ᾽ ἔχει διαφορὰν πολλήν·
2 a καὶ δοκεῖ ὁ τὰ περὶ αὑτὸν εἰδὼς καὶ διατρίβων φρόνιμος
εἶναι, οἱ δὲ πολιτικοὶ πολυπράγμονες· διὸ Εὐριπίδης

πῶς δ᾽ ἂν φρονοίην, ᾧ παρῆν ἀπραγμόνως
ἐν τοῖσι πολλοῖς ἠριθμημένον στρατοῦ
ἴσον μετασχεῖν ;
τοὺς γὰρ περισσοὺς καί τι πράσσοντας πλέον...

ζητοῦσι γὰρ τὸ αὑτοῖς ἀγαθόν, καὶ οἴονται τοῦτο δεῖν
πράττειν. ἐκ ταύτης οὖν τῆς δόξης ἐλήλυθεν τὸ τούτους
φρονίμους εἶναι· καίτοι ἴσως οὐκ ἔστι τὸ αὑτοῦ εὖ ἄνευ
10 οἰκονομίας οὐδ᾽ ἄνευ πολιτείας. ἔτι δὲ τὰ αὑτοῦ πῶς δεῖ
διοικεῖν, ἄδηλον καὶ σκεπτέον. σημεῖον δ᾽ ἐστὶ τοῦ εἰρημένου καὶ διότι γεωμετρικοὶ μὲν νέοι καὶ μαθηματικοὶ

1141 b 25 φρόνησις seclusit Scaliger, Susemihl
    26 τὰ seclusit Stewart, Burnet
    28 μόνον Κ Μ Sus Byw : μόνους L Bek Burnet.
    34 τὸ αὑτῷ Κ Bek Sus Byw : τὸ τὰ αὑτῷ L M Coraes Fritzsche :
        corruptum putat Ramsauer
1142 a 1 ὁ τὰ περὶ L M Bek Sus Byw : ὁ τὸ περὶ pr. Κ Burnet
    4 ἠριθμημένον Κ Γ Byw : ἠριθμημένῳ L M Bek Sus

cannot have both kinds of knowledge, to have the latter rather than the former[1]

But here too[2] there must be a supreme directing form of wisdom.

VIII

Political wisdom and practical wisdom are in practice the same quality, though the words do not really mean the same 25 thing. Of the practical wisdom that is concerned with the state as a whole, the supreme directing kind is legislative wisdom, the kind concerned with particular occurrences has the name, political wisdom, which is common to both. This latter is concerned[3] with action and deliberation: for the parliamentary enactment is a thing to be done[4], like the particular action. Hence people say that it is only those who deal with particular occurrences who 'take part in politics': for it is only these who perform actions, like workmen in a 30 trade.

It is also held that practical wisdom is most properly the kind that concerns a man's own single self: and this kind is given the name, practical wisdom, which belongs to all the kinds. The other kinds are household wisdom, legislative wisdom, and political wisdom ; and the latter includes parliamentary and judicial wisdom.

To know what is good for one's self must certainly be one kind of knowledge ; but it is very different from other kinds ; and people hold that the man who knows and occupies himself 11 with his own concerns is practically wise, and that the politicians are restless meddlers ; thus Euripides says—

> My practice wisdom ? when I might have been
> At peace, accounted one among the many,
> Equal with others ?...   5
> They that aspire too high, and strive too hard...

Such persons aim at their own good, and suppose that to be a man's chief duty. It is, therefore, this opinion that leads to the statement that these men are practically wise. And yet no doubt one's personal prosperity cannot exist without household and political wisdom.   10

Further, the proper way of managing one's own affairs is not easy to discover and requires much learning. A proof of this statement is the fact that young men may become good at geometry and mathematics and in such matters philo-

---

[1] i.e. the knowledge of particular facts rather than that of general principles.
[2] sc. in practical as in philosophic wisdom.
[3] i.e. specially concerned.
[4] i.e. it is a statement of the thing to be done.

γίνονται καὶ σοφοὶ τὰ τοιαῦτα, φρόνιμος δ᾽ οὐ δοκεῖ
γίνεσθαι. αἴτιον δ᾽ ὅτι καὶ τῶν καθ᾽ ἕκαστά ἐστιν ἡ
15 φρόνησις, ἃ γίνεται γνώριμα ἐξ ἐμπειρίας, νέος δὲ ἔμπειρος
οὐκ ἔστιν—πλῆθος γὰρ χρόνου ποιεῖ τὴν ἐμπειρίαν.
ἐπεὶ καὶ τοῦτ᾽ ἄν τις σκέψαιτο, διὰ τί δὴ μαθηματικὸς
μὲν παῖς γένοιτ᾽ ἄν, σοφὸς δ᾽ ἢ φυσικὸς οὔ. ἢ ὅτι τὰ
μὲν δι᾽ ἀφαιρέσεώς ἐστιν, τῶν δ᾽ αἱ ἀρχαὶ ἐξ ἐμπειρίας·
20 καὶ τὰ μὲν οὐ πιστεύουσιν οἱ νέοι ἀλλὰ λέγουσιν, τῶν δὲ
τὸ τί ἐστιν οὐκ ἄδηλον; ἔτι ἡ ἁμαρτία ἢ περὶ τὸ καθόλου
ἐν τῷ βουλεύσασθαι ἢ περὶ τὸ καθ᾽ ἕκαστον· ἢ γὰρ ὅτι
πάντα τὰ βαρύσταθμα ὕδατα φαῦλα, ἢ ὅτι τοδὶ βαρύσταθμον. ὅτι δ᾽ ἡ φρόνησις οὐκ ἐπιστήμη, φανερόν·
25 τοῦ γὰρ ἐσχάτου ἐστίν, ὥσπερ εἴρηται· τὸ γὰρ πρακτὸν
τοιοῦτον. ἀντίκειται μὲν δὴ τῷ νῷ· ὁ μὲν γὰρ νοῦς τῶν
ὅρων, ὧν οὐκ ἔστι λόγος, ἡ δὲ τοῦ ἐσχάτου, οὗ οὐκ ἔστιν
ἐπιστήμη ἀλλ᾽ αἴσθησις, οὐχ ἡ τῶν ἰδίων, ἀλλ᾽ οἵᾳ
αἰσθανόμεθα ὅτι τὸ ἐν τοῖς μαθηματικοῖς ἔσχατον τρίγω-
30 νον· στήσεται γὰρ κἀκεῖ. ἀλλ᾽ αὕτη μᾶλλον αἴσθησις
ἢ φρόνησις, ἐκείνης δὲ ἄλλο εἶδος.

IX

τὸ ζητεῖν δὲ καὶ τὸ βουλεύεσθαι διαφέρει· τὸ γὰρ
βουλεύεσθαι ζητεῖν τι ἐστίν. δεῖ δὲ λαβεῖν καὶ περὶ
εὐβουλίας τί ἐστιν, πότερον ἐπιστήμη τις ἢ δόξα ἢ
εὐστοχία ἢ ἄλλο τι γένος. ἐπιστήμη μὲν δὴ οὐκ ἔστιν·
2 b οὐ γὰρ ζητοῦσι περὶ ὧν ἴσασιν, ἡ δ᾽ εὐβουλία βουλή τις,
ὁ δὲ βουλευόμενος ζητεῖ καὶ λογίζεται. ἀλλὰ μὴν οὐδ᾽

1142 a 14 ὅτι καὶ τῶν K L Sus Byw : ὅτι τῶν M Bek
28 ἐν τοῖς μαθηματικοῖς seclusit Bywater, nec tamen Burnet
30 ἢ K edd : ἡ L M Γ : ἢ ἡ conj. Burnet

sophically wise, but do not seem to become practically wise. The reason is that practical wisdom is concerned with practical facts, which become known through experience, whereas a young man has no great experience, since it is only the progress of time that can produce experience.

Indeed, it may also be asked, Why, then, may a boy be good at mathematics, but not at metaphysics or natural science? No doubt the reason is that mathematics deals with abstractions, whereas the first principles of metaphysics and natural science can only be reached by experience, and young persons do not believe these with conviction, but merely repeat them, whereas the real meaning of mathematical first principles is quite plain.

Moreover, error may occur in deliberation either with regard to the universal or with regard to the particular: one may say either that all heavy water is unwholesome or that this particular water is heavy.

And it is plain that practical wisdom is not scientific knowledge: for it is, as has been said, concerned with particulars, since actions are always particulars.

It corresponds therefore to inductive reason: for inductive reason leads to axioms of which no demonstration is possible, while practical wisdom deals with particulars, of which there can be no scientific knowledge, but only sense-perception, not the perception of the several senses, but that whereby in mathematics we perceive that the particular figure before us is[1] a triangle: for here too[2] one must come to a stop somewhere. This perception[3] however is rather sensation than practical wisdom, but it is a different species of sensation from the other one mentioned[4].

IX

Now search and deliberation are not the same thing: deliberation is a particular kind of search. We ought also to ascertain what deliberative excellence is, whether it is some kind of knowledge, or opinion, or success in conjecturing, or some other kind of thing.

It is, in the first place, not knowledge: for people do not search for what they know already: but deliberative excellence is a kind of deliberation[5], and the man who deliberates searches and makes calculations. Neither, again, is it success

---

[1] sc. for instance.   [2] i.e. in mathematics as in problems of conduct.
[3] i.e. that in problems of conduct.
[4] i.e. the sensation of the several senses.
[5] perhaps βουλή may be translated 'deliberative quality' here.

εὐστοχία· ἄνευ τε γὰρ λόγου καὶ ταχύ τι ἡ εὐστοχία,
βουλεύονται δὲ πολὺν χρόνον, καὶ φασὶ πράττειν μὲν
5 δεῖν ταχὺ τὰ βουλευθέντα, βουλεύεσθαι δὲ βραδέως. ἔτι
ἡ ἀγχίνοια ἕτερον καὶ ἡ εὐβουλία· ἔστι δὲ εὐστοχία τις ἡ
ἀγχίνοια. οὐδὲ δὴ δόξα ἡ εὐβουλία οὐδεμία. ἀλλ' ἐπεὶ
ὁ μὲν κακῶς βουλευόμενος ἁμαρτάνει, ὁ δ' εὖ ὀρθῶς
βουλεύεται, δῆλον ὅτι. ὀρθότης τις ἡ εὐβουλία ἐστίν, οὔτε
10 ἐπιστήμης δὲ οὔτε δόξης· ἐπιστήμης μὲν γὰρ οὐκ ἔστιν
ὀρθότης (οὐδὲ γὰρ ἁμαρτία), δόξης δ' ὀρθότης ἀλήθεια·
ἅμα δὲ καὶ ὥρισται ἤδη πᾶν οὗ δόξα ἔστιν. ἀλλὰ μὴν
οὐδ' ἄνευ λόγου ἡ εὐβουλία. διανοίας ἄρα λείπεται· αὕτη
γὰρ οὔπω φάσις· καὶ γὰρ ἡ δόξα οὐ ζήτησις ἀλλὰ φάσις
15 τις ἤδη, ὁ δὲ βουλευόμενος, ἐάν τε εὖ ἐάν τε καὶ κακῶς
βουλεύηται, ζητεῖ τι καὶ λογίζεται. ἀλλ' ὀρθότης τίς
ἐστιν ἡ εὐβουλία βουλῆς· διὸ ἡ βουλὴ ζητητέα πρῶτον
τί καὶ περὶ τί. ἐπεὶ δ' ἡ ὀρθότης πλεοναχῶς, δῆλον ὅτι
οὐ πᾶσα· ὁ γὰρ ἀκρατὴς καὶ ὁ φαῦλος ὃ προτίθεται ἰδεῖν
20 ἐκ τοῦ λογισμοῦ τεύξεται, ὥστε ὀρθῶς ἔσται βεβουλευ-
μένος, κακὸν δὲ μέγα εἰληφώς· δοκεῖ δὲ ἀγαθόν τι τὸ εὖ
βεβουλεῦσθαι. ἡ γὰρ τοιαύτη ὀρθότης βουλῆς εὐβουλία,
ἡ ἀγαθοῦ τευκτική. ἀλλ' ἔστι καὶ τούτου ψευδεῖ συλλογισμῷ τυχεῖν, καὶ ὃ μὲν δεῖ ποιῆσαι τυχεῖν, δι' οὗ δὲ οὔ,
25 ἀλλὰ ψευδῆ τὸν μέσον ὅρον εἶναι· ὥστε οὐδ' αὕτη πω
εὐβουλία, καθ' ἣν οὗ δεῖ μὲν τυγχάνει, οὐ μέντοι δι' οὗ
ἔδει. ἔτι ἔστι πολὺν χρόνον βουλευόμενον τυχεῖν, τὸν δὲ

1142 b 15 ἐάν τε καὶ K M Sus Byw : ἐάν τε L O Bek
  18 ὃ codd. edd : οὗ conj. Rassow
  19 ἰδεῖν codd. (δεῖν Γ) : ἰδεῖν Bek Fritzsche Ramsauer : †ἰδεῖν† Grant
      Byw Sus : δεῖν Madvig Jackson Grant Burnet : λαβεῖν conj.
      Stewart : τυχεῖν conj. Rassow : τούτου conj. Byw : εἰ δεινός conj.
      Apelt
  21 τι K M Sus Byw : τι εἶναι L O Bek
      γὰρ codd. edd : ἄρα conj. Spengel

in conjecturing: for success in conjecturing is attained without reasoning, and is a rapid sort of thing, whereas a man deliberates for a long time, and people say that one should act quickly when deliberation is over, but deliberate slowly.   5

Quickness of judgment also is different from deliberative excellence: in fact quickness of judgment is a particular kind of success in conjecture. Nor again is deliberative excellence any kind of opinion.

But since the man who deliberates badly goes wrong, and the man who deliberates well does it rightly, it is plain that deliberative excellence is some kind of rightness: but a rightness neither of knowledge nor of opinion: there cannot 10 be a rightness of knowledge, since there cannot be a wrongness of knowledge: while rightness of opinion is truth[1], and moreover, everything about which we have an opinion is already marked off from all other things. At the same time, deliberative excellence implies the power of reasoning. It must therefore be rightness of the inquiring intellect: for the intellect while inquiring has not yet arrived at assertion; whereas opinion is not a search, but an assertion of something 15 already discovered; but the man who deliberates, whether he deliberates well or badly, makes some kind of search or calculation.

But deliberative excellence is rightness in deliberation: we must therefore first know what deliberation is and what it is about. And whereas the word 'rightness' can be used in more senses than one, it is plain that not all the senses are appropriate here. For the man without self-control, or the wicked man, will reach through his calculation the conclusion 20 which it lies before him to discover, so that he will have deliberated rightly[2], but will have procured himself a great evil: but to have deliberated well is evidently something good, for deliberative excellence is that sort of rightness in deliberating which leads to the gaining of some good.

But it is possible to gain even this by a false reasoning process, and it is possible that the conclusion as to what ought to be done may be right, but that the reason which led 25 to the conclusion may be wrong, and the middle term may be the wrong one[3]. That quality then is still not deliberative excellence which leads a man to arrive at the right conclusion, but yet not by the right means. Moreover, it is possible to arrive at a conclusion by means of long deliberation, while another man may do it quickly. With the former, then, even

---

[1] i.e. simply truth and nothing more.
[2] i.e. in one sense of the word 'rightly.'
[3] lit. false.

ταχύ· οὐκοῦν οὐδ᾽ ἐκείνη πω εὐβουλία, ἀλλ᾽ ὀρθότης ἡ
κατὰ τὸ ὠφέλιμον, καὶ οὗ δεῖ καὶ ὡς καὶ ὅτε. ἔτι ἔστι
30 καὶ ἁπλῶς εὖ βεβουλεῦσθαι καὶ πρός τι τέλος. ἡ μὲν δὴ
ἁπλῶς ἡ πρὸς τὸ τέλος τὸ ἁπλῶς κατορθοῦσα, τὶς δὲ
ἡ πρός τι τέλος. εἰ δὴ τῶν φρονίμων τὸ εὖ βεβουλεῦσθαι,
ἡ εὐβουλία εἴη ἂν ὀρθότης ἡ κατὰ τὸ συμφέρον πρὸς
τὸ τέλος, οὗ ἡ φρόνησις ἀληθὴς ὑπόληψίς ἐστιν.

X

ἔστι δὲ καὶ ἡ σύνεσις καὶ ἡ εὐσυνεσία, καθ᾽ ἃς λέ-
3 a γομεν συνετοὺς καὶ εὐσυνέτους, οὔτε ὅλως τὸ αὐτὸ ἐπιστήμῃ ἢ δόξῃ (πάντες γὰρ ἂν ἦσαν συνετοί) οὔτε τις μία
τῶν κατὰ μέρος ἐπιστημῶν, οἷον ἡ ἰατρικὴ περὶ ὑγιεινῶν,
ἡ γεωμετρία περὶ μεγέθη· οὔτε γὰρ περὶ τῶν ἀεὶ ὄντων
5 καὶ ἀκινήτων ἡ σύνεσίς ἐστιν οὔτε περὶ τῶν γινομένων
ὁτουοῦν, ἀλλὰ περὶ ὧν ἀπορήσειεν ἄν τις καὶ βουλεύσαιτο.
διὸ περὶ τὰ αὐτὰ μὲν τῇ φρονήσει ἐστίν· οὐκ ἔστι δὲ
τὸ αὐτὸ σύνεσις καὶ φρόνησις· ἡ μὲν γὰρ φρόνησις
ἐπιτακτική ἐστιν· τί γὰρ δεῖ πράττειν ἢ μή, τὸ τέλος
10 αὐτῆς ἐστίν· ἡ δὲ σύνεσις κριτικὴ μόνον. ταὐτὸ γὰρ
σύνεσις καὶ εὐσυνεσία καὶ συνετοὶ καὶ εὐσύνετοι. ἔστι δ᾽
οὔτε τὸ ἔχειν τὴν φρόνησιν οὔτε τὸ λαμβάνειν ἡ σύνεσις·
ἀλλ᾽ ὥσπερ τὸ μανθάνειν λέγεται συνιέναι, ὅταν χρῆται
τῇ ἐπιστήμῃ, οὕτως ἐν τῷ χρῆσθαι τῇ δόξῃ ἐπὶ τὸ κρίνειν
15 περὶ τούτων περὶ ὧν ἡ φρόνησίς ἐστιν, ἄλλου λέγοντος,
καὶ κρίνειν καλῶς· τὸ γὰρ εὖ τῷ καλῶς τὸ αὐτό. καὶ

1142 b 31 τὶς δὲ K M Sus Byw : ἡ δέ τις L O Bek
33 πρὸς τὸ τέλος K Byw : πρός τι τέλος LM Bek Sus
35 εὐσυνεσία H. Stephanus Spengel Sus Byw : ἀσυνεσία codd. Bek
1143 a 1 εὐσυνέτους H. Stephanus Spengel Sus Byw : ἀσυνέτους codd. Bek
3 οἷον ἡ K M Sus Byw : οἷον L Bek Burnet
4 ἡ γεωμετρία K Sus Byw : ἢ γεωμετρία L M Bek Burnet
μεγέθη K M Ramsauer Sus Byw : μεγέθους L Bek
14 ἐπὶ τὸ codd. Bek Sus Byw : ἐπὶ τῷ Coraes Fritzsche

now we have not deliberative excellence[1], but only when we have rightness of a beneficial kind, and have the right conclusion reached by the right means and at the right time.

Once more, it is possible to deliberate[2] well in general or 30 with a view to some particular end. Deliberative excellence in general, therefore, is that which leads to success with regard to the general end, while that deliberative excellence which leads to success with regard to some special end is a special kind of deliberative excellence.

If therefore to deliberate[2] well is characteristic of the practically wise man, deliberative excellence must be that rightness which declares what is profitable as a means to the end, of which[3] practical wisdom is the true conception.

X

Judgment, too, or sound judgment, the quality whose possessor we call judicious or a sound judge, is not the same 11 thing as scientific knowledge in general: nor as opinion, for in that case everyone would be judicious: nor is it any one special kind of knowledge, such as medicine the knowledge of restoratives of health, or geometry the knowledge of magnitudes. For judgment is not concerned with the things that exist eternally and cannot be affected, nor with all and any of 5 the things that come into existence, but only with the things about which one may feel doubt and deliberate. Judgment is therefore concerned with the same things as practical wisdom, but yet judgment and practical wisdom are not identical.

Practical wisdom gives commands; its conclusion is the statement of what we ought or ought not to do: but judgment 10 is simply critical. [4](For judgment and sound judgment are the same, the judicious person is the same as the sound judge.)

Judgment is not the having of practical wisdom, nor yet the acquiring of it: but just as learning is called judgment, when a man uses his faculty of scientific knowledge, so too when a man uses his faculty of opinion, to criticise what another man says, about the matters with which practical 15 wisdom is concerned: that is to say, to criticise well— 'soundly' and 'well' meaning the same thing.

[1] lit. so not even that is yet deliberative excellence.
[2] lit. to have deliberated.
[3] the reference of the relative pronoun is doubtful.
[4] sc. there is no need to go on repeating both the words 'judgment' and 'sound judgment'....

ἐντεῦθεν ἐλήλυθεν τοὔνομα ἡ σύνεσις, καθ' ἣν εὐσύνετοι, ἐκ τῆς ἐν τῷ μανθάνειν· λέγομεν γὰρ τὸ μανθάνειν συνιέναι πολλάκις.

XI

20   ἡ δὲ καλουμένη γνώμη, καθ' ἣν συγγνώμονας καὶ ἔχειν φαμὲν γνώμην, ἡ τοῦ ἐπιεικοῦς ἐστι κρίσις ὀρθή. σημεῖον δέ· τὸν γὰρ ἐπιεικῆ μάλιστά φαμεν εἶναι συγγνωμονικόν, καὶ ἐπιεικὲς τὸ ἔχειν περὶ ἔνια συγγνώμην. ἡ δὲ συγγνώμη γνώμη ἐστὶ κριτικὴ τοῦ ἐπιεικοῦς ὀρθή· ὀρθὴ δ' ἡ τοῦ ἀληθοῦς.

25   εἰσὶ δὲ πᾶσαι αἱ ἕξεις εὐλόγως εἰς ταὐτὸ τείνουσαι· λέγομεν γὰρ γνώμην καὶ σύνεσιν καὶ φρόνησιν καὶ νοῦν ἐπὶ τοὺς αὐτοὺς ἐπιφέροντες γνώμην ἔχειν καὶ νοῦν ἤδη καὶ φρονίμους καὶ συνετούς. πᾶσαι γὰρ αἱ δυνάμεις αὗται τῶν ἐσχάτων εἰσὶ καὶ τῶν καθ' ἕκαστον· καὶ ἐν 30 μὲν τῷ κριτικὸς εἶναι περὶ ὧν ὁ φρόνιμος, συνετός, καὶ εὐγνώμων ἢ συγγνώμων—τὰ γὰρ ἐπιεικῆ κοινὰ τῶν ἀγαθῶν ἁπάντων ἐστὶν ἐν τῷ πρὸς ἄλλον. ἔστι δὲ τῶν καθ' ἕκαστα καὶ τῶν ἐσχάτων ἅπαντα τὰ πρακτά· καὶ γὰρ τὸν φρόνιμον δεῖ γινώσκειν αὐτά, καὶ ἡ σύνεσις καὶ 35 ἡ γνώμη περὶ τὰ πρακτά, ταῦτα δ' ἔσχατα. καὶ ὁ νοῦς τῶν ἐσχάτων ἐπ' ἀμφότερα· καὶ γὰρ τῶν πρώτων ὅρων 3 b καὶ τῶν ἐσχάτων νοῦς ἐστι καὶ οὐ λόγος, καὶ ὁ μὲν κατὰ τὰς ἀποδείξεις τῶν ἀκινήτων ὅρων καὶ πρώτων, ὁ δ' ἐν ταῖς πρακτικαῖς τοῦ ἐσχάτου καὶ ἐνδεχομένου καὶ τῆς ἑτέρας προτάσεως· ἀρχαὶ γὰρ τοῦ οὗ ἕνεκα αὗται· ἐκ

1143 a 19 συγγνώμονας K M Byw : εὐγνώμονας L Bek Sus
30 εὐγνώμων ἢ seclusit Burnet
33 τὰ πρακτά seclusit Ramsauer

Indeed this name of judgment, the quality that makes people sound judges, is used in a sense transferred from that which is applied to learning: we often give learning the name of judgment[1].

XI

Consideration, as it is called, the quality whose possessors 20 we call considerate[2], and say that they have consideration[3], is the correct critical judgment of what is fair. This is proved by the fact that we describe the fair-minded man as particularly considerate[2], and it is fair to take certain facts into consideration[4]. Sympathetic considerateness[5] is the correct critical consideration of what is fair: and correct consideration is that which reaches truth.

All the qualities mentioned[6] may fairly be said to have a 25 common tendency. We attribute consideration[7], judgment, practical wisdom, and intelligence to the same people, and say that they 'have consideration,' 'have intelligence by this time,' and are practically wise and judicious. For all these faculties are concerned with ultimates, that is to say, particulars: and in judging of others' opinions about matters with which the practically wise man deals, a man may show himself judicious, and also a good considerer or a considerate 30 man—for the quality of fairness belongs to all good behaviour towards other persons.

All actions belong to the class of particulars or ultimates, for the practically wise man must understand them[8]: and judgment and consideration are concerned with actions, and these are ultimates[9].

Νοῦς (Inductive reason or Intelligence) is also concerned 35 with ultimates, in both senses[10]: for it is this, and not deductive 11 reason, which leads to knowledge of both the primary and the ultimate propositions. This it is which leads to the unassailable primary propositions that are the foundation of deductions[11]: and this it is which in practical deductions[12] leads to the particular, a not invariable fact, which forms the minor premiss: these particular facts are the foundation of the end

---

[1] the word σύνεσις translated 'judgment,' can also mean 'intelligence,' as here.
[2] more properly 'forgiving.'   [3] more properly 'have good sense,' 'are right.'
[4] properly 'to make allowances for,' 'to forgive.'
[5] συγγνώμη is the ordinary word for 'forgiveness.'
[6] sc. the four φρόνησις εὐβουλία σύνεσις γνώμη.
[7] the word here = 'sense,' 'understanding.'   [8] i.e. actions.
[9] sc. hence practical wisdom, judgment, and consideration are all concerned with ultimates.
[10] sc. 'both senses of the word ultimate': (though two senses of νοῦς are also implied).   [11] sc. deductions properly so called.   [12] only loosely so called.

5 τῶν καθ᾽ ἕκαστα γὰρ τὰ καθόλου· τούτων οὖν ἔχειν δεῖ
αἴσθησιν, αὕτη δ᾽ ἐστὶ νοῦς. διὸ καὶ φυσικὰ δοκεῖ εἶναι
ταῦτα, καὶ φύσει σοφὸς μὲν οὐδείς, γνώμην δ᾽ ἔχειν καὶ
σύνεσιν καὶ νοῦν. σημεῖον δ᾽ ὅτι καὶ ταῖς ἡλικίαις
οἰόμεθα ἀκολουθεῖν, καὶ ἥδε ἡ ἡλικία νοῦν ἔχει καὶ
10 γνώμην, ὡς τῆς φύσεως αἰτίας οὔσης. διὸ καὶ ἀρχὴ καὶ
τέλος νοῦς· ἐκ τούτων γὰρ αἱ ἀποδείξεις καὶ περὶ τούτων.
ὥστε δεῖ προσέχειν τῶν ἐμπείρων καὶ πρεσβυτέρων ἢ
φρονίμων ταῖς ἀναποδείκτοις φάσεσι καὶ δόξαις οὐχ
ἧττον τῶν ἀποδείξεων· διὰ γὰρ τὸ ἔχειν ἐκ τῆς ἐμπειρίας
15 ὄμμα ὁρῶσιν ὀρθῶς. τί μὲν οὖν ἐστιν ἡ φρόνησις καὶ ἡ
σοφία, καὶ περὶ τί ἑκατέρα τυγχάνει οὖσα, καὶ ὅτι ἄλλου
τῆς ψυχῆς μορίου ἀρετὴ ἑκατέρα, εἴρηται.

XII

διαπορήσειε δ᾽ ἄν τις περὶ αὐτῶν τί χρήσιμοι εἰσίν.
ἡ μὲν γὰρ σοφία οὐδὲν θεωρήσει ἐξ ὧν ἔσται εὐδαίμων
20 ἄνθρωπος (οὐδεμιᾶς γάρ ἐστι γενέσεως), ἡ δὲ φρόνησις
τοῦτο μὲν ἔχει, ἀλλὰ τίνος ἕνεκα δεῖ αὐτῆς; εἴπερ ἡ μὲν
φρόνησίς ἐστιν ἡ περὶ τὰ δίκαια καὶ καλὰ καὶ ἀγαθὰ
ἀνθρώπῳ, ταῦτα δ᾽ ἐστὶν ἃ τοῦ ἀγαθοῦ ἐστὶν ἀνδρὸς
πράττειν, οὐδὲν δὲ πρακτικώτεροι τῷ εἰδέναι αὐτά ἐσμεν,
25 εἴπερ ἕξεις αἱ ἀρεταί εἰσιν, ὥσπερ οὐδὲ τὰ ὑγιεινὰ οὐδὲ
τὰ εὐεκτικά—ὅσα μὴ τῷ ποιεῖν ἀλλὰ τῷ ἀπὸ τῆς ἕξεως
εἶναι λέγεται—οὐδὲν γὰρ πρακτικώτεροι τῷ ἔχειν τὴν
ἰατρικὴν καὶ γυμναστικήν ἐσμεν. εἰ δὲ μὴ τούτων χάριν

1143 b 5 τὰ καθόλου K Byw : τὸ καθόλου L M Bek Sus
15 περὶ τί K M Byw : περὶ τίνα L Bek Sus Burnet
19 θεωρήσει K M Byw : θεωρεῖ L Bek Sus Stewart Burnet
22 ἡ περὶ K M Bek Byw : περὶ L Rassow Sus Stewart

in view: for universals are constructed out of particulars: 5
therefore we must have perception of these particulars, and
this perception is νοῦς (Inductive Reason or Intelligence).
That is why people look upon these qualities[1] as natural, and
hold that no one is by nature philosophically wise, but that
the possession of consideration and judgment and inductive
reason does come by nature.

A testimony to this view is the fact that we hold our
characters[2] to correspond to our periods of life: and those of
a particular age are said to possess intelligence and con‐
sideration, nature being looked upon as the cause of this.

[Therefore Inductive reason is the beginning and the end: 10
for deductions start from these[3] and are concerned with these[4].]

Hence it is necessary to give heed to the undemonstrable
statements and opinions of experienced and elderly or prac‐
tically wise men no less than to their demonstrations: for
they see correctly, because they have acquired the power of
vision through experience.

We have, then, defined practical wisdom and philosophic 15
wisdom, and said whàt each of them is in fact concerned with,
and shown that they are the excellences of two separate parts
of the soul.

XII

But an objection may be raised by asking what the use of
them is. Philosophic wisdom, it will be said, will not attempt
to discover anything that will lead to a human being's
happiness, since it is not concerned with the coming into 20
existence of anything. Practical wisdom on the other hand
has this advantage, it is true[5]; but for what is it necessary?
Practical wisdom is the quality concerned with what is just
and beautiful and good for man: and these are the things
which the good man naturally does: because we know about
them, we are not therefore in a better position to perform
them, for the virtues are permanent qualities: just as we 25
cannot perform healthy and vigorous acts any better for
knowing about them (using the words healthy and vigorous
in the sense not of producing, but of springing from, a state
of health and vigour): for we are not made more able to do
what is healthy and vigorous by understanding medicine and
physical culture.

---

[1] i.e. practical wisdom, judgment, etc.   [2] lit. ourselves.
[3] sc. ultimates with which Inductive Reason deals.
[4] i.e. practical 'deductions' lead finally to the statement of particular things
to be done.
[5] i.e. the advantage of at least *attempting* to discover the means to happiness.

φρόνιμον ῥητέον ἀλλὰ τοῦ γίνεσθαι, τοῖς οὖσι σπουδαίοις
30 οὐδὲν ἂν εἴη χρήσιμος· ἔτι δ' οὐδὲ τοῖς μὴ ἔχουσιν· οὐδὲν
γὰρ διοίσει αὐτοὺς ἔχειν ἢ ἄλλοις ἔχουσι πείθεσθαι,
ἱκανῶς τ' ἔχοι ἂν ἡμῖν ὥσπερ καὶ περὶ τὴν ὑγίειαν·
βουλόμενοι γὰρ ὑγιαίνειν ὅμως οὐ μανθάνομεν ἰατρικήν.
πρὸς δὲ τούτοις ἄτοπον ἂν εἶναι δόξειεν, εἰ χείρων τῆς
35 σοφίας οὖσα κυριωτέρα αὐτῆς ἔσται· ἡ γὰρ ποιοῦσα
ἄρχει καὶ ἐπιτάττει περὶ ἕκαστον. περὶ δὴ τούτων λεκ-
τέον· νῦν μὲν γὰρ ἠπόρηται περὶ αὐτῶν μόνον.

4a   πρῶτον μὲν οὖν λέγωμεν ὅτι καθ' αὐτὰς ἀναγκαῖον
αἱρετὰς αὐτὰς εἶναι, ἀρετάς γ' οὔσας ἑκατέραν ἑκατέρου
τοῦ μορίου, καὶ εἰ μὴ ποιοῦσι μηδὲν μηδετέρα αὐτῶν.
ἔπειτα καὶ ποιοῦσι μέν, οὐχ ὡς ἡ ἰατρικὴ δὲ ὑγίειαν, ἀλλ'
5 ὡς ἡ ὑγίεια, οὕτως ἡ σοφία εὐδαιμονίαν· μέρος γὰρ οὖσα
τῆς ὅλης ἀρετῆς τῷ ἔχεσθαι ποιεῖ καὶ τῷ ἐνεργεῖν εὐδαίμονα. ἔτι τὸ ἔργον ἀποτελεῖται κατὰ τὴν φρόνησιν καὶ
τὴν ἠθικὴν ἀρετήν· ἡ μὲν γὰρ ἀρετὴ τὸν σκοπὸν ποιεῖ
ὀρθόν, ἡ δὲ φρόνησις τὰ πρὸς τοῦτον. τοῦ δὲ τετάρτου
10 μορίου τῆς ψυχῆς οὐκ ἔστιν ἀρετὴ τοιαύτη, τοῦ θρεπτικοῦ·
οὐδὲν γὰρ ἐπ' αὐτῷ πράττειν ἢ μὴ πράττειν. περὶ δὲ
τοῦ μηθὲν εἶναι πρακτικωτέρους διὰ τὴν φρόνησιν τῶν
καλῶν καὶ δικαίων, μικρὸν ἄνωθεν ἀρκτέον, λαβόντας
ἀρχὴν ταύτην. ὥσπερ γὰρ καὶ τὰ δίκαια λέγομεν πράτ-
15 τοντάς τινας οὔπω δικαίους εἶναι, οἷον τοὺς τὰ ὑπὸ τῶν
νόμων τεταγμένα ποιοῦντας ἢ ἄκοντας ἢ δι' ἄγνοιαν ἢ
δι' ἕτερόν τι καὶ μὴ δι' αὐτά (καίτοι πράττουσί γε ἃ
δεῖ καὶ ὅσα χρὴ τὸν σπουδαῖον), οὕτως, ὡς ἔοικεν, ἔστι

1143 b 28 ῥητέον Κ Μ Byw : θετέον L Γ Bek Sus Burnet
      30 ἔχουσιν codd. Bek Sus Byw : οὖσιν Argyropylus Ramsauer
1144 a 1 λέγωμεν Κ Byw : λέγομεν L M Bek Sus
        4 ἡ ἰατρικὴ Κ Byw : ἰατρικὴ L M Bek Sus
        6 τῷ ἐνεργεῖν εὐδαίμονα edd. (sed cum obelis Byw): ἐνέργεια εὐδαιμονία
           Κ, τῷ ἐνεργεῖν εὐδαιμονίαν L, τῷ ἐνεργεῖν τὸν εὐδαίμονα Μ Γ,
           ἐνεργεῖ εὐδαιμονίαν Ο

But if we are to say that a man should be practically wise, not for the reason given[1], but in order to *become* able to do good actions; then, it may be objected, practical wisdom can be of no use to those who are already good persons; nor can it be of any use to those who have not got this goodness: for it will make no difference whether they have it themselves or are controlled by others who have it: it would be enough for us to do as we do with regard to health: we want to be healthy, but we do not therefore learn medicine.

A further possible objection is, that it is absurd for practical wisdom to be inferior to philosophic wisdom and at the same time to be in a position of greater authority, ruling and giving orders about every detail as it does, being the quality that is connected with action.

So far we have been stating difficulties: now therefore we must discuss them.

In the first place, then, let us reply that these qualities are bound to be in themselves desirable, simply because they are the respective good qualities of the two parts of the intellect, whether either does or does not produce any positive result.

In the next place, they do produce results: philosophic wisdom produces happiness, not indeed in the sense in which medicine produces health, but in the sense in which health produces happiness: it is a part of complete excellence, and makes a man happy by being possessed and exercised.

Further, the proper function of a man is completely performed by[2] the joint operation of practical wisdom and moral excellence. Moral excellence makes the end in view right, practical wisdom makes the means to it right. (The fourth part of the mind, the nutritive, has no excellence of this kind[3]: for there is nothing that it lies in its power to do or not to do.)

But to deal with the objection that we are not because of practical wisdom any the more in a position to perform beautiful and just acts, we must go a little deeper into the question. We ground our answer on the following consideration. We say that some of those persons who do just acts are still not just persons: for example those who do what is commanded by law either unwillingly, or in ignorance, or for some other reason than for the sake of the action itself: and this in spite of the fact that they do the things which they ought to do and which the good man is bound to do. In the same way, it appears, it is possible for a man to be in

[1] i.e. to *be* able to do good actions. [2] i.e. *only* by....
[3] i.e. no excellence relating to the *peculiar* function of man.

τὸ πῶς ἔχοντα πράττειν ἕκαστα ὥστ᾽ εἶναι ἀγαθόν, λέγω
20 δ᾽ οἷον διὰ προαίρεσιν καὶ αὐτῶν ἕνεκα τῶν πραττομένων.
τὴν μὲν οὖν προαίρεσιν ὀρθὴν ποιεῖ ἡ ἀρετή, τὸ δ᾽ ὅσα
ἐκείνης ἕνεκα πέφυκε πράττεσθαι οὐκ ἔστι τῆς ἀρετῆς
ἀλλ᾽ ἑτέρας δυνάμεως. λεκτέον δ᾽ ἐπιστήσασι σαφέστερον περὶ αὐτῶν. ἔστι δὴ δύναμις ἣν καλοῦσι δει-
νότητα· αὕτη δ᾽ ἐστὶ τοιαύτη ὥστε τὰ πρὸς τὸν ὑπο-
25 τεθέντα σκοπὸν συντείνοντα δύνασθαι ταῦτα πράττειν
καὶ τυγχάνειν αὐτοῦ. ἂν μὲν οὖν ὁ σκοπὸς ᾖ καλός,
ἐπαινετή ἐστιν, ἂν δὲ φαῦλος, πανουργία· διὸ καὶ τοὺς
φρονίμους δεινοὺς καὶ πανούργους φαμὲν εἶναι. ἔστι δ᾽
ἡ φρόνησις οὐχ ἡ δύναμις, ἀλλ᾽ οὐκ ἄνευ τῆς δυνάμεως
30 ταύτης. ἡ δὲ ἕξις τῷ ὄμματι τούτῳ γίνεται τῆς ψυχῆς
οὐκ ἄνευ ἀρετῆς, ὡς εἴρηταί τε καὶ ἔστι δῆλον· οἱ γὰρ
συλλογισμοὶ τῶν πρακτῶν ἀρχὴν ἔχοντές εἰσιν, ἐπειδὴ
τοιόνδε τὸ τέλος καὶ τὸ ἄριστον, ὁτιδήποτε ὄν—ἔστω γὰρ
λόγου χάριν τὸ τυχόν. τοῦτο δ᾽ εἰ μὴ τῷ ἀγαθῷ, οὐ
35 φαίνεται· διαστρέφει γὰρ ἡ μοχθηρία καὶ διαψεύδεσθαι
ποιεῖ περὶ τὰς πρακτικὰς ἀρχάς. ὥστε φανερὸν ὅτι
ἀδύνατον φρόνιμον εἶναι μὴ ὄντα ἀγαθόν.

XIII

4 b σκεπτέον δὴ πάλιν καὶ περὶ ἀρετῆς. καὶ γὰρ ἡ
ἀρετὴ παραπλησίως ἔχει, ὡς ἡ φρόνησις πρὸς τὴν
δεινότητα—οὐ ταὐτὸ μέν, ὅμοιον δέ—οὕτω καὶ ἡ φυσικὴ
ἀρετὴ πρὸς τὴν κυρίαν. πᾶσι γὰρ δοκεῖ ἕκαστα τῶν
5 ἠθῶν ὑπάρχειν φύσει πως· καὶ γὰρ δίκαιοι καὶ σωφρονικοὶ καὶ ἀνδρεῖοι καὶ τἆλλα ἔχομεν εὐθὺς ἐκ γενετῆς·

1144 a 23 δύναμις K M Byw : τις δύναμις L Bek Sus
26 αὐτῶν codd. Bek Sus Stewart : αὐτοῦ Byw
28 καὶ πανούργους codd. Bek Byw : καὶ τοὺς πανούργους Klein Ram-
      sauer Sus
29 δύναμις K L Michelet Fritzsche Rassow Byw Burnet : δεινότης
      M Bek Grant Ramsauer Stewart

such a condition when doing all his actions as to be a really good man; I mean the condition in which he purposes those actions and does them for their own sake.   20

Now moral goodness causes the purpose to be right: but to understand what the nature of things requires should be done in order to achieve that purpose is the work not of moral goodness but of another faculty, which we must discuss with careful attention.

There is a faculty which is called Ability, which is such as to be able to put into practice the means to any proposed end in view, and to discover what those means are[1]. 25 Now if the end in view is a noble one, the ability is praiseworthy; but if the end in view is bad, the ability is villainy. Hence we call able men practically wise or villainous[2].

Practical wisdom is not identical with this faculty, but it cannot exist without it. The fixed quality[3] cannot come to belong to this eye of the mind without moral virtue. This 30 has been said, and it is clearly true: for deductive arguments about conduct always have as their premiss 'Since so-and-so is the end and the greatest good'—whatever so-and-so may be, for we may take it as anything for the sake of argument: and this cannot be seen correctly except by the good man: for wickedness causes perversion and deception about the 35 premisses of arguments as to conduct. Plainly therefore it is impossible that a man who is not good should be practically wise.

XIII

Accordingly we must also further discuss moral excellence. 114 The fact is that moral excellence shows very much the same relation that practical wisdom bears to ability: these two are not identical, but are similar: and it is in just this way that natural moral excellence is related to true moral excellence. All are agreed that in some sense or other the several moral qualities are natural and inborn: from the very moment of 5 our birth we are just and self-controlled and brave, and possess the other qualities.

---

[1] reading αὑτῶν codd. not αὑτοῦ Bywater.   [2] sc. as the case may be.
[3] sc. the good quality of practical wisdom.

ἀλλ' ὅμως ζητοῦμεν ἕτερόν τι τὸ κυρίως ἀγαθὸν καὶ τὰ
τοιαῦτα ἄλλον τρόπον ὑπάρχειν. καὶ γὰρ παισὶ καὶ
θηρίοις αἱ φυσικαὶ ὑπάρχουσιν ἕξεις, ἀλλ' ἄνευ νοῦ
10 βλαβεραὶ φαίνονται οὖσαι. πλὴν τοσοῦτον ἔοικεν
ὁρᾶσθαι, ὅτι ὥσπερ σώματι ἰσχυρῷ ἄνευ ὄψεως κινου-
μένῳ συμβαίνει σφάλλεσθαι ἰσχυρῶς διὰ τὸ μὴ ἔχειν
ὄψιν, οὕτω καὶ ἐνταῦθα· ἐὰν δὲ λάβῃ νοῦν, ἐν τῷ πράττειν διαφέρει· ἡ δ' ἕξις ὁμοία οὖσα τότ' ἔσται κυρίως
ἀρετή. ὥστε καθάπερ ἐπὶ τοῦ δοξαστικοῦ δύο ἐστὶν
15 εἴδη, δεινότης καὶ φρόνησις, οὕτως καὶ ἐπὶ τοῦ ἠθικοῦ
δύο ἐστίν, τὸ μὲν ἀρετὴ φυσικὴ τὸ δ' ἡ κυρία, καὶ τούτων
ἡ κυρία οὐ γίνεται ἄνευ φρονήσεως. διόπερ τινές φασι
πάσας τὰς ἀρετὰς φρονήσεις εἶναι. καὶ Σωκράτης τῇ
μὲν ὀρθῶς ἐζήτει τῇ δ' ἡμάρτανεν· ὅτι μὲν γὰρ φρονήσεις
20 ᾤετο εἶναι πάσας τὰς ἀρετάς, ἡμάρτανεν, ὅτι δ' οὐκ ἄνευ
φρονήσεως, καλῶς ἔλεγεν. σημεῖον δέ· καὶ γὰρ νῦν
πάντες, ὅταν ὁρίζωνται τὴν ἀρετήν, προστιθέασι, τὴν ἕξιν
εἰπόντες καὶ πρὸς ἅ ἐστιν, τὴν κατὰ τὸν ὀρθὸν λόγον·
ὀρθὸς δ' ὁ κατὰ τὴν φρόνησιν. ἐοίκασι δὴ μαντεύεσθαί
25 πως ἅπαντες ὅτι ἡ τοιαύτη ἕξις ἀρετή ἐστιν, ἡ κατὰ τὴν
φρόνησιν. δεῖ δὲ μικρὸν μεταβῆναι· ἔστι γὰρ οὐ μόνον
ἡ κατὰ τὸν ὀρθὸν λόγον, ἀλλ' ἡ μετὰ τοῦ ὀρθοῦ λόγου
ἕξις ἀρετή [ἐστιν]. ὀρθὸς δὲ λόγος περὶ τῶν τοιούτων ἡ
φρόνησίς ἐστιν. Σωκράτης μὲν οὖν λόγους τὰς ἀρετὰς
30 ᾤετο εἶναι (ἐπιστήμας γὰρ εἶναι πάσας), ἡμεῖς δὲ μετὰ
λόγου. δῆλον οὖν ἐκ τῶν εἰρημένων ὅτι οὐχ οἷόν τε
ἀγαθὸν εἶναι κυρίως ἄνευ φρονήσεως, οὐδὲ φρόνιμον ἄνευ
τῆς ἠθικῆς ἀρετῆς. ἀλλὰ καὶ ὁ λόγος ταύτῃ λύοιτ' ἄν, ᾧ

1144 b 6 ζητοῦμεν codd. edd : ἡγούμεθ' ooni. Rassow
26 ἔστι γὰρ οὐ K M Byw : οὐ γὰρ L Bek Sus
27 ἐστιν K L Bek Sus Byw : om. M O : seclusit Burnet

Nevertheless, we desire to find that true moral excellence is something other than this, and that the moral qualities mentioned belong to us in some other way. The fact is that even children and the lower animals possess these natural qualities, which however are evidently harmful when separated from intelligence. We may surely observe, at any rate, that just as a body of great strength but without sight meets with great falls, when put in motion, just because it is without sight, so also it happens in this case[1]. But if a man acquires intelligence also, he acts particularly well: and his moral character, though it will be much what it was before, will then be moral excellence truly so called.

So that just as in the case of the intellectual part of the soul that deals with the contingent there are two kinds of quality, ability and practical wisdom, so also there are two kinds in the case of the moral part, the one natural and the other true excellence; and of these it is the true excellence which cannot be produced without practical wisdom.

Hence it is that some say that all the moral excellences are forms of practical wisdom: and Socrates was right to some extent, but also to some extent wrong: he was wrong in supposing all the moral excellences to *be* forms of practical wisdom, but quite right in teaching that these excellences cannot exist without practical wisdom.

A proof of this is that even now everyone in defining a moral excellence, after stating the quality and the things with which it is concerned, adds that it is the quality determined by right reason. And that reason is right which is the result of practical wisdom. It appears then that all thinkers have somehow or other hit upon the truth, that moral excellence is a quality which is in accordance with practical wisdom.

We must however, slightly change the wording of this statement: for moral excellence is a quality that is not only in accordance with, but in conjunction with, right reason. And practical wisdom *is* right reason about such matters. Socrates, then, supposed the moral excellences to be kinds of reason (for they were all, he said, forms of knowledge) but we hold that they are conjoined with reason.

It is plain, then, after what has been said, that it is not possible without practical wisdom to be really good morally, nor without moral excellence to be practically wise.

Moreover, this result may provide an answer to the argument by which a person might object that the moral

---

[1] i.e. to the person with great moral qualities without intelligence.

διαλεχθείη τις ἂν ὅτι χωρίζονται ἀλλήλων αἱ ἀρεταί· οὐ
35 γὰρ ὁ αὐτὸς εὐφυέστατος πρὸς ἁπάσας, ὥστε τὴν μὲν
ἤδη τὴν δ᾽ οὔπω εἰληφὼς ἔσται· τοῦτο γὰρ κατὰ μὲν τὰς
5 a φυσικὰς ἀρετὰς ἐνδέχεται, καθ᾽ ἃς δὲ ἁπλῶς λέγεται
ἀγαθός, οὐκ ἐνδέχεται· ἅμα γὰρ τῇ φρονήσει μιᾷ ὑπαρχούσῃ πᾶσαι ὑπάρξουσιν. δῆλον δέ, κἂν εἰ μὴ πρακτικὴ
ἦν, ὅτι ἔδει ἂν αὐτῆς διὰ τὸ τοῦ μορίου ἀρετὴν εἶναι· καὶ
5 ὅτι οὐκ ἔσται ἡ προαίρεσις ὀρθὴ ἄνευ φρονήσεως οὐδ᾽
ἄνευ ἀρετῆς· ἡ μὲν γὰρ τὸ τέλος ἡ δὲ τὰ πρὸς τὸ τέλος
ποιεῖ πράττειν. ἀλλὰ μὴν οὐδὲ κυρία γ᾽ ἐστὶ τῆς σοφίας
οὐδὲ τοῦ βελτίονος μορίου, ὥσπερ οὐδὲ τῆς ὑγιείας ἡ
ἰατρική· οὐ γὰρ χρῆται αὐτῇ, ἀλλ᾽ ὁρᾷ ὅπως γένηται·
10 ἐκείνης οὖν ἕνεκα ἐπιτάττει, ἀλλ᾽ οὐκ ἐκείνη. ἔτι ὅμοιον
κἂν εἴ τις τὴν πολιτικὴν φαίη ἄρχειν τῶν θεῶν, ὅτι
ἐπιτάττει περὶ πάντα τὰ ἐν τῇ πόλει.

1145 a 2 ὑπαρχούσῃ Κ Μ Byw : οὔσῃ L Bek Sus Burnet
   3 τοῦ μορίου codd. Bek Byw : τοῦ ⁎ ⁎ μορίου Sus : τοῦ ἑτέρου μορίου
    coni. Spengel

excellences are separable from each other : any one man, he may say, is not equally disposed towards all of them, so that he will have already achieved one of them when he has not 35 yet achieved another. This, it is true, is possible with regard to the natural moral excellences, but with regard to those excellences which entitle a man to be called morally good, 11 without qualification, it is not possible : for as soon as a man has the single excellence of practical wisdom he will have all the moral excellences along with it.

And it is now plain that, even if practical wisdom had no effect on action, it would nevertheless be desirable because it is the excellence of that part of the mind to which it belongs: and also that purpose will not be right without practical 5 wisdom or without moral excellence[1] : for the one makes the end right, and the other causes the doing of the means to the end.

At the same time practical wisdom is not in a position of authority over philosophic wisdom or over the nobler part of the mind : just as medicine is not in a position of authority over our health : for it does not make use of it, but takes measures for its existence : it does not therefore command it, 10 but commands for it. It is, we may add, as if one were to say that political science is in authority over the gods because it orders everything that is done in the country.

[1] i.e. without practical wisdom any more than without moral excellence.

DIALECTIC METHOD IN THE SIXTH BOOK.

In his edition of the NE Professor Burnet says in some places, and implies in many others, that many misunderstandings of the Ethics have sprung from a failure to see how dialectic Aristotle's method is[1]. It will be well to see how far his contentions are justified in so far as they apply to book VI: and generally to see what Aristotle understands by the dialectical method, and what he takes to be its place in ethical discussion.

The dialectic method is referred to by name in many different passages of the Aristotelian writings[2], and it has not been seen how complex a notion the name conveys, and to what different conceptions of it the various references must lead us. But it is possible to distinguish at least three elements, which sometimes combine to give διαλεκτική its complex meaning, whereas at other times one or other of them is prominent to the partial or entire exclusion of the others.

1. The words διαλέγεσθαι, διαλεκτικός, as is well known, mean 'conversation' 'conversational' in the first place[3]. They became restricted, during the century or so that followed Socrates, to conversation of a certain kind. A dialectic discussion was not desultory, but concerned with one topic, in fact with the truth or falsity of a given proposition. It took place not between a number of persons speaking in any order, but between two persons only. These persons either held actually, or for the purposes of the argument were supposed to hold, opposite views about the question under discussion, the one denying what the other affirmed to be true. The formal object of the discussion was not to find out what the truth really was: there was indeed no common object, but each disputant attempted

---

[1] See his edition of N.E. Introd. xxxix—xlvi and the *Preface.*

[2] See Bonitz Index s. v. διαλεκτικός.

[3] I have not thought it necessary to give an accurate or full account of the history of the word.

to prove the other wrong and himself right. The common ground of argument was certain propositions, admitted by both disputants to be true, whether as a matter of fact they were true or not. The immediate result of such a discussion could never be an increased knowledge of truth about the subject discussed, though indirectly it might lead to such knowledge by giving a man keener insight into the subject. The method was essentially oral. There was no arbiter: neither party had won till he had forced the other to confess himself in the wrong or at least defeated. Dialectic in this sense was a kind of intellectual game, pleasant for the clever and active-minded, and useful as a training in subtilty and readiness—it was in fact, as Aristotle calls it, γυμναστική[1]   2.   But the dialectic method is not confined to debate between two persons. A single person may employ it, and in his hands it becomes something very different, and it is most important to observe what the differences are. Of course it is quite possible to invent and to record in writing a debate between two persons of the kind that has just been described. In this case the author is simply a dramatist: he takes no side himself, is not interested in the result, cares no more for the truth of the matter (so far as anything he says in his own person goes) than either of the disputants, and at the same time is not desirous, as the disputants are, of winning a victory. The author of such a composition is not really himself discussing the subject dialectically—he is merely recording a discussion on the part of others ; only those others are not real people, but the creatures of the author's brain. But putting aside such compositions as being merely a sort of literary and artificial form of the first kind of dialectic, there is another kind of dialectic argument employed by a single thinker. In any reasoning, whether inductive or deductive, the premisses may be true statements known to be true, or they may be statements which many people regard as certainly true but as to which the reasoner himself is uncertain. There are certain subjects, about which it is evidently possible to reason, and to learn better by doing so, concerning which it is nevertheless impossible to discover any true statement known to be true to start with. In the absence of certainly true premisses it is necessary to take such premisses as seem most probably true. There are two tests of the probability of any statement, the external test of

---

[1] Topics 101 a 27. The usefulness of it πρὸς τὰς ἐντεύξεις is different, but similarly practical, and like it opposed to the third use of it, mentioned in the same passage, πρὸς τὰς κατὰ φιλοσοφίαν ἐπιστήμας.

its acceptance by other people, the internal test of its seeming to the reasoner himself to correspond with facts. The statements about the subject to be discussed that appear, after undergoing this double test, to be most probably true, are the proper premises for the reasoning to follow. Now this reasoning is dialectic and not demonstrative, for the uncertainty of the original premises makes all the conclusions founded on them uncertain. 3. The process of reasoning from probable premises is quite different from the process of obtaining those probable premises : and the latter process is also dialectical. If, whenever the truth about a thing cannot be ascertained, everyone were agreed on the probable truth about it, this latter process would not be needed. But when it is asked what the probable truth is, it is commonly found that different people give different answers. If in these various answers there were no common element, no trace of agreement, it would be useless to investigate them : the only thing to do would be to reject all authority whatsoever, and follow the view that seems best in itself, whether anyone else holds it or not. But there is, Aristotle thinks, an a priori likelihood of public opinion being not wholly wrong, and of the cleverest thinkers being not wholly wrong either[1] : and in practice it is commonly found that public opinion is at least partly right, and that the cleverest thinkers are at least partly right ; and moreover, if one takes the trouble to see exactly what they mean, that they do not so entirely disagree with each other as appears at first sight. Various ἔνδοξα or received views that seem incompatible to begin with may be shown compatible by means of careful examination. If, for instance, the cause of the existence of what error there is in any given ἔνδοξον can be assigned, it is easier to feel certain how far that ἔνδοξον is false and how far it is true : or again a formal restatement of an ἔνδοξον, involving no change in its meaning, may remove an inconsistency with another ἔνδοξον that was after all only a formal inconsistency. In these and in various other ways ἔνδοξα may be wholly or partly reconciled. All this will make it clearer what view is most probable (ἐνδοξότατον) and ought to be started with : and the process is called dialectic. It is plainly preparatory for the second process, already described.

---

[1] NE 1098 b 27—29 τὰ μὲν πολλοὶ καὶ παλαιοὶ λέγουσιν τὰ δὲ ὀλίγοι καὶ ἔνδοξοι ἄνδρες. οὐδετέρους δὲ τούτων εὔλογον διαμαρτάνειν τοῖς ὅλοις, ἀλλ' ἔν γέ τι ἢ καὶ τὰ πλεῖστα κατορθοῦν. This is plainer than 1153 b 32 (quoted by Burnet) πάντα γὰρ φύσει ἔχει τι θεῖον.

The last of these three processes is related in different ways to each of the two former ones. It is like the first, especially like the literary recorded form of the first, in that the author actually brings the disputants, though he may not dramatically personify them, on to the debating stage, and makes them speak their parts and do the best they can. The soundness of any ἔνδοξον can best be tested and approved by the reader if he is allowed to see all the objections that can fairly be urged against it, and the answers that can be made against those objections in defence of it. But the author is no longer merely passive, and cannot allow his reader to be passive either. He is anxious to arbitrate between the rival views, to decide which of them is the truest, and to take the truest for his own, modified it may be by some element of truth that is contained in the others and yet is rejected or neglected in that which is truest on the whole. It is important for him to reach a view of his own on the questions at issue, in order that he may have material for further reasoning, and so ultimately solve the problems that most press for solution and acquire the knowledge that is most desirable. And it is important that his view should be as near as possible to that truth which from the nature of the subject he can never discover with exactness and certainty: for his conclusions can be no more true or convincing than are the grounds on which they are based. He is thus in a position quite different from that taken by either of the disputants whose merits he has to judge: and he is a dialectician (διαλεκτικός) in quite another sense. It does not follow that the man who is cleverest at devising arguments to support his view and repel the opponent's attacks is the most acute or impartial judge of what the real merits of the case are. To become the former may be more useful in practical life: it may enable one to defend against skilful attacks some truth that is not strong enough to defend itself: it certainly is one of the best means to become the latter. But it is the latter who will be capable of discovering truth for himself, and of distinguishing the false from the true in the opinions of others.

The third process is different also from the second, though they are alike in certain respects that distinguish them from the first. They are processes carried on by a single thinker and not the combination of the processes carried on by two thinkers. Their end is not victory but truth, not mental training for future efforts but the present attainment of valuable results. They are in fact parts of a single whole process, that by which the philosopher (to use the word in its broadest sense) investigates those questions which are naturally incapable of being answered with exact precision because they concern variable and not invariable things. But the two parts are different in themselves. The one consists in securing the right materials to work with, and the other in making the right use of those materials when secured. The one starts with a number of statements that are not exactly the same, that may be very different, that are sometimes formally incompatible and sometimes inconsistent in substance: from which medley, by whatever means the dialectical ability of the reasoner can devise, the truth must be sorted out, or at least what is as near the truth as it seems possible to go. The other follows out the method of exact science. The premisses are not indeed scientifically certain, and the conclusions can be no more certain than the premisses: but the procedure is exact and well-defined. These two processes are plainly very different, and must not be confused because they have the common name 'dialectic,' or because Aristotle in no place formally states the distinction between them. They may be more mixed up with each other in the practical setting out of an argument than the logical priority of the one to the other makes strictly correct: thus an objection to the premisses may be raised at any point where its force can best be felt or where it can most conveniently be answered, and need not in practice necessarily be forestalled before the constructive argument begins.

The common feature of these three forms of dialectic, in virtue of which they deserve their common name, is that they are all forms of reasoning about views that are not certainly true but are to some extent probable. Dialectic is thus as a whole opposed to exact scientific reasoning, to which it is in one sense inferior and in another sense not so: for it is, or is capable of being, the best possible way of reasoning about subjects that are in themselves variable and inexact, and so is as good of its kind (i.e. in relation to its subject-matter) as scientific reasoning can be: but as its subject-matter is in itself inferior because of this variableness, and as the results produced are at best less certainly true than those of science, it is as a whole definitely inferior to science as a whole. Dialectic is also opposed to Sophistic and Eristic, for these latter are marked either by the premisses not being probable as they are asserted to be or by the reasoning from the premisses not being well conducted as it pretends to be: that is to say, either the third or the second of the three dialectic processes distinguished above is not properly carried out, but an inferior imitation is substituted, containing statements that are not only not certainly true—for that can be said of the statements of dialectic too—but are less true than other statements that might and therefore ought to have been made in their place. Grote observes[1] that this latter distinction is not so sound as that of dialectic from scientific reasoning, seeing that it concerns not the arguments themselves but the minds of the persons who use them. But Aristotle would no doubt reply to this, that there is an objective difference between a sound and an unsound deduction from any given premisses, and between premisses that are and premisses that are not accepted by the majority of intelligent people ; that it is this difference rather than the difference in moral character of the reasoners that really separates dialectic from sophistic and eristic, though in practice it is found that the bad moral motives of greed or vanity or the like are what induce men deliberately to pervert the truth as they do, the sophist aiming at making a fortune by his profession, and the eristic, who is not a sophist, desiring to win admiration by a display of his talent. The distinction is therefore that of good from bad in the same sphere, whereas the distinction of dialectic from exact scientific reasoning is that of good from good in different spheres : both distinctions are sound, but the latter is plainly the more radical[2].

The way is now open for considering the question of how far in the Ethics generally, and in VI particularly, the method Aristotle employs is, in any of the above senses, dialectical. It is not difficult to return the general answer, that in the first sense the Ethics is not dialectical, in the second sense it is, in the third sense it is to some extent but by no means altogether. For the treatise is plainly no mere piece of mental gymnastic like the Socratic dialogues of Plato : it aims at positive results, and is to all appearance continually reaching them, and is not forced by any later turn of the argument to abandon what it has reached : it does not, like the first book of the Republic, show two contending sides and one finally victorious, but a single body of doctrine gradually shaping itself out of a chaos of loose ill-defined opinions. But dialectical in the second sense it is plain that on Aristotle's principles this and any other ethical

---

[1] 'Aristotle' i 387.

[2] Aristotle was no doubt aware of the latter's being the more radical, as indeed he indicates (if his editors have carried out his intentions) by separating the Topics from the Analytics more completely than he separates the Sophistic Fallacies from the other books of the Topics.

treatise is bound to be: for since it deals with that contingent unknowable thing human conduct its general principles must be rough and not truly universal (τύπῳ καὶ ὡς ἐπὶ τὸ πολύ), and its particulars must always have a number of peculiarities that have to be reckoned with in reasoning on the subject and yet are not to be classified beforehand or brought under the general rule. The most fundamental of all ethical general principles can only be the most probable of ἔνδοξα on the subject; though that principle is not necessarily an ἔνδοξον in the sense that it is actually accepted either by people in general or by experts and wise men—it may be a new opinion of the author's own.

The question at issue is just this, How far is the Ethics dialectical in the third sense above mentioned? This question may well be stated in the words Professor Burnet employs in his preface. There are some who have tried to find in the Ethics 'the scientific and metaphysical basis of Aristotle's moral philosophy.' Such a basis Professor Burnet is quite unable to discover there. He regards the treatise as 'dialectical throughout,' because 'the foundations of the doctrine here set forth' are 'of the most shifting character, taken as they are at one time from the opinions of ordinary people, at another from popular Platonism.' Finding a large number of hitherto unnoticed striking resemblances, if not direct references, to Isocrates and Plato, he infers that Aristotle in the Ethics accepts, like a practical dialectician (in the first of our three senses of the word), views from his opponents that he does not hold himself and could not square with many of his fundamental philosophic principles, and deduces from them conclusions which his opponents are thus more forced to accept than if the same conclusions had been deduced from strict Aristotelian principles. Finding that the methods of argument, of sustaining a θέσις or destroying an ἔνστασις or solving an ἀπορία, are those prescribed in the Topics as rules for the game of dialectic, he infers that the whole treatise is handled in the spirit of the contemporary players of the game at Athens. Seeing however that the external form of the work is not very different from that of other works of Aristotle which cannot be regarded as anything but strictly scientific in their methods and results, and that there is the appearance at least of results obtained to which the author himself attaches as much validity as the nature of the subject-matter allows of and which form the basis of that comparatively scientific treatise, the Politics, it would appear that Professor Burnet, while rightly denying

_–what indeed Aristotle himself disclaims repeatedly—the exactness and certainty of Aristotle's conclusions on ethical subjects, has gone too far in the opposite direction. The fact is that it is not impossible that the foundations of the doctrine of the Ethics should be current popular or philosophic opinions, and at the same time the Ethics contain the scientific and metaphysical basis of Aristotle's moral philosophy in so far as moral philosophy admits of such a basis. It is true that neither pure metaphysics nor pure psychology is allowed to come into the treatise to any great extent. Professor Burnet himself insists in ·vi on a meaning of λόγος, familiar in Aristotle's metaphysical discussions but alien to common usage, which I cannot see any reason to attribute to it there[1]. But the comparative neglect of metaphysics and psychology does not imply Aristotle's adoption of views in any way inconsistent with his metaphysical and psychological doctrines : such considerations are simply regarded as inappropriate to the subject in hand, either because they do not throw light on the questions to which an answer is sought, or because the subject is essentially foreign to them and does not permit of any direct application of them. Nowhere in the Ethics, I believe, does Aristotle ever accept for the purposes of argument a view with which he anywhere else expresses or implies his disagreement. That he founds his own opinions about ethical subjects, and especially his axioms and premisses, on the opinions of others, does not show that the opinions he appears to accept, with or without investigation, are not accepted in reality. Though he always considers the opinions of particular thinkers and of men in general wherever they are to the point, and though those opinions that he declares to be his own he seems always to regard as placed on a firmer footing if shown to be in harmony with or the same as the opinions of others : yet his deference to others is neither invariable nor complete, especially not in matters of substantial importance—in terminology he is more ready to follow established usage—and he is not always content to select and adopt the most plausible of current views, even in a modified form ; the preliminary examination of those views may simply show how unsatisfactory they all are, and so justify the author in striking out a line for himself. In the first book, for instance, the preliminary definition of Happiness is reached directly, by an argument to which the previous discussion of current views of happiness does not, formally at least, contribute anything at all.

[1] See the Miscellaneous Notes.

Professor Burnet admits indeed[1] that Aristotle's 'attitude toward these beliefs' of the many and the wise 'is by no means uncritical'; but he does not appear to regard the critical attitude as containing the possibility of complete rejection of any of the beliefs of the many or the wise, even in part. Aristotle does not, according to him, judge for himself how far the wise and the many are right or wrong: he only finds out how it is that the wise and the many, who are both right, appear to contradict each other, though they do not do so in reality. In spite of what he says about Aristotle's being a convinced intuitionalist in moral judgments[2], this does amount to holding that he would have us take our first principles on trust[3]. But it is clear that if our premisses are taken on trust, our conclusions must be taken on trust too, though less directly. Yet plainly the great result of the Ethics, the view obtained of the greatest good for man, is not taken on trust. The argument is not 'If such-and-such people are right in their views about human life, it must follow that happiness is so-and-so : and since we cannot do better than suppose those people to be right in their views, it follows that we cannot do better than suppose happiness to be so-and-so.' Nor, to put it rather differently is it this—'You say this and that : well, if this and that are true, happiness is so-and-so : you are therefore obliged to admit happiness to be so-and-so : but whether it is so-and-so or not I have not shown nor even stated what I believe about it.' No : Aristotle's line is rather to consider first what current opinions are; to show by comparison, or re-statement, or consideration of their history and causes, how far they are true; to form, partly but not entirely by their help, as correct opinions as possible on the points at issue; to argue from these opinions thus formed, as from true premisses; and to test the conclusions produced by such argument by further appeals to such current opinions as previous consideration has shown to be at all plausible. So much for the dialectic question as far as it concerns the Ethics as a whole: I will now try to determine the extent and nature of the dialectic element in VI.

In the first place it will be allowed that VI is, like the other books of the Ethics, dialectic in so far as its subject-matter is the variable and contingent (τὰ ἐνδεχόμενα ἄλλως ἔχειν), since neither its conclusions nor its premisses can be statements of what is universally and always true. To reason about such a subject as the intellectual goodness of man must be to reason ἐξ ἐνδόξων, for no certain and

---

[1] Introd. xl.   [2] xlii.   [3] xli.

sure premises can be got on such a subject, but only such as are probably or generally true. Reasoning ἐξ ἐνδόξων is dialectic, as the opening words of the Topics show. Hence the whole of VI, as well as the rest of the treatise, must be dialectic in this sense. It should be hardly necessary to point out that σοφία with its divisions ἐπιστήμη and νοῦς, though they give rise to activities that are not dialectical but scientific, since they have to do with the truly knowable and exact, are yet considered in the Ethics from an outside point of view, in their relation to the chief good for man, a question that is not directly within their province, and concerning which no exact and scientific statements can be made : these parts of the whole subject form therefore no exception to the general rule, that the subject-matter of the Ethics is not the eternal but the contingent.

Again, the form of the last two chapters, if not their spirit, is obviously dialectical. The previous arguments had led to the belief (1) that σοφία and φρόνησις are highly valuable and useful qualities, (2) that σοφία is a better quality than φρόνησις is. Two ἐνστάσεις or objections are now raised in the regular disputants' fashion, giving reasons to support the view (1) that σοφία and φρόνησις are useless, (2) that φρόνησις is better than σοφία. The result is the ἀπορία that occurs when two disputants support opposite views with reasons, and for a time neither can refute the other. The ἀπορία is removed by a corresponding two-fold λύσις, which breaks down the objections and sustains the original θέσεις. In what respect are these two chapters less dialectical than any other argument between the supporters of two opposite views ? In the first place it must be noted that the same form of argument may and does occur in reasoning about scientific subjects, and has no necessary connection with the un-certainty of the premises : an excellent instance is chapter iii of Analytica Posteriora I, which passage, and many others like it, is distinguished from ordinary popular dialectical arguments by the fact that truth and not victory is the end in view, and that the objections are in consequence genuine and substantial, not captious and verbal, the answers to the objections really satisfactory (at least in the author's view) and not merely good enough for the kind of objection they meet or to convince the kind of person who would raise such an objection. The two chapters in question have therefore the dialectic form, but not the dialectic spirit, and their substance might have been expressed without the use of the dialectic form, though that happens to be a convenient form for the purpose.

Again, there is in this book much examination of popular and philosophical (especially Platonic) doctrines and usages of words, and much correction of both where the author considers them wrong. As has been pointed out elsewhere, Aristotle is especially anxious to introduce a correcter terminology, and many of his arguments chiefly concern the proper use of words, showing that other people rather use certain words wrongly than are wrong on points of fact. This applies to the usage of every one of the eight names of intellectual virtues (excluding the minor virtues εὐστοχία and ἀγχίνοια) with which Aristotle deals: and he also introduces correcter usages of the words λογιστικόν and πολιτική. Besides improving terminology he corrects the substance of others' views: thus he shows the error of the common suppositions, (1) that moral virtue is knowledge, (2) that moral virtue is merely κατὰ τὸν ὀρθὸν λόγον, (3) that politics are a higher and better study than science, (4) that practical is superior to theoretic statesmanship, (5) that selfish prudence is the highest kind of φρόνησις, (6) that the intellectual excellences are of no use, (7) that φρόνησις is superior to σοφία. Now all this correction of others' mistakes is in a sense dialectical, for it is not direct reasoning from premisses, as scientific reasoning (the opposite of dialectical reasoning) usually is, but has to do with the opinions of opponents. But the correction of others is done not to defeat or humble them but to produce truth and prevent the spread of falsehood: and moreover it is made by means of contentions regarded not merely as what the adversary will accept but as really probable in themselves. These corrections are in fact not dialectical in just the same respect as that in which the last two chapters of VI are not dialectical—the higher and more philosophical spirit in which they are made, and the consequent greater soundness of the contentions that are supported. It is of course in this consequent greater soundness that the superiority of those arguments that are not in this sense dialectical to those that are consists. It is this fact that Grote overlooks in his criticism of Aristotle's distinction of dialectic from sophistic and eristic as lying entirely in the motives of the disputants and not at all in the objective character of their arguments. In practice it is found that the motives of the disputants invariably affect the objective character of the arguments.

So far it is probable that the account I have given of the extent to which VI is dialectic would be more or less agreed to by everyone; but now comes the point on which I understand Professor Burnet to disagree with previous commentators; as I must think, mistakenly. There are certain statements made, in VI as in other books of the Ethics, which the author appears to accept as true and not to reject or substantially modify afterwards, which Professor Burnet considers are made dialectically. By this he seems to mean that Aristotle at best only puts them forward tentatively and probably is conscious of his disbelief in them: that in no case, at any rate, has he made up his mind that they are probably true: that he afterwards tacitly or openly rejects many of them, wholly or in part: and that he only mentions them to show that the ethical views he supports, though they could be made to rest on other grounds, on axioms with which he would agree, can nevertheless rest securely enough on the axioms that are accepted by his opponents though by him rejected or at least considered inappropriate. There are moreover certain usages of words which Professor Burnet considers to be not Aristotelian but Platonic or popular, and which he therefore holds to be dialectically used, accepted that is from the opponent, in order to have the satisfaction of fighting him not only with his own arguments but with his own words. I shall try to show that with one doubtful exception none of the statements or usages referred to by Professor Burnet in VI as in this sense dialectical really are so: that is to say, that they do not imply that Aristotle has adopted, even temporarily, any view that is not actually his own.

1.   1139 a 3—6 refers to the previous division of the soul into two parts, and proposes to subdivide one of these parts into two further parts. When the former division was made[1], it was stated that the ἐξωτερικοὶ λόγοι made it rightly, and ought to be followed in this matter. The ἐξωτερικοὶ λόγοι, Professor Burnet says following Diels, are discourses extraneous to the Aristotelian school: and he adds that nearly always the expression means the writings of the Academic school, and certainly has that meaning here (1102 a 26)[2]. The former division would on this showing be a piece of current Academic psychology. But (a) it is far from certain that ἐξωτερικοὶ λόγοι means 'discourses extraneous to the Aristotelian school'; (b) τὸν αὐτὸν τρόπον in 1139 a 5 need not mean that the ἐξωτερικοὶ λόγοι are being followed in the second division as they were in the first— it would naturally mean only 'into two parts'; (c) if the ἐξωτερικοὶ λόγοι represent the opinions of some other person or persons than

[1]   1102 a 26—28.

[2]   See his note on this passage, page 58.

Aristotle, yet it does not follow that he disagrees at all with the conclusions he proposes to adopt from them, even from the strictly scientific point of view. Moreover, it is too much to say that 'Aristotle himself did not believe in parts of the soul at all' (Burnet, page 58 note). Such an expression as 1102 b 16 φαίνεται δ᾽ ἐν αὐτοῖς (sc. ἐν τοῖς ἐγκρατέσι καὶ ἀκρατέσι) ἄλλο τι παρὰ τὸν λόγον πεφυκὸς ὃ μάχεται καὶ ἀντιτείνει τῷ λόγῳ implies that in some real sense there are parts of the soul. The point is not settled in the Psychology one way or the other : it is only shown there that in whatever sense the soul may be considered to have parts, these parts do not at any rate correspond in space to parts of the body. So that this dividing of the soul into parts is not a dialectical adoption of a piece of Academic psychology in which Aristotle does not himself believe.

2. Professor Burnet holds that the argument that difference of subject-matter implies a corresponding difference in the parts of the soul (see his note on 1139 a 8—10) is un-Aristotelian and is dialectically adopted from Plato. It is one thing to admit that Plato held this opinion when he wrote the Republic, and another thing to deny that Aristotle held it when he wrote the Ethics. Even without considering the ὅμοιον ὁμοίῳ theory of knowledge on which it is made here to depend, the general principle that difference between two things implies a corresponding difference between things similarly related to them is upheld elsewhere in this same book of the Ethics. Thus φρόνησις is said to be inferior to σοφία because its objects are inferior to the objects of σοφία : 1141 a 20 ἄτοπον εἴ τις τὴν πολιτικὴν ἢ τὴν φρόνησιν σπουδαιοτάτην οἴεται εἶναι, εἰ μὴ τὸ ἄριστον τῶν ἐν τῷ κόσμῳ ἄνθρωπός ἐστιν : cf. also the rather different argument that follows about ταὐτὸν and ἕτερόν. Also the ποιητικὴ ἕξις is said to be different from the πρακτικὴ ἕξις as ποίησις is different from πρᾶξις : 1140 a 2—5. And in x there is the argument 1177 a 12 εὔλογον κατὰ τὴν κρατίστην (sc. ἀρετὴν τὴν εὐδαιμονίαν εἶναι ἐνέργειαν) αὕτη δ᾽ ἂν εἴη τοῦ ἀρίστου—which latter inference is not explicitly justified, evidently because it is considered obviously true. There is therefore no reason to suppose the view of this passage 1139 a 8—10—the view that difference of subject-matter implies a corresponding difference in the parts of the soul—is a view that Aristotle does not really take, even if no proof of that view were given at the same time.

3. 1139 a 10 καθ᾽ ὁμοιότητά τινα καὶ οἰκειότητα ἡ γνῶσις ὑπάρχει. 'Aristotle himself,' says Professor Burnet, 'did not hold the similia

similibus theory of knowledge in this naked form: the argument still proceeds on Platonic lines.' But the form is not particularly naked : τινα helps substantially to clothe it, implying dissent from such crude forms of the theory as Empedocles held (γαίᾳ γαῖαν ὀπώπαμεν) and making a reservation in favour of Aristotle's own view. Moreover, Aristotle's own view is definitely a similia similibus one, as Professor Stewart very plainly shows (Notes vol. ii p. 12—14) by a careful examination of the teaching of the Psychology. 'On Aristotelian principles the faculties in exercise are not merely like but identical with the objects as perceived' (ii 14), and the objects as perceived are the forms of things without their matter (εἴδη ἄνευ τῆς ὕλης). The argument of 1139 a 10 thus proceeds along lines that may be and indeed are Platonic, but are also Aristotelian enough.

4. The use of λογιστικόν (1139 a 12) to describe one part only of what Plato called by this name can hardly be a dialectic use in Professor Burnet's sense : it is rather a usage to which the Academic opponent would demur.

5. Professor Burnet maintains that the use of the imperative in 1139 a 6 ὑποκείσθω, 1139 a 11 λεγέσθω, 1139 b 15 ἔστω is dialectical. This can only be proved by showing that the positions taken up in those passages are afterwards given up or considerably changed, or that they are inconsistent with Aristotle's doctrines clearly expressed elsewhere. I have already defended the first two positions as really Aristotelian : I will show below that the view of 1139 b 15 is also maintained, so that ἔστω is really equivalent to ἔστι. For the usage compare 1103 b 31 τὸ μὲν οὖν κατὰ τὸν ὀρθὸν λόγον πράττειν κοινὸν καὶ ὑποκείσθω—a position not afterwards abandoned. The imperative appears to lay down, not a position which Aristotle really disagrees with but accepts for the sake of argument, but one which it is not considered necessary to prove because it either is obviously more or less true, or has been proved elsewhere.

6. The list of five ἀρεταί in 1139 b 16, τέχνη ἐπιστήμη φρόνησις σοφία νοῦς, is said to be not Aristotle's own list but 'a mere preliminary enumeration of states with a prima facie claim to be regarded as διανοητικαὶ ἀρεταί (Burnet 257 med.): we shall find that he reduces them to two, φρόνησις and σοφία.' It is said, moreover, that ὑπόληψις and δόξα 'are introduced as co-ordinate, quite in accordance with the tentative character of the present discussion' (Burnet 257). Now there is no need to read into this passage the implication that the five ἀρεταί on the one hand, or ὑπόληψις and δόξα on the other, are

regarded as co-ordinate : such a position is not here taken up, and so has not to be surrendered afterwards. Again, there is nothing to show that the prima facie claim of τέχνη νοῦς and ἐπιστήμη to be intellectual ἀρεταί is not sustained afterwards : because the various intellectual ἀρεταί can be classed in two groups each with a single name, it does not follow they are not true and distinct intellectual ἀρεταί in themselves. Φρόνησις is afterwards shown to include the divisions εὐστοχία ἀγχίνοια εὐβουλία σύνεσις γνώμη νοῦς πρακτικός as well as τέχνη here mentioned : but there is no reason to deny the name of ἀρετή to the smallest of these subdivisions any more than to the largest combination. Aristotle was above the pedantry (which it is apparently desired to force on him) of supposing that everything called an ἀρετή must be co-ordinate with everything else called an ἀρετή. This important point, which I have referred to elsewhere, is here mentioned simply with reference to the alleged dialectic character of the present passage. As to ὑπόληψις and δόξα, there is no difficulty in the fact that ὑπόληψις is the genus that includes ἐπιστήμη : the statement that ὑπολήψει ἐνδέχεται διαψεύδεσθαι is perfectly true, for it means not that *any* ὑπόληψις may be false or wrong, but that the name ὑπόληψις applies to what is wrong and what is right alike. That ὑπόληψις and δόξα are here regarded as co-ordinate is, as I have said, an unfounded assumption.

7. Chapter iv (about τέχνη) Professor Burnet declares to be highly dialectic in character. But again I maintain that it contains no statement that is not entirely in accordance with Aristotle's real opinions. That ποίησις and πρᾶξις are different is a doctrine that Aristotle does indeed say that he takes from the ἐξωτερικοὶ λόγοι, but this does not imply that he has any fault to find, from the most strictly scientific point of view, with the ἐξωτερικοὶ λόγοι and their teaching on this point. When he says πιστεύομεν he presumably means that he thinks them to be correct in this matter and not that, whether they are correct or mistaken, they may be followed in the present discussion. The rest of the chapter is fair deduction on strict Aristotelian principles, from this initial fact, or (as regards the correct usage of the *word* τέχνη) from the observed facts of ordinary speech.

8. The definition of νοῦς is said to be obtained dialectically (Burnet, page 265, last note). If this means that it rests on premisses that Aristotle does not agree to, the statement is incorrect, for there is no reason to suppose that Aristotle does not consider the five ἀρεταί

of 1139 b 16 as a valid and exhaustive list. Nor is there anything unscientific about the process of proof by exhaustion here employed. It is true that the validity of the argument depends on the fact, yet to be proved, that τοῦ σοφοῦ περὶ ἐνίων ἔχειν ἀπόδειξίν ἐστιν: but that statement Aristotle really holds to be true, and if the words ὡς δειχθήσεται or the like were inserted after ἀπόδειξίν ἐστιν the argument would be as valid formally as it is already valid in substance.

9. The argument about εὐβουλία is, it is said (Burnet, page 275, 1st note), on strictly Academic lines. This does not follow from the doubtless true position, that Aristotle discusses εὐβουλία in its relation to ἐπιστήμη because Plato (Republic 428 b) had said that εὐβουλία was 'clearly a kind of ἐπιστήμη.' Aristotle is continually correcting the errors of others as he does here, but he is not obliged to assume even their phraseology to do so to advantage. Nor is there anything obviously Academic about the phraseology here, with one possible exception (διάνοια) to be noticed later.

10. Professor Burnet has a curious note on 1143 b 4 ἀρχαὶ γὰρ τοῦ οὗ ἕνεκα αὗται. 'The universal rules of conduct and the definition of εὐδαιμονία can only be found by a dialectical process which starts from particular moral judgments.' Now there is nothing obviously dialectical about the moral induction by which particular moral judgments are generalised into universal moral judgments, except in the sense in which a moral induction and a moral deduction are both dialectical—namely, that they are processes concerned with τὰ ἐνδεχόμενα ἄλλως ἔχειν and so must consist of reasoning ἐξ ἐνδόξων. But Professor Burnet can hardly mean, by his use of the word 'dialectical,' to point only to what is common to all moral reasoning. He seems rather to suggest that there is an important likeness between the system of investigation into ethical questions here conducted in the Ethics and the investigations into ethical questions that we each of us conduct in our practical life. But this Aristotle never says; and it is hardly true.

The above are the principal passages in book VI that appear to Professor Burnet to be of a dialectical nature. He believes indeed that the entire treatise is tentative, and that it contains a great number of assumptions in the truth of which Aristotle does not himself really believe, and which are the opinions either of the contemporary Academy or of ordinary people. If he fails—as I have tried to show that he does fail—to show that those particular passages, which he thinks most strikingly support his view, really do support it, a fortiori it may be argued that the rest of the reasoning, which has on the face of it more of the scientific expository character that marks all Aristotle's other works, is not dialectic at all in the sense of the word 'dialectic' in question. Professor Burnet further makes a more definite though less important allegation, that Aristotle, in the same dialectic spirit, uses words, not with the meanings he would himself naturally attach to them, but with those attached to them by the persons whose opinions he is supposed to be accepting. Now it is undoubtedly true, as I have shown elsewhere, that Aristotle sometimes accepts popular usages alongside of others which he regards as more correct and which he wishes to introduce: thus he is willing to use both πολιτική and φρόνησις, and certainly also νοῦς, in the popular sense of those words, as well as with a wider and more correct meaning peculiar to himself. But in nearly all cases he distinguishes the sense that he holds strictly correct from that which he holds merely allowable because established. There are one or two cases in which he is said to use words in the latter sense without saying anything to show he is not using them in the former, and misunderstandings on the part of Aristotle's readers are said to have arisen in consequence.

1. About λογιστικόν and δοξαστικόν I have already said something. Professor Burnet supposes λογιστικόν to be used by Aristotle because Plato used the word, though admittedly Plato used it in quite a different sense: and he supposes δοξαστικόν to be used by Aristotle because Plato opposes ἐπιστήμη to δόξα, and therefore δοξαστικόν is the suitable antithesis to ἐπιστημονικόν. But the usage of λογιστικόν constitutes not an acceptance but a rejection of the Platonic usage: and since Aristotle's classification of διάνοια into θεωρητική and πρακτική is not the same as Plato's distinction of ἐπιστήμη and δόξα (a fact that Professor Burnet admits, but says must be lightly passed over) it is hard to suppose that, whatever reason Aristotle has for using the term δοξαστικόν, it is because he is dialectically accepting the Platonic psychology and the Platonic phraseology therewith. I have shown elsewhere the reasons I suppose Aristotle to have had for using both λογιστικόν and δοξαστικόν as he does.

2. In 1143 b 5 αἴσθησις is used in the general sense of 'perception,' and includes the activity of the intellect. This is said to be a dialectical acceptance of vague everyday language. But Aristotle often makes a vague and loose use of words even in his

most scientific and expository treatises, simply because he is careless of formal precision when he thinks his meaning is plain, and also in some cases because he is without the word he wants and so has to make another do. The latter as well as the former is the cause of the use of αἴσθησις here: it is hard to see what other word could have been used: and it is plain that αἴσθησις in the strict sense cannot be meant, so that there is no danger of confusion of meaning, or Aristotle thought there was none. There is then nothing dialectical about the usage of αἴσθησις here.

3. In 1142 b 12 the use of διάνοια in διανοίας ἄρα λείπεται is possibly the only instance in VI of a real acceptance of a Platonic usage with which Aristotle disagrees. Διάνοια here plainly means the intellect considered as unsatisfied, searching, actively inquiring but not contemplating the results of inquiry. That Plato uses διάνοια in this sense is plain[1], though he certainly does not so use it always. It is not so plain, however, that Aristotle never uses it in this sense. Cf. for instance, Metaphysics 1074 b 36 ἀεὶ ἄλλου ἡ ἐπιστήμη καὶ ἡ αἴσθησις καὶ ἡ δόξα καὶ ἡ διάνοια (compare this list with that of this chapter on εὐβουλία): Interpretation 16 b 20 ἵστησι γὰρ ὁ λέγων (sc. τὰ ὀνόματα) τὴν διάνοιαν 'he stops his reasoning activity': and διάνοια is elsewhere used in a sense narrower than that in which it is used in the early part of VI: thus in Metaphysics 1027 b 25 it is definitely said to make propositions and not to apprehend simple notions or ἀδιαίρετα: and it seems confined to the meaning διάνοια πρακτική in Ethics 1148 a 9 παρὰ τὴν προαίρεσιν καὶ τὴν διάνοιαν ἀκράτης λέγεται, and Topics 151 a 3 οἷον εἰ τὴν ἀνδρίαν ὡρίσατο τόλμαν μετὰ διανοίας ὀρθῆς. So that all that can be fairly said is that διάνοια is here used in a sense that is more regularly Platonic than it is regularly Aristotelian, and not that Aristotle would not have admitted the present sense as a possible and correct one. This single instance of a dialectical attitude that Professor Burnet maintains pervades the whole of VI cannot prove much, and could not even if it were more unmistakeable than it is: μία γὰρ χελιδὼν ἔαρ οὐ ποιεῖ.

---

[1] See Professor Burnet's references (page 276 of his edition).

ON FORMAL ACCURACY IN ARISTOTLE, ILLUSTRATED BY THE SIXTH BOOK.

Aristotle's originality is shown by this among other things, that he first conceived how desirable it is for the philosopher to be formally accurate in the use of his terms and in the arrangement of his arguments. Like most original conceptions, whether Aristotle's or other people's, this one was imperfectly formed, and much less perfectly embodied in practice. To the modern reader the result is a kind of perplexity comparatively absent from the writings alike of those who have not formed the conception of accuracy at all, and of those who have not only formed it but been able to work it out properly. Such difficulties have usually been attacked without the help of any general principles, and because singly, very often unsuccessfully. Some consideration of this question of accuracy should help towards the immediate object of understanding book VI, and also serve as a basis for similar investigation of other works. The principles it is here desired to establish are not shown to rest on anything but this single book: but that they are in fact of very general application it does not seem easy to deny, and this should give them a wider significance than will in this essay definitely be claimed for them.

It must at once strike every student of to-day, it may also have struck the students of those times, that Aristotle's attempts at carefulness and consistency are in some things greater than need be, and in other things less. Pedantic precision seems to alternate with unscientific slovenliness: and he is often, it appears, slovenly where the subject is of great importance, and precise where it is trivial. The view some scholars are ready to accept, that in the corpus of Aristotelian writings we have to do with mere lecture notes, and not with such finished work as the Platonic dialogues, may be to some extent true, though nothing can prove it; and if it is true it may serve to account for much that is puzzling in the writings as they have come down to us. But apart from the fact that even considered as lecture notes they are inconsistent and irregular enough to demand explanation, and sufficiently unlike what one would expect to find the lecture notes of a modern philosopher, it is dangerous to make such doubtful applications of a doubtful fact as many editors are apt to make, explaining for instance the omission of what seems to be urgently necessary by the hypothesis that the lecturer meant to trust his memory to fill the gap when actually addressing his audience. There is nothing for it but to take the text as it stands; to suppose that the form in which we have it, however imperfect we may think it, was considered by the Peripatetic school satisfactory enough to remain as the permanent form and to be slavishly imitated even in details; and to explain away as well as possible the difficulties to which the peculiarities of this form give rise.

The question may be considered under two heads, not so distinct as not to shade into each other and present many features in common: (i) the undoubted variation, and the alleged inconsistency, in the use of particular words and phrases: (ii) the apparent or real imperfections of argument. The latter shades off on the one hand into the former, on the other into the larger questions of matter and substance, as distinguished from pure form, a distinction which, it may be remarked, it is often exceedingly hard to make, just as it is hard, when the distinction between the two is easy to make in itself, to know which of the two is really to the fore in any given passage. It will be convenient to proceed from the more to the less definite of the above two questions, and first to consider the problems that arise from the usage of particular words and phrases.

The claim already made for Aristotle, that he was the first to aim consciously at formal accuracy of language, must be modified, so far as the usage of particular words and phrases is concerned, by a recognition of what he owes in this matter to certain of his predecessors, who gave him some materials which he had only to put into place in his system. Prodicus, according to a tradition preserved among other places in a well-known passage in the Protagoras (337 A—C), attached the greatest importance to a correct use of words (ὀρθοέπεια), drawing fine and not always justifiable distinctions between what every-day people regarded as complete synonyms.

Socrates, who was familiar with the teaching of Prodicus, was anxious to fix the meanings of important or ambiguous words and to establish a consistent usage of them accordingly: it is doubtful whether he regarded words as having meanings attaching to them in the unchangeable nature of things, so that each distinct word must correspond to a real thing, and the only task is to discover what the thing is; or whether he saw dimly, what Aristotle saw more clearly, that words are a sort of spontaneous convention, rather instruments of thought than guides to truth, and showing what people actually think rather than whether in so thinking they are right or not. Plato was curiously careless of form. He was a poet not only in mind but in expression: and because he was a poet, and not a man of science like Aristotle, he could feel no reluctance to sacrifice formal exactness to beauty. It is this far more than his dialectic method that makes him inexact. It is not the experience of the modern dialectician that a vague use of terms is unobjectionable, and it must be held a weakness on the part of Plato, though scarcely one to be regretted, that he did not see how far consistency of language may be of service in the search for material truth. Not that he is indifferent to terminology: he is always glad to fix a conception with a name, and if the name is not ready to his hand he does not hesitate to coin a new word or give an old one a technical meaning. The form his inquiries take is nearly always the search for the definition of some word. But his theory of ideas taught him to distinguish words from things, it is not words but things that really interest him, and so long as he can make it clear that he is talking about a certain thing he does not trouble himself to describe it always in the same words.

Aristotle as well as Plato could see the difference between things and the words describing them. It is hardly more than an accident that some of his most important works take the Socratic shape of search for the meaning of words—that the object of the Ethics, for instance, seems to be a definition of the word εὐδαιμονία, and the object of the 6th book the definition of a number of words likely to be confused with each other—for precision and consistency in language is never his end in view, never anything more than the most subordinate of means to reaching the truth about real things. But he saw how important it is as such a means, and not only in the search for truth but in its exposition to others when found. The result is that his works are crowded with technical terms, and with discussions as to the meaning and right use of particular words. Like Plato he now and then regrets the fact that there is no name to describe some class of things determined by some induction or analysis, and is at pains to account for the fact. He far exceeds Plato in the boldness with which he invents new words and phrases, or uses old words and phrases with new meanings. The former process was hard for the Greeks. The flexibility of their language was a small compensation for their lack of the advantage that modern thinkers possess in two dead languages with a large and varied vocabulary which may be drawn upon to any extent without fear of confusion with common speech. New coinages were accordingly rare, though the need for them was never greater, even in our own day. Consequently the other process, adaptation of terms already existing, was common with all thinkers, and for the greatest thinkers inevitable : Aristotle found himself driven to it at every turn. But whereas the more recondite sciences demanded new terms to express ideas that were at once novel and abstruse : in the Ethics the subject dealt with is too closely connected with the common experience of men to demand them to the same extent, for the main ideas are not wholly novel. What new terms there are nearly all belong to such other sciences as logic, metaphysics or psychology, and occur when these sciences are touched upon in some ethical connection. Here and there an unfamiliar vice or virtue, to which people are not in practice addicted, is held worthy of a new name : but sometimes its namelessness is merely remarked and not remedied. To the special use of terms already in use Aristotle was led by inclination almost as much as by necessity. It was one of his cardinal principles that the mass of mankind is not likely to be wholly wrong on any subject, and that, as they are on the whole capable of expressing their opinions correctly in speech, the ordinary usage of words is apt to be more or less the right one. He paid a similar respect, genuine though discriminating, to the language as well as to the opinions of earlier philosophers. He was therefore glad to adopt an old term whenever he could, feeling it a testimonial to the soundness of his own conclusions. He kept as nearly as he could to the old meaning, and if he was obliged to enlarge, to restrict, or altogether to change the meaning, he tried his best to exhibit some justifying analogy of the new meaning with the old, beyond what would at first sight appear.

The sixth book contains instances of (a) popular and (β) philosophic terms, which Aristotle has adopted, fixing upon them a special meaning of his own. A third important but complicated class is (γ) those terms that have been previously adopted by philosophers from common speech and by them modified in meaning, now taken over by Aristotle, who modifies their meaning still further.

(a) *Popular Terms.*

(1) Τέχνη. This term is modified from popular usage in two ways : (1) its application is restricted to the actual making of things, (2) it is regarded as a necessarily good state of mind and not as one that may be either good or bad and yet deserve the name. As to the first point, it is carefully distinguished from the intellectual excellence that applies to πρᾶξις or the doing of things. Ποίησις and πρᾶξις, it is affirmed, are entirely different things, and it is with ποίησις only that τέχνη can be concerned. The sphere of ποίησις is certainly not well-defined—it does not seem clear under which head divination and rhetoric, for instance, would come ; but restriction in the meaning of τέχνη there is, and in spite of the fact that the definition of τέχνη is obtained (1140 a 6—10) by induction from popular usage, it seems clear that popular usage is to some extent being set aside. The other modification, whereby τέχνη is made to connote what is necessarily excellent, scarcely needs proof : it will be shown later that Aristotle himself takes account of it.

(2) Πολιτική. Aristotle broadens the meaning of this word. It means, he says, the architectonic practical science, under which all the others come, and by which all the others must be determined. People in general regard it as something that chiefly concerns the magistrate or the demagogue : but it has to do with everything from the most trivial details of civic administration to the widest generalities concerning the end of human life or the nature of law.

(3) Γνώμη. Whereas people use γνώμη to mean merely 'opinion,' or at best 'common sense' about anything, Aristotle infers from its derivation that it has a restricted and good meaning. It is ὀρθὴ κρίσις, not any sort of κρίσις, and κρίσις τοῦ ἐπιεικοῦς, not κρίσις of anything and everything.

(β) *Philosophic Terms.*

(1) Ὀρθὸς λόγος. This means various things in the mouths of various philosophers : all are agreed that it is ὀρθὸς λόγος that fixes

what is good, but they are vague or wrong about what it is. Socrates identifies it with virtue, Protagoras judges it fluctuating with the utility of the moment, Plato makes it the transcendental knowledge of the ideas. It is really, Aristotle says, the excellence of the lower reasoning part of the soul, that concerned with such ἐνδεχόμενα ἄλλως ἔχειν as affect the actions of men: or rather it is that part of the soul when possessed of that excellence. The formula that states its connection with moral virtue is to be adopted but modified— moral virtue must be said to be neither ὀρθὸς λόγος itself nor merely κατὰ τὸν ὀρθὸν λόγον but μετὰ τοῦ ὀρθοῦ λόγου.

(2) Λογιστικόν. Plato used this word to denote the reasoning part of the soul as a whole (e.g. in Republic 439 D), but Aristotle restricts it to mean the lower of the two parts of the reasoning part of the soul (1139 a 12 τὸ μὲν ἐπιστημονικὸν τὸ δὲ λογιστικόν· τὸ γὰρ βουλεύεσθαι καὶ λογίζεσθαι ταὐτόν).

(3) Εὐβουλία. Plato identified this with σοφία and ἐπιστήμη (Republic 428 B), but Aristotle restricts it greatly: with him it is only one aspect or division of the practical excellence φρόνησις.

(γ)   *Terms both popular and philosophic.*

Under this head come four out of the five of the most important terms of this 6th book—ἐπιστήμη νοῦς σοφία and φρόνησις.

(1) The popular use of ἐπιστήμη distinguished it little from τέχνη. The skill of a statesman or doctor or general could be called either. It was only philosophers who took a stricter view of it. They narrowed its meaning too much, Aristotle thinks: it is absurd to think with Parmenides that nothing but pure being, or with Plato that nothing but the ideas, can be known. But it is true that only those things can be known, in the strict sense, which μὴ ἐνδέχεται ἄλλως ἔχειν: this view is insisted on constantly in NE VI, cutting out the popular ἐπιστῆμαι from their right to the name, but including, in opposition to Parmenides, Plato, and most other philosophers, physics as well as metaphysics and mathematics, and more of mathematics than the barren methods of many earlier thinkers would allow.

(2) Νοῦς in the popular usage was usually equivalent to common sense or intelligence. Philosophers on the other hand exalted it as they exalted ἐπιστήμη. Aristotle, who admires Anaxagoras and his elevated conception of νοῦς, joins with him and Plato in giving the word great dignity. In VI ii he uses it for a moment in the broad

sense of 'the intellect.' But in VI vi he quite definitely applies it, in a restricted sense, to the intellectual excellence that leads the mind by induction to the grasp of necessary axiomatic truth : a use on the whole quite consistent with the last section of the Posterior Analytics.

(3) Σοφία in the popular usage meant either the practical wisdom of a legislator or moralist[1] or the skill of an artist of high merit[2]. The philosophers used it variously to mean the highest kind of intellectual excellence of which they held a man capable. Their ideas not squaring with those of Aristotle, their application of the word was different also, to anything from practical wisdom in the popular sense to the lofty knowledge of reality conceived by Plato. Aristotle carries on the philosophic tradition, adapting the meaning of σοφία to his own views in making it composite of νοῦς and ἐπιστήμη, and by an ingenious analogy connecting his definition with the popular meaning as well (1141 a 16).

(4) Φρόνησις. The philosophers never distinguished between φρόνησις and σοφία. People in general, says Aristotle, do not always distinguish them, but tend to call the man who knows his interests φρόνιμος, and the clever artist σοφός. Aristotle adopts this distinction, but with important modifications. His idea of the σοφός is more the philosophers', his idea of the φρόνιμος more the ordinary person's. Φρόνησις is to be concerned with practical matters only : the popular view is only wrong in narrowing the notion down to that of a selfish unsocial consideration of one's own individual interests, whereas the φρόνιμος must act as what Nature intends him to be, the member of a community.

It should now be clear that Aristotle finds no difficulty in supplying his terminology with the forms of common speech or of other philosophers, or in modifying their meanings to suit the peculiarities of his own doctrines, while adhering as far as may be to the common meanings, and justifying his departures therefrom by tracing analogies between old meanings and new.

This would not in itself be a source of serious confusion to anyone. But unfortunately, though quite naturally, Aristotle is often not content to use words only in the new senses he has imposed upon them, but at other times reverts to the senses more familiar to people in general or to other schools of philosophers. It will be

---

[1] e.g. the seven sages were σοφοί.

[2] 1141 a 9 τὴν σοφίαν ἐν ταῖς τέχναις τοῖς ἀκριβεστάτοις τὰς τέχνας ἀποδίδομεν.

best to give such examples of this as occur in NE vi before trying to explain why it happens.

(1) Τέχνη is used in two places not in the new sense of an ἀρετή but in the old sense of a field of intellectual activity in which goodness or badness can be shown. These are 1140 b 22 τέχνης μὲν ἔστιν ἀρετή, φρονήσεως δ' οὐκ ἔστιν, 1141 a 11 οὐθὲν ἄλλο σημαίνοντες τὴν σοφίαν ἢ ὅτι ἀρετὴ τέχνης ἐστίν. Compare this with the contrast of τέχνη with ἀτεχνία 1140 a 20 ἡ μὲν οὖν τέχνη...ἕξις τις μετὰ λόγου ἀληθοῦς ποιητική ἐστιν, ἡ δ' ἀτεχνία τοὐναντίον μετὰ λόγου ψευδοῦς ποιητικὴ ἕξις: the difference of meaning is plain[1]. It may also be noted that in other works Aristotle uses τέχνη in a very loose sense, e.g. Analytics 71 a 4 αἵ τε μαθηματικαὶ τῶν ἐπιστημῶν...καὶ τῶν ἄλλων ἑκάστη τεχνῶν, Metaphysics 981 b 23 αἱ μαθηματικαὶ τέχναι, Topics 170 a 31 καθ' ἑκάστην τέχνην...οἷον κατὰ γεωμετρίαν.

(2) Πολιτική is applied to a section of what in Aristotle's special usage[2] is meant by πολιτική. This use is quite definitely distinguished from the special one as being the popular one: 1141 b 28 διὸ πολιτεύεσθαι τούτους μόνους λέγουσιν. It is accepted in the popular sense as adequately patching the gap caused by the want of a special name for this division of πολιτική in the broad sense: only it is intimated that the popular judgment, that practical are better than theoretical politics, to which the popular usage of the word πολιτική is due, is mistaken, for νομοθετική is ἀρχιτεκτονικὴ and so better than πολιτική in the narrow sense. With this caution the narrow sense is allowed to pass[3].

(3) Ἐπιστήμη. This word is used in NE vi, as elsewhere, in the loose sense of 'art,' 'practical science,' sometimes almost 'profession': which is the popular usage. Thus 1138 b 26 ἐν ταῖς ἄλλαις ἐπιμελείαις περὶ ὅσας ἐστὶν ἐπιστήμη, where the examples following of such ἐπιμέλειαι are γυμναστική and ἰατρική, with which of course ἐπιστήμη in the strict sense has nothing to do. Also 1141 a 16 ἀκριβεστάτη ἂν τῶν ἐπιστημῶν εἴη ἡ σοφία, where the strict use follows, εἴη ἂν ἡ σοφία νοῦς καὶ ἐπιστήμη. Also 1143 a 2 (ἡ σύνεσις οὐκ ἔστι) τις μία τῶν κατὰ μέρος ἐπιστημῶν, οἷον ἡ ἰατρικὴ περὶ ὑγιεινῶν ἢ γεωμετρία περὶ μεγέθη, where one of the examples, ἰατρική, is περὶ τῶν ἐνδεχομένων ἄλλως ἔχειν.

---

[1] This point is discussed more fully in the Notes.

[2] Illustrated by 1141 b 24 τῆς δὲ περὶ πόλιν ἡ μὲν ὡς ἀρχιτεκτονικὴ φρόνησις νομοθετική, ἡ δὲ ὡς τὰ καθ' ἕκαστα τὸ κοινὸν ἔχει ὄνομα, πολιτική.

[3] Classical Review Feb. 1905 page 17 (note 8).

(4) Νοῦς is used in four senses in NE vi. Besides the strict meaning determined in the chapter devoted to it, vi vi, it may mean :—(a) the intellect as a whole: 1139 a 17 τρία δή ἐστιν ἐν τῇ ψυχῇ τὰ κύρια πράξεως καὶ ἀληθείας, αἴσθησις νοῦς ὄρεξις, where νοῦς = διάνοια, cf. a 33 ἄνευ νοῦ καὶ διανοίας, a 21 ὅπερ ἐν διανοίᾳ κατάφασις καὶ ἀπόφασις τοῦτ᾽ ἐν ὀρέξει δίωξις καὶ φυγή, b 4 ἢ ὀρεκτικὸς νοῦς ἢ ὄρεξις διανοητική. (b) that particular sort of φρόνησις which apprehends particular facts either as minor premisses for practical syllogisms or as materials for inductively-reached major premisses of the same sort of syllogisms ; see the whole passage 1143 a 25—b 5, particularly a 35—b 5. (c) φρόνησις in general, 1144 b 12 ἐὰν δὲ λάβῃ νοῦν ἐν τῷ πράττειν διαφέρει. Of these three usages the first is that of previous philosophers, especially Anaxagoras, the other two popular, as in the common phrase νοῦν ἔχειν 'to have good sense[1].'

(5) Φρόνησις. The usage of Socrates, Plato and other philosophers, whereby φρόνησις is a synonym of σοφία and means the highest wisdom, is not adopted by Aristotle (though it is, in several places, by Eudemus in the undisputedly Eudemian books). But its use in a less elevated sense than the strict one, that is to say in the ordinary sense of common speech, is accepted with a reserve, just as πολιτική is accepted, 1141 b 29 δοκεῖ δὲ καὶ φρόνησις μάλιστ᾽ εἶναι ἡ περὶ αὐτὸν καὶ ἕνα, καὶ ἔχει αὕτη τὸ κοινὸν ὄνομα, φρόνησις : the reserve being, as with πολιτική, that the popular ethical judgment on which the usage is founded is a wrong one: for φρόνησις περὶ αὐτὸν καὶ ἕνα is the lowest, and not the highest, of the three divisions of φρόνησις in the strict sense, πολιτική οἰκονομική and φρόνησις περὶ ἕνα.

Besides the variations in usage where there is a strict usage and also one or more loose ones, there are certain terms used in several senses none of which can be said to be more the strict one or more accurate than the others : such as διάνοια, βουλευτική, λόγος.

(1) διάνοια in the 2nd chapter is a synonym of νοῦς, and means the intellect as a whole, but in 1142 b 12, διανοίας ἄρα λείπεται (sc. ὀρθότητα εἶναι τὴν εὐβουλίαν)· αὕτη γὰρ οὔπω φάσις, it is plain διάνοια is the intellect considered as searching for and not as possessing truth, or as the activity itself that consists in such searching.

(2) βουλευτική in its broadest sense is the distinguishing epithet of φρόνησις as a whole, as distinguished from σοφία[2], or of the λογιστικὸν μέρος as distinguished from the ἐπιστημονικὸν μέρος

---

[1] 1143 a 27, b 7.
[2] 1140 a 30 ὅλος ἂν εἴη φρόνιμος ὁ βουλευτικός.

(1139 a 12)[1]: more narrowly it is applied (1141 b 27) to πολιτική[2] (in the narrower sense of that word as distinguished from νομοθετική): most narrowly of all to parliamentary as distinguished from judicial πολιτική (1141 b 33 ἡ μὲν βουλευτικὴ ἡ δὲ δικαστική).

(3) λόγος means (a) the reasoning part of the soul, τὸ διανοητικὸν μέρος, not clearly distinguished from the ἐνέργεια of that part. In this sense it is used in the often-repeated phrase ὀρθὸς λόγος, which means 'the reason in its excellent condition.' (Professor Burnet indeed maintains that the metaphysical meaning of εἶδος, as opposed to ὕλη, belongs properly to ὀρθὸς λόγος, and speaks of the φρόνιμος as having the form of goodness in his soul; but such metaphysical subtilty is foreign to the methods of the Ethics, except for such definite metaphysical digressions as that in Book 1 on the Platonic idea of the good.) So too λόγος is a synonym of νοῦς and διάνοια, 1139 a 24 δεῖ τόν τε λόγον ἀληθῆ εἶναι καὶ τὴν ὄρεξιν ὀρθήν, a 32 προαιρέσεως δὲ (sc. ἀρχαί εἰσιν) ὄρεξις καὶ λόγος ὁ ἕνεκά τινος, 1140 b 28 ἀλλὰ μὴν οὐδ' ἕξις μετὰ λόγου μόνον· σημεῖον δ' ὅτι κτλ. and in all the definitions of intellectual virtues ἕξις μετὰ λόγου ἀληθοῦς κτλ. Λόγος also means (b) 'the argument' 1144 a 33 ἔστω γὰρ λόγου χάριν τὸ τυχόν, 1144 b 32 ἀλλὰ καὶ ὁ λόγος ταύτῃ λύοιτ' ἂν ᾧ διαλεχθείη τις ἂν ὅτι χωρίζονται ἀλλήλων αἱ ἀρεταί: also in the phrase ἐξωτερικοὶ λόγοι, which occurs in this book at 1140 a 2: (c) 'syllogism' as distinguished from induction (ἐπαγωγή). So 1140 b 33 μετὰ λόγου γὰρ ἡ ἐπιστήμη, 1142 a 25 ὁ μὲν γὰρ νοῦς τῶν ὅρων, ὧν οὐκ ἔστι λόγος, 1142 b 12 ἀλλὰ μὴν οὐδ' ἄνευ λόγου ἡ εὐβουλία (where it suggests the first meaning also), 1143 a 36 καὶ γὰρ τῶν πρώτων ὅρων καὶ τῶν ἐσχάτων νοῦς ἐστι καὶ οὐ λόγος.

The above are I think all the important variations in the meaning of terms to be found in NE vi. The list is a considerable one, and though there are probably more in NE vi than in any other part of Aristotle's writings, to a greater or less extent they occur everywhere. The fact is the more remarkable because Aristotle does nevertheless at times attach great importance to the use of names, as may be shown from this very book. He is most careful, for instance, to lay down the principle that πρᾶξις and ποίησις are different (1140 a 2, again a 5—6, again a 16—17, again b 3—4). He carefully states that σύνεσις and εὐσυνεσία are different names for the same thing, and also συνετός and εὐσύνετος 1143 a 10. And there is the

---

[1] 1139 a 12 τὸ μὲν ἐπιστημονικὸν τὸ δὲ λογιστικόν.
[2] 1141 b 26 αὕτη γὰρ πρακτικὴ καὶ βουλευτική.

remarkable variation of epithets given to the part of the διανοητικόν concerned with ἐνδεχόμενα ἄλλως ἔχειν. At 1139 a 12 the apparently natural epithet βουλευτικόν is rejected in favour of λογιστικόν, in order, as I have elsewhere tried to show, tacitly to allow for non‑practical θεωρία τῶν ἐνδεχομένων ἄλλως ἔχειν, and in two other passages, 1140 b 26 and 1144 b 14, the word δοξαστικόν is substituted for λογιστικόν, in the first passage if not in both apparently to insist on the same point, that θεωρία of ἐνδεχόμενα is not necessarily practical. Even if this were not the true explanation of the variation in terms, it would still be plain that Aristotle for some reason or other does attach much importance to the use of the right term in this connection.

The variations in the meaning of terms have not all the same explanation. There can be little doubt that one or two of them are due to sheer confusion of thought on the author's part. Just as Aristotle was capable of producing confused arguments, so he was capable of confusing various meanings of single words. The extra‑ordinary change in the sense of τέχνη, quite unmarked as it is by any observation or explanation, can hardly be explained otherwise. But of no other change in this book can it be definitely asserted with any confidence, only in a few other cases can it even plausibly be conjectured, that the author did not clearly separate his meanings and successfully avoid real confusion of thought. As a general rule it is easy to suppose that he was not only clear in his own mind that he meant different things by the same word at different times, but certain that his hearers or readers also would quite understand what his meaning was. It has to be remembered how unlikely it is that the formal difficulties that give most trouble to‑day are just the same as those which gave most trouble then. Even people speaking the same language and of the same age and training and general ability will be variously disconcerted by various ellipses or obscure transi‑tions in argument, or by various instances of this particular practice of changing the meanings of words. The view that these variations were clear to Aristotle and his hearers is not the less but the more plausible that in other passages in this work there may be observed what seems exaggerated carefulness to define a not always very important point, already it would seem defined clearly enough: e.g. 1140 a 16—17 in spite of the previous a 1—10, 1142 a 23—25 in spite of the previous 1140 b 1—3, and such repeated definitions as 1140 b 20—21 (of φρόνησις) after the previous 1140 b 4—6, 1140 a

20—21 (of τέχνη) after the previous 1140 a 9—10, 1141 b 2—3 (of σοφία) after the previous 1141 a 19—20. It is, then, confidence that the variations in usage are clear and will not lead to confusion that has probably caused Aristotle to admit them, without as a rule commenting on them at all; though he sometimes does comment on them, e.g. 1139 b 18 εἰ δεῖ ἀκριβολογεῖσθαι καὶ μὴ ἀκολουθεῖν ταῖς ὁμοιότησιν, which plainly marks a departure from his use of the word ἐπιστήμη elsewhere. It is perhaps more literary purism than anything else that makes modern philosophical writers avoid similar variations where the sense is not endangered; an avoidance that is in any case easier for them than for Aristotle because of the larger vocabulary on which they can draw for synonyms. They are not always more successful than Aristotle in avoiding that material confusion of thought which comes from confusing the meaning of words. One explanation of Aristotle's variations, the simple fact of his limited vocabulary, will not serve to explain his varying without comment in places where comment seems needed: for it was his practice to comment where he felt the danger of confusion; of this there is a good instance (besides 1139 b 18 already quoted) in 1143 b 25 ὥσπερ οὐδὲ τὰ ὑγιεινὰ οὐδὲ τὰ εὐεκτικά, ὅσα μὴ τῷ ποιεῖν ἀλλὰ τῷ ἀπὸ τῆς ἕξεως εἶναι λέγεται. We are thus obliged to suppose that he only withholds explanatory comment because it seems to him superfluous, and so that all the difficult variations are more difficult now than they seemed at the time, except in one or two cases where real confusion of thought may be causing the trouble. There is seldom any good reason either for straining the meaning of a word into consistency with its meaning in other places, or for regarding it as a meaning dialectically accepted for the purposes of argument but in no way stamped with permanent approval.

Before turning to the kindred question of how far NE VI is logically accurate and well-arranged in its arguments, it will be worth while to notice certain points that turn, altogether or very largely, on questions that are purely terminological. (i) Much difficulty has been needlessly made about the opening of the 3rd chapter in respect of the remark ὑπολήψει γὰρ καὶ δόξῃ ἐνδέχεται ψεύδεσθαι. This has been held to imply that the five virtues mentioned just before, τέχνη ἐπιστήμη φρόνησις σοφία νοῦς, are infallible; that is to say, that they are states of soul that prevent their possessors from ever making any false judgments about the matters with which they are severally concerned. In a sense this is true, but the infallibility of these virtues is quite a different thing from the infallibility of that νοῦς which is concerned with simple concepts as distinguished from propositions. In this latter there is indeed no possibility of error, but neither is there in the strict sense any possibility of truth ; however, since there is no possibility of error in that kind of νόησις, the statement of the 'Psychology' that this kind of νοῦς is infallible may be regarded as a significant and correct one ; and it is correct in this sense, that everyone who exercises this kind of νόησις at all is as right as anyone else at all can be. But it is not true that everyone who exercises his mind in various ways in such a manner that the virtues τέχνη ἐπιστήμη φρόνησις σοφία νοῦς would belong to him if he exercised it rightly ipso facto does exercise it rightly and so has those virtues belonging to him. For example, a man may attempt to be φρόνιμος, but may fail, either partly or altogether. In so far as he fails he does not deserve the name of φρόνιμος, but on the other hand in so far as he succeeds he does deserve that name ; and the case is the same with the other virtues. The name φρόνιμος really belongs without qualification only to the perfect man, who is of course infallible in the strict sense of that word. But a man can be more or less φρόνιμος ; it is absurd to deny the name to anyone who is very wise in practical matters simply because he is not perfectly or invariably wise. Yet such a person is not infallible : it may be said of his φρόνησις (or more accurately perhaps of his mind) ἐνδέχεται ψεύδεσθαι. Plainly then this is a question of terminology : τέχνη and the other four are virtues, good states, states that lead the mind to truth : ὑπόληψις and δόξα are states that may be good or may be bad, the names indicating neither quality. (ii) A smaller point is raised by 1140 b 28 ἀλλὰ μὴν οὐδ' ἕξις μετὰ λόγου μόνον· σημεῖον δ' ὅτι λήθη μὲν τῆς τοιαύτης ἕξεως ἔστι, φρονήσεως δ' οὐκ ἔστιν. This does not mean that φρόνησις is indestructible, as some have explained, but that its destruction is not of the kind called λήθη or forgetfulness, and that since only that can be forgotten which is purely intellectual, φρόνησις which cannot be forgotten is not purely intellectual—with which conclusion, incomplete as it is, the subject breaks off for the time : the argument is completed in the last chapter of the book by showing the connection between φρόνησις and ἠθικὴ ἀρετή. (iii) When it is said 1144 b 31 οὐχ οἷόν τε ἀγαθὸν εἶναι κυρίως ἄνευ φρονήσεως, οὐδὲ φρόνιμον ἄνευ τῆς ἠθικῆς ἀρετῆς, this statement is pronounced a circular argument, and therefore a difficulty to those who find it hard to credit Aristotle with such an argument. Yet there is no sign that Aristotle feels any difficulty himself. The fact is that the circle is only apparent, being a merely terminological one. A parallel statement would be 'A man cannot be a husband without a wife, nor a woman a wife without a husband.' For just as the man by marrying becomes a man of a special kind, a husband, and a woman by marrying becomes a woman of a special kind, a wife, so δεινότης by its association with φυσικὴ ἀρετή becomes δεινότης of a special kind, φρόνησις, and φυσικὴ ἀρετή by association with δεινότης becomes ἀρετή of a special kind, κυρία ἀρετή. Δεινότης and φυκικὴ ἀρετή may either of them exist without the other, but when this is the case δεινότης does not deserve the *name φρόνησις* nor ἀρετή the *name κυρία ἀρετή*. Questions such as the above, turning partly or altogether on the meaning and proper usage of particular words, are so common in Aristotle that great care should always be taken to see how far an argument really concerns the matter of the subject under discussion and how far merely the form in which the matter is expressed : commentators as a rule seem too ready to assume the former alone to be in question. But it is often the latter. This fact is not only of importance in itself, but helps to show the importance Aristotle attaches to the right use of words and so to justify the attempt to find method and purpose in his variations of terminology that seem on the surface slipshod and unmethodical.

There is one more question yet of interest and importance that has to do with accuracy in the use of words as distinguished from arguments. It was the inevitable consequence of the fact that the Hellenes had no language but their own, none at least in which any but the most ordinary thoughts could be expressed by them, that the forms of the Greek tongue very often led them astray on points of material fact; and one of the common stumbling-blocks was etymology. The meaning of a compound word was held to be made up of the separate meanings of the elements of the compound; or the meaning of one word was held to fix that of another derived from it. The result was that the things themselves which these words were most commonly taken to represent were forced into an unnatural connection with each other. In the Cratylus dialogue, and in isolated passages elsewhere, Plato illustrates this tendency, to which it is a matter of some doubt how far he was subject himself. In NE VI the force of etymology is evident in two cases, an examination of which, desirable in itself as an attempt to explain two difficult passages, will serve to typify Aristotle's attitude towards etymology as a guide to fact, and to show further the amount of importance he attaches to names and their correct use. (i) In the chapter on εὐβουλία it is decided that εὐβουλία must be an ὀρθότης τῆς διανοίας (1142 b 12). Then the statement is suddenly made (b 16) ἀλλ' ὀρθότης τίς ἐστιν ἡ εὐβουλία βουλῆς, which nothing further is said to justify. Evidently the argument is that the εὐ- in εὐβουλία implies ὀρθότης, and the -βουλία implies βουλή. Derivation is allowed to have as much weight as this, that the name εὐβουλία cannot properly be used of anything that is not ὀρθότης βουλῆς. The consistency of this formula with the previous formula ὀρθότης διανοίας is assumed. The one was reached by etymology, the other by considering what εὐβουλία is in practice used to mean. Common usage is thus maintained to pay due respect to the derivation of a word, and not to attach to a word any meaning inconsistent with its derivation.

(ii) The section on γνώμη seems to contain a real confusion of thought that is due to an improper use of etymology. Γνώμη (as in the phrase γνώμην ἔχειν) may mean either 'opinion' or 'right opinion' about anything, occasionally even 'good sense.' Συγγνώμη, though derived from γνώμη, means 'consideration,' 'fair-mindedness,' 'readiness to make allowances and to forgive': more a moral than an intellectual quality (or rather activity) and more a consequent than an antecedent of the moral virtue ἐπιείκεια. These two very distinct notions are fused into one, or rather a sort of mean between them is taken, and the name γνώμη is given to the condition the definition of which is reached by this compromise. This meaning of γνώμη is wholly artificial, though it may attach rightly to the name of a class or kind of intellectual excellence really important and otherwise nameless. There is room to doubt whether Aristotle did not see quite well what he was doing, aware of the real distinctness of γνώμη and συγγνώμη, and using etymology more as a pretext for his artificial meaning for γνώμη than as a real argument to show what γνώμη is actually used to mean. But it is more consistent with his respect for common usage and for the public opinion on which that usage is based to suppose there is real confusion here and that he does suppose γνώμη and συγγνώμη to be as closely connected in meaning as they are closely connected in name.

To turn now to the other branch of the subject, in the matter of arrangement of the argument the sixth book has been charged with as much looseness and inaccuracy as in its use of particular words. The want of formal symmetry, even the want of formal correctness, must be admitted : but it is quite another thing to admit that this want is due to confusion of thought and veils material inaccuracy. Occasionally the latter is true, but hardly oftener, in my opinion, than I have allowed it true as regards particular words.

The first question is that of Order : both the order of words in lists, and of subjects in the whole discussion. As to the first, if significance is to be attributed to the order of words in lists, Aristotle can only be called slipshod for his carelessness about this in the sixth book : but if, as appears really to be the case, in spite of arguments which editors have brought forward to support the contrary view, such order is practically never significant either in this book or elsewhere, the undoubted fact that such order often varies greatly is a fact of no importance, and proves no real carelessness on the author's part even as regards the form in which he expresses himself. Consider the examples that occur in VI—

(*a*) 1139 a 18 αἴσθησις νοῦς ὄρεξις. Here Professor Burnet suggests that the position of νοῦς between αἴσθησις and ὄρεξις indicates that it is to be taken with both : to which there are doctrinal objections as well as the want of any parallel to this particular kind of significance of order, a significance which here at least is not obvious at first sight.

(*b*) 1139 b 16 τέχνη ἐπιστήμη φρόνησις σοφία νοῦς. This is not the order in which these five virtues are discussed in detail, and so can hardly be significant. There is a parallel passage Analytics 89 b 7 Τὰ δὲ λοιπὰ πῶς δεῖ διανεῖμαι ἐπί τε διανοίας καὶ νοῦ καὶ ἐπιστήμης καὶ τέχνης καὶ φρονήσεως καὶ σοφίας κτλ, where the order can hardly (pace Stewart) be more significant than here. The order in 1141 a 5 ἐπιστήμη φρόνησις σοφία νοῦς is just that of the previous discussion, and since τέχνη is left out altogether can hardly be supposed significant.

(*c*) 1143 a 26 γνώμην καὶ σύνεσιν καὶ φρόνησιν καὶ νοῦν. The order is not suggestive, and is not the same as what follows, a 27 γνώμην ἔχειν καὶ νοῦν ἤδη καὶ φρονίμους καὶ συνετούς, nor as that of b 7 γνώμην δ᾽ ἔχειν καὶ σύνεσιν καὶ νοῦν : there is thus no significance of order in any of these cases.

None of the above instances of haphazard order spring from confusion in the author's mind, or can naturally lead to confusion in the student's mind, provided no attempt is made to find a significance in the order which the author never attempted to put into it.

The order in which the subjects of the sixth book are discussed is hardly of greater importance than the order in which words in lists are arranged. A certain rough practical convenience deter. mines it, rather than the obviousness or importance of the subjects themselves. This refers especially to the accounts of the various intellectual virtues, both the five main ones and the three or four subordinate ones. Ἐπιστήμη and νοῦς must plainly be defined before σοφία can be defined, since the latter is composite of the two former. Τέχνη is more intelligible in itself than is φρόνησις, which is more easily explained by contrast with τέχνη than τέχνη by contrast with it: therefore τέχνη is discussed before φρόνησις. The full discussion of φρόνησις is deferred till some view of all the five main virtues is got, in order that the general outline of the argument of the book may be indicated as soon as possible. The three or four subordinate virtues (εὐβουλία σύνεσις γνώμη, also νοῦς in one sense, besides the barely-mentioned sub-species εὐστοχία and ἀγχίνοια) are clearly best explained when the main virtue φρόνησις, to which they are subordinate, has itself been explained for the most part. It thus appears that the order of the discussion is rather practically convenient than theoretically significant. Even where practical convenience cannot be traced, there is no reason to suppose the order of subjects, as of words, is not purely haphazard. This principle may be applied, though it does not always hold good, to Aristotle's writings in general, even to the more severely didactic.

The sixth book further contains many instances of formal inaccuracy of expression in small points, such as are not very easy to distinguish from the variation from strict meaning in particular words that has already been discussed, but may be said to consist less in the meaning of a word or phrase itself than in its relations with the context. They may be roughly classified into instances of vagueness, looseness, and incompleteness.

i. *Vagueness.*

(*a*) 1139 a 2 περὶ ψυχῆς πρῶτον εἰπόντες. In discussing the virtues of the ψυχή of course one περὶ ψυχῆς λέγει : see the preceding sentence, τὰς τῆς ψυχῆς ἀρετὰς διελόμενοι. But the vague phrase περὶ ψυχῆς is evidently intended to bear a strictly psychological meaning, as in the title of the ' Psychology '—Περὶ Ψυχῆς.

(*b*) 1139 a 8—10 describes the difference between the two main divisions of the intellect as generic (γένει). 1140 b 3 describes the difference between the two main divisions of one of the previous divisions as also generic.

διανοητικόν

ἐπιστημονικόν.........λογιστικόν (γένει ἕτερα)

ποιητικόν...............πρακτικόν (also γένει ἕτερα)

Generic difference is regarded as something quite vague, and the meaning would hardly have been changed if εἴδει ('specific') had been written for γένει.

ii.   Looseness.

(a) 1142 a 12 γεωμετρικοὶ μὲν νέοι καὶ μαθηματικοὶ γίνονται. This seems to imply that the γεωμετρικός is, whereas in fact he is not, wholly different from the μαθηματικός. Geometry is of course one branch of mathematics, as it is elsewhere said to be. Correct writing would place ἄλλως or ὅλως before μαθηματικοί. But the sense is clear.

(b) 1142 a 17 διὰ τί δὴ μαθηματικὸς μὲν παῖς γένοιτ' ἄν, σοφὸς δ' ἢ φυσικὸς οὔ. By σοφός is plainly meant φιλόσοφος or θεολογικός: but there is formal inconsistency with the previous inclusion of μαθηματική and φυσική under σοφία.

(c) No less than four formulae describing εὐβουλία are given successively in chapter ix : 1142 b 1 βουλή τις, b 8 ὀρθότης τις, b 12 διανοίας ὀρθότης, b 16 βουλῆς ὀρθότης. Formally, βουλή τις is inconsistent with ὀρθότης τις and the other two, and the last two with each other.

(d) Ἀρετή is used without qualification to mean ἠθικὴ ἀρετή, though the intellectual ἕξεις that are the subject of the book are just as much ἀρεταί as are the ἠθικαὶ ἀρεταί. For this see chapter xiii passim.

(e) Φρόνησις and its subordinates (σύνεσις γνώμη etc.) are called ἕξεις in 1143 a 25, δυνάμεις immediately afterwards a 28.

(f) 1144 a 24 δεινότης defined as τοιαύτη ὥστε τὰ πρὸς τὸν ὑποτεθέντα σκοπὸν συντείνοντα δύνασθαι ταῦτα πράττειν καὶ τυγχάνειν αὐτοῦ. Here the word πράττειν is used with remarkable looseness of a purely intellectual act.

(g) In dealing with the ὀρθὸς λόγος in chapter xiii these two formally inconsistent statements occur : 1144 b 23 ὀρθὸς δὲ (sc. λόγος) ὁ κατὰ τὴν φρόνησιν, 1144 b 27 ὀρθὸς δὲ λόγος περὶ τῶν τοιούτων ἡ φρόνησίς ἐστιν.

iii. *Incompleteness.*

(a) 1141 a 3 εἰ δὴ οἷς ἀληθεύομεν καὶ μηδέποτε διαψευδόμεθα ... ἐπιστήμη καὶ φρόνησίς ἐστι καὶ σοφία καὶ νοῦς, τούτων δὲ κτλ. Why is τέχνη left out of the list? Many reasons have been given: (a) we may have the list of another editor here (Stewart): (b) the omission may be a pure accident (Burnet): (c) τέχνη was shown in chapter v to be a ἕξις ἧς ἐστι λήθη (Stewart): (d) τέχνη is included in φρόνησις, both being περὶ τὰ ἐνδεχόμενα ἄλλως ἔχειν (Eustratius): (e) τέχνη may be included in ἐπιστήμη (Stewart): (f) τέχνη may be included in σοφία, which is the ἀρετὴ τέχνης (Burnet). Now Ramsauer well says that Aristotle does not mind going without formal symmetry and precision so long as his meaning is plain. But the meaning is quite plain. τέχνη had its proper place in the argument at 1140 b 34 τῆς ἀρχῆς τοῦ ἐπιστητοῦ οὔτ᾽ ἂν ἐπιστήμη εἴη οὔτε τέχνη οὔτε φρόνησις κτλ. It is therefore probably left out of the formal list because there is no possibility of confusing the use of τέχνη with the use of νοῦς, whereas it is easy to see that νοῦς might, in certain connections, be used as a synonym of either ἐπιστήμη φρόνησις or σοφία.

(b) 1143 a 25 Εἰσὶ δὲ πᾶσαι...συνετούς. The list of virtues εἰς ταὐτὸ τείνουσαι is incomplete to begin with, for εὐβουλία is left out. Lower down at 1143 b 7 the list is reduced to three by leaving out φρόνησις, and at b 9 to two by leaving out σύνεσις. There being no assignable reason why any of these three should be purposely omitted, it must be supposed due to the author's being careless of formal accuracy and intending the full list of five to be understood in each place. The original omission of εὐβουλία is the most remarkable, for πᾶσαι αἱ ἕξεις—whether αὗται is read or not—agrees ill with its intentional omission in a list that includes φρόνησις, and at the same time εὐβουλία was discussed at such length that it cannot be considered of minor importance. Burnet's explanation, that the ἕξεις here mentioned all apprehend their object immediately, that in this way they are εἰς ταὐτὸ τείνουσαι, and that therefore εὐβουλία is purposely excluded as being μετὰ λόγου, could not hold. For this would make it necessary to exclude φρόνησις also, since φρόνησις is ἕξις ἀληθὴς μετὰ λόγου πρακτική (1140 b 5). As a matter of fact the meaning of εἰς ταὐτὸ τείνουσαι is given quite clearly in line 28, πᾶσαι γὰρ αἱ δυνάμεις αὗται τῶν ἐσχάτων εἰσὶ καὶ τῶν καθ᾽ ἕκαστον: and of course εὐβουλία is also τῶν ἐσχάτων καὶ τῶν καθ᾽ ἕκαστον. It seems possible that the reason of the omission of εὐβουλία is that it is so closely connected with φρόνησις that whatever is said here of φρόνησις applies to it also. But it is surely more likely that εὐβουλία is not omitted of any set purpose at all, but simply through carelessness of formal completeness. The other omissions are to be explained in the same way. They are less remarkable, for it is easy to see that the omitted terms, since they have been definitely mentioned once, are to be understood again.

The sixth book contains at least one remarkable instance of the assumption of a statement as proved when the proof has not been explicitly set forth. This is the sentence 1143 b 14—17 τί μὲν οὖν ἐστὶν ἡ φρόνησις καὶ ἡ σοφία, καὶ περὶ τί ἑκατέρα τυγχάνει οὖσα, καὶ ὅτι ἄλλου τῆς ψυχῆς μορίου ἀρετὴ ἑκατέρα, εἴρηται. All the premisses necessary for these conclusions have been collected in the previous discussion, but the conclusions themselves have not been explicitly drawn, and yet here they are referred to in a recapitulatory fashion that seems to advance no new proposition at all. This fact, it may be pointed out, is of considerable importance in relation to the question whether the reference in x, 1177 a 18 ὅτι δ' ἐστὶ θεωρητική (sc. ἡ ἐνέργεια ἡ τοῦ ἀρίστου ἐν ἡμῖν), εἴρηται, implies that the author had something else than NE vi in his mind. It is undeniable that the statement is not explicitly made anywhere in vi. But (1) the distinction of σοφία from φρόνησις as μὴ πρακτική from πρακτική is substantially the same as that of θεωρητική from πρακτική, (2) σοφία has distinctly been declared in vi to be better than φρόνησις and so to be the best of ἀρεταί. Here again, therefore, we find a conclusion referred to as drawn when it has not been drawn explicitly, though all the necessary premisses for it have been collected—a mere terminological note, to point out that θεωρητική is a fit adjective to apply to σοφία in consideration of its character as already set forth, is all that would have been needed: less indeed than is needed to formally justify the statement of 1143 b 14—17 about φρόνησις and σοφία, as to the connection of which with the rest of vi there can be no reasonable doubt.

NE vi contains some instances of very badly stated arguments. (A) That by which in 1140 a 31 seq. φρόνησις is distinguished from ἐπιστήμη, though stated very fully, is very far from clear. It has several steps :

(1)   φρόνησις is a ἕξις βουλευτική.

But βούλευσις is not περὶ τῶν μὴ ἐνδεχομένων (this is twice said, a 31—33 and a 35—36).

∴ βούλευσις *is* περὶ τῶν ἐνδεχομένων.

∴ φρόνησις *is* περὶ τῶν ἐνδεχομένων.

(2) There is no ἀπόδειξις of ἐνδεχόμενα.

But φρόνησις is περὶ τῶν ἐνδεχομένων.

∴ φρόνησις is not μετ᾽ ἀποδείξεως.

(3) ἐπιστήμη *is* μετ᾽ ἀποδείξεως.

But φρόνησις is *not* μετ᾽ ἀποδείξεως.

∴ φρόνησις is distinct from ἐπιστήμη.

The course of the argument is confused by :

(a) the use of three nearly synonymous phrases, τῶν ἀδυνάτων ἄλλως ἔχειν, τῶν μὴ ἐνδεχομένων αὐτῷ πρᾶξαι, τῶν ἐξ ἀνάγκης ὄντων.

(b) the wrapping up of syllogism within syllogism.

(c) the introduction of the proof (πάντα γὰρ ἐνδέχεται καὶ ἄλλως ἔχειν) of what is already known (οὐκ ἔστιν ἀπόδειξις τῶν ἐνδεχομένων ἄλλως ἔχειν).

(d) the mention of τέχνη before ἐπιστήμη is done with.

(e) the substitution of πρακτόν in 1140 b 3 for βουλευτόν.

(B) The argument by which εὐβουλία is distinguished from ἐπιστήμη and δόξα (1142 a 34—b 12) is also very badly stated: it begins by alleging one reason why εὐβουλία is not ἐπιστήμη: then follows an awkwardly-placed distinction of εὐβουλία from εὐστοχία and ἀγχίνοια: then the bare statement that εὐβουλία is distinct from δόξα is made and not supported : then with a slight but confusing change of formula the argument returns to ἐπιστήμη, showing that εὐβουλία is not ὀρθότης ἐπιστήμης (a wholly needless step considering the material grounds on which εὐβουλία has already been shown not to be ἐπιστήμη itself) : then εὐβουλία is *shown* to be distinct from δόξα —for to show that it is not ὀρθότης δόξης is to show that it is not ὀρθὴ δόξα and a fortiori not δόξα of any other sort, though this inference is not expressed as it should have been :—could anything be much worse than all this from the point of view of arrangement? (C) It is possible that the text of certain passages ought to be re-arranged, and that the author is not to be blamed for what is really the result of subsequent dislocation. The most striking passage of this kind is 1139 a 21—b 10, a re-arrangement of which I have suggested in another place. Unless re-arrangement is allowed Aristotle cannot be acquitted of great carelessness in the writing of this passage. Another passage is 1141 a 20—b 2, where the argument that φρόνησις or πολιτική cannot be the best intellectual excellence is badly broken by the proof that φρόνησις and σοφία are not the same, which is an awkward interruption even if considered as in parenthesis.

If it is asked how Aristotle can be justified in his disregard of logical precision and clear systematic arrangement, the answer is in part that it is impossible to justify him for it altogether.   It is easy to excuse him for it, and to point out that in an age which had not conceived the ideal of formal precision as the fit vehicle for precise thought it is too much to expect that the first exponent of that ideal[1] should be able to go as far towards its attainment as he has since taught others to go.   But to excuse a fault is not to deny its existence, and some of the apparent faults that have been mentioned cannot be disregarded on the ground that they are not real.   Others, however, are probably more apparent than real.   Just as many variations in the use of words that are a puzzle to us to-day were most likely matters of course to Aristotle's immediate followers, so the formal inconsistencies and incompletenesses and haphazard arrangements of argument were in many cases far less troublesome at the time than they have since come to be, and conversely certain points needed elaboration at the time which would now be passed over lightly enough.   Aristotle's contemporaries had the advantage of thoroughly understanding their own language as a living and spoken one, and also of being fully conversant with the phraseology of both the Academic and the Peripatetic schools and aware of the relation between the two : so that suggestion could often take the place of formal exposition, and gaps in argument be readily, almost instinctively, filled up by the hearers or readers.   Helped by that comparison of languages which enables us to see in detail the difference between facts and the words that describe them, and enlightened by the progress philosophy has made since the age that gave it birth, we are better able now than any previous generation has been to discern certain real mistakes of expression and argument that Aristotle has made : but we are more likely than those of his own time to condemn other expressions and arguments as faulty which the general intelligence of the time must rightly have regarded as adequate and satisfactory.   Whatever the formal difficulties of such a book as NE vi may be, whether due to the author's fault or our own ignorance, the material doctrine, in its main features and in nearly all its details, will be found to stand out with as much clearness and consistency as can reasonably be desired.

[1] The last part of the *Parmenides* shows indeed that Plato had conceived the ideal, but is hardly enough to constitute him its first exponent.

1138 b 18—34.

What is the meaning of the word λόγος in chapter i of book VI, as it occurs in the phrases ὡς ὁ ὀρθὸς λόγος, κατὰ τὸν ὀρθὸν λόγον, ὁ τὸν λόγον ἔχων?

Professor Burnet holds that λόγος means 'form,' in the strict metaphysical sense, in which it is equivalent to εἶδος: and that the ὀρθὸς λόγος is 'the form of goodness in the soul.' The objections to this are: (1) 1103 b 31 τὸ κατὰ τὸν ὀρθὸν λόγον κοινὸν καὶ ὑποκείσθω, and 1144 b 21 πάντες ὅταν ὁρίζωνται τὴν ἀρετὴν προστιθέασι...τὴν κατὰ τὸν ὀρθὸν λόγον, imply a meaning of the word λόγος that is not confined to the Aristotelian school but common to all schools of philosophy: but the metaphysical meaning 'form' is purely Aristotelian. (2) Pure metaphysical questions are avoided in the Ethics as much as possible, and words are not likely to be used there in purely metaphysical senses. Otherwise it would not be very improbable that Aristotle should use the common formula ὀρθὸς λόγος in a special sense of his own. But as it is, the special sense is not appropriate to the method of the Ethics. In any case, the change to the special sense would be so violent that it could hardly have been made without some explanation. (3) In the context, the 'form of goodness in the soul' could only mean the form of *moral* goodness. The subject of book VI is certainly not moral but intellectual goodness. But book VI no less certainly answers the question at the end of chapter i τίς ἐστιν ὁ ὀρθὸς λόγος; Therefore ὁ ὀρθὸς λόγος must be intellectual goodness rather than moral: and this is in fact stated in 1144 b 27 ὀρθὸς λόγος περὶ τῶν τοιούτων φρόνησίς ἐστιν.

These difficulties are avoided by taking λόγος in its ordinary though vaguer sense of 'reason[1].' There is no need to press the

---

[1] Ramsauer appears to do so, Peters and Welldon translate rightly, and Eustratius is on the right track.

question whether by 'reason' is meant a part of the soul, or a faculty, or a process, or a quality. The distinction between these four things is often neglected, in book VI and elsewhere : thus in chapter xiii the ὀρθὸς λόγος is said to be φρόνησις and also to be κατὰ φρόνησιν. Ὁ ὀρθὸς λόγος means therefore 'the reasoning part of the soul in its good condition,' or 'the good quality of the reasoning part of the soul,' or 'the faculty of good reasoning,' or 'the process of good reasoning.' This view is supported by the following considerations : (*a*) No change of meaning is thus required : for all schools of philosophy would understand something of the kind by ὀρθὸς λόγος : the same meaning therefore fits the passages in VI where the phrase occurs and the two passages already quoted 1103 b 31 and 1144 b 21. (*b*) VI is in this view what the wording of chapter i requires that it should be, a fulfilment of the resolution 1138 b 20 τοῦτο (sc. τὸν ὀρθὸν λόγον) διελῶμεν, and an answer to the question 1138 b 34 τίς ἐστιν ὁ ὀρθὸς λόγος ; (*c*) This meaning best suits the phrases ὡς ὁ λόγος or ὡς ὁ ὀρθὸς λόγος κελεύει, which occur repeatedly in the discussion of the moral virtues (see 1114 b 29, 1115 b 12 and 19, 1117 a 8, 1119 a 20, 1125 b 35). The personification involved in the use of the word κελεύει is far more natural than if the λόγος were a pure abstraction. (*d*) The identification of the ὀρθὸς λόγος with φρόνησις in 1144 b 27 becomes easier in this view. The passage 1103 b 31—34, where it is implied that the ὀρθὸς λόγος is an ἀρετή (τί ἐστιν ὁ ὀρθὸς λόγος καὶ πῶς ἔχει πρὸς τὰς ἄλλας ἀρετάς), agrees with this view, and need not be rejected, as most editors wish to do, on the ground of inconsistency of doctrine with VI.

Two views of other editors may be noticed briefly. Grant supposes the ὀρθὸς λόγος to be identical with the σκοπός and the ὅρος of 1138 b 22 and 23, and naturally complains that this chapter merely confuses the question with a cloud of formulae. But he is wrong, for it would be absurd, if the ὅρος and the λόγος were identical, to ask the question at the end of the chapter in the form there given, τούτου (*i.e.* τοῦ ὀρθοῦ λόγου) τίς ὅρος.—Professor Stewart says that the λόγος is at once the subjective faculty and the objective order. This is no doubt true, for the thinking mind and its thought are (according to Aristotle's metaphysics) the same. But if, as I have maintained, metaphysics are not in place in the Ethics, there is no reason to suppose that this identity of mind and thought, true as it is, is at all referred to in this book : the subjective faculty alone is meant.

1138 b 18.

Ἐπεὶ δὲ τυγχάνομεν etc.

The argument of this opening paragraph of vi may be stated more or less as follows :—Moral virtue was defined as a mean between too much and too little. Since the mean is relative to the various characters and circumstances of different people, it fluctuates, and must be fixed by each man for himself, whether on the advice of another or not. All are agreed that it is the reason which must do this fixing of the mean, and that it is the reason in its good state (ὀρθὸς λόγος) that will do it rightly, *i.e.* that will declare for a given person in given circumstances that to be the mean which really is so for that person in those circumstances. It is plain that of this ὀρθὸς λόγος, an important subject, as much should be known as possible : for though to know about it is not to have it, yet to know about it is a necessary first step to having it : just as, though to know what medical skill is does not amount to being a successful or skilful doctor, to know what medical skill is must be a necessary first step towards becoming a skilful doctor. ' You should do the right thing ' is a maxim very generally true of any line of activity : if it be asked ' What is the right thing ? ' it is a correct answer to say ' That which the expert in that line holds to be right ' : but this answer is not explicit enough to be useful : it must further be asked ' Who is the expert, and what is the nature of his knowledge ? ' It is the full answer to this question that will both decide whose advice is to be taken about the right thing to do, and serve as the first step towards becoming one's self an expert and adviser. Moreover, it is by referring to the grand final end of all action that the expert fixes the nature of any particular mean ; for any given state is truly a mean, and not an excess or a defect, simply because it contributes better than any excess over it or defect from it would contribute to the grand final end. This end is of course happiness : to ask what happiness is is to ask the main question of the Ethics, which is thus for a moment brought forward to show the connection of this part of the treatise with the treatise as a whole. At the end of the paragraph the two questions are summed up and put side by side : (1) the more immediate problem, What is the ὀρθὸς λόγος? (2) the final and supremely important problem, What is the grand final end, which is the standard to which the ὀρθὸς λόγος refers ? The former question is answered in book vi, the latter in book x.

Professor Burnet rightly says[1] 'There is nothing in Rassow's view that an independent introduction to book VI begins' at 1138 b 35 Τὰς δὴ τῆς ψυχῆς ἀρετὰς....But the connection of thought that he discovers between the first and the second paragraph is not obvious and not necessary. As.he admits himself[2], Aristotle has two reasons for the discussion of Goodness of Intellect. (1) It is necessary in order to understand Moral Goodness: (2) it is necessary in order to discover what the best and completest goodness is, for that best and completest goodness may be not moral but intellectual, as indeed the sequel shows. The first paragraph sets forth the first reason, and the second paragraph the second reason. The transition is certainly not more abrupt than that to the discussion of moral virtue at 1103 a 18. But neither is there any specific connection of thought.

Is however the general substance of the first paragraph of VI inconsistent either with the second paragraph or with any preceding part of the Ethics? Both questions have been wrongly answered in the affirmative.

(*A*) That the first paragraph gives a different reason from that given by the second paragraph for discussing intellectual goodness is no sign that the two paragraphs are inconsistent. Both reasons are, as has been said, valid—intellectual virtue ought to be understood both for its own sake and also in order that we may understand moral virtue. All the fault that can fairly be found with the two paragraphs is that their wording does not clearly bring out the connection of these two reasons with each other, but presents each reason in turn as if it were the only one. But the last two chapters of the book unmistakably bring up the question of the first paragraph again when they discuss the relation of ἠθικὴ ἀρετή (the moral μεσότης) to φρόνησις (the ὀρθὸς λόγος concerned with the moral μεσότης): and the seeming inconsistency of the first two paragraphs then disappears.

(*B*) Ramsauer holds that the first paragraph only sets out to do what has been done already. In II ix, he says, directions have already been given for finding the mean in moral action, such as to avoid the extreme that is more contrary to the mean, the extreme to which we are more prone, the extreme that is pleasanter, and so on: and the process of ἐπιτείνειν καὶ ἀνιέναι (1138 b 23) recommended in the first paragraph of VI is the same as the process of inclining now towards the excess and now towards the defect recommended in

---

[1] Note on 1138 b 35.   [2] Introduction to Book VI, § 1.

II ix. This is true: but all those suggestions of II ix are practical, and take for granted knowledge of the nature of the mean. They are meant as helps towards making use of that knowledge and applying it to conduct rather than towards acquiring it in the first instance. The way is therefore still open for a discussion of the means of knowing what the moral mean is. The suggestions of II ix answered not the question 'How am I to find out the best thing to do?' but the question 'How am I to get myself into the way of doing it?' The first paragraph of VI is therefore not inconsistent with II ix.

1139 a 12—15.

Why is the word λογιστικόν, rather than βουλευτικόν or δοξαστικόν, chosen as the name of the part of the intellect concerned with variables? And why is δοξαστικόν nevertheless used twice in VI instead of λογιστικόν?

The objections to the use of λογιστικόν are as follows :—

(a) the word is generally used by Aristotle and also by Plato in the general sense of 'reasoning,' as a synonym for διανοητικόν as Aristotle uses that word. See Republic 439 D τὸ μὲν ᾧ λογίζεται λογιστικὸν προσαγορεύοντες τῆς ψυχῆς, τὸ δὲ ᾧ ἐρᾷ τε καὶ πεινῇ...ἀλόγιστόν τε καὶ ἐπιθυμητικόν : and Psychology 432 a 24 (referring to Plato's doctrine) λογιστικὸν καὶ θυμικὸν καὶ ἐπιθυμητικόν. For Aristotle's own use of λογιστικὸν in this general sense see Psychology 433 b 29 φαντασία πᾶσα ἢ λογιστικὴ ἢ αἰσθητική, 434 a 7 ἡ βουλευτικὴ ἐν τοῖς λογιστικοῖς ζῴοις, Rhetoric 1369 a 1 τὰ μὲν διὰ λογιστικὴν ὄρεξιν τὰ δὲ δι' ἀλόγιστον, Topics 128 b 39 (sc. ἡ ἀρετή) ἐν πλείοσιν, ἐπιστήμη δ' ἐν λογιστικῷ μόνον καὶ τοῖς ἔχουσι λογιστικὸν πέφυκε γίνεσθαι, and see also Topics 134 a 34, 136 b 11, 138 b 13, 145 a 29, 147 b 32.

(b) Βουλευτικός is a word commonly used, apparently in just the sense wanted here, both in the Ethics and elsewhere in Aristotle, and also by Plato. See Ethics 1113 a 10 ἡ προαίρεσις ἂν εἴη βουλευτικὴ ὄρεξις τῶν ἐφ' ἡμῖν, 1152 a 19 ὁ μελαγχολικὸς οὐδὲ βουλευτικὸς ὅλως, and three other passages of VI, 1139 a 23, 1140 a 30, 1141 b 27 : also Rhetoric 1383 a 7 ὁ φόβος βουλευτικοὺς ποιεῖ· καίτοι οὐδεὶς βουλεύεται περὶ τῶν ἀνελπίστων, Psychology 434 a 7 ἡ βουλευτικὴ φαντασία ἐν τοῖς λογιστικοῖς ζῴοις ὑπάρχει· πότερον γὰρ πράξει τόδε ἢ τόδε λογισμοῦ ἤδη ἐστὶν ἔργον, Politics 1260 a 10 f. Plato uses the word, as in Republic 434 B and 441 A. So that βουλευτικόν on its own merits would seem a better word to have used here.

(c) But further than this, the passage 1139 a 12 τὸ γὰρ βουλεύεσθαι καὶ λογίζεσθαι ταὐτόν, οὐδεὶς δὲ βουλεύεται περὶ τῶν μὴ ἐνδεχομένων ἄλλως ἔχειν· ὥστε τὸ λογιστικόν ἐστιν ἕν τι μέρος τοῦ λόγον ἔχοντος appears to make the correctness of the use of λογιστικόν here entirely dependent on its meaning the same thing as βουλευτικόν. Why therefore is βουλευτικόν not simply used at once?

(d) In spite of what is said in 1139 a 12, τὸ γὰρ βουλεύεσθαι καὶ λογίζεσθαι ταὐτόν, it does not appear that in common speech (which is obviously referred to here) the terms βουλεύεσθαι and λογίζεσθαι have in fact the same meaning. The meanings of λογίζεσθαι that come nearest to those of βουλεύεσθαι, such as 'reckon, calculate, take into account, infer from calculation,' are quite distinct from 'take counsel, deliberate, seek to find what the right course of action is.'

To these objections it may be replied :—

(a) It is quite in accordance with Aristotle's custom to use the same word in a generic and also in a specific sense : and he would not be likely to object to the specific use here simply because elsewhere he had used or meant to use the word in the wider sense, especially as he is not here obliged to use it in the generic as well as the specific sense, but has the term διανοητικόν to fall back upon.

(b) βουλευτικός is indeed a more suitable word to describe that part of the soul which is concerned with practical conduct. But it appears to me that the non-practical contemplation of variables is not altogether lost sight of by Aristotle, although he does not discuss it. Now λογιστικόν is a word suited to the lower part of the intellect considered as purely theoretic, while βουλευτικόν is not. Λογιστικόν is therefore employed here as being the more inclusive term.

(c) The argument τὸ γὰρ βουλεύεσθαι καὶ λογίζεσθαι ταὐτόν need only be supposed to justify the use of the word λογιστικόν as applied to the inferior part of the intellect considered as practical. As applied to that part of the intellect considered as non-practical, the use of λογιστικόν is accepted without justification, just as the use of ἐπιστημονικόν applied to the higher part of the intellect is accepted without justification. The very fact that βουλευτικόν is more appropriate than λογιστικόν as the name of the practical intellect is what makes the justification desirable.

(d) It must be admitted that in common speech βουλευτικόν and λογιστικόν do not mean the same thing. But they are not so far apart that the gap cannot be bridged well enough for the purpose in hand. And it must be noticed that all that is required is that it should be possible, in ordinary speech, to use λογιστικόν in the sense of βουλευτικόν, even if it can be used in other senses too : it is not required (as the sense of the passage shows) that the words should be exact synonyms or co-extensive in their meaning.

Why then is the word δοξαστικόν twice used (1140 b 26 and 1144 b 14) instead of λογιστικόν ? In the former case, I believe, to call attention to the two-fold nature of the lower part of the intellect, which can be purely theoretic as well as practical. Just as βουλευτικόν was the right name for it considered as practical, so δοξαστικόν is the right name for it considered as theoretic, and λογιστικόν is the right name for it considered as both. In the latter case (1144 b 14) the object seems to be to emphasize the purely intellectual nature of δεινότης as opposed to ἠθικὴ ἀρετή. This emphasis really is conveyed by the use of δοξαστικόν, for in so far as the λογιστικὸν μέρος is βουλευτικόν it is associated with, and dependent upon, moral ἀρετή to some extent.

1139 a 15.

ληπτέον ἄρ᾿ ἑκατέρου τούτων τίς ἡ βελτίστη ἕξις· αὕτη γὰρ ἀρετὴ ἑκατέρου.

No such peculiar and detailed definition of intellectual goodness is here given as was given of moral goodness. The virtues of the parts of the soul are, it is said, their best conditions : this statement needs no proof, for it would readily be agreed that by the ἀρετή of anything at all is meant its best condition : this is as true of ἠθικὴ ἀρετή as of anything else, though of this particular kind of ἀρετή a special definition was obtained.

The usual punctuation—αὕτη γὰρ ἀρετὴ ἑκατέρου, ἡ δ᾿ ἀρετὴ πρὸς τὸ ἔργον τὸ οἰκεῖον—hides the sense. I have placed a full stop after ἑκατέρου. The words ἡ δ᾿ ἀρετὴ πρὸς τὸ ἔργον τὸ οἰκεῖον have nothing to do with what precedes, and a great deal to do with the whole of the following chapter, which is devoted to discovering the ἔργον of each of the two intellectual faculties with a view to discovering the ἀρετή of each thereby. This is quite clearly brought out by the conclusion 1139 b 12 ἀμφοτέρων δὴ τῶν νοητικῶν μορίων ἀλήθεια τὸ ἔργον. καθ᾿ ἃς οὖν μάλιστα ἕξεις ἀληθεύσει ἑκάτερον, αὗται ἀρεταὶ ἀμφοῖν.

1139 a 17.

Τρία δή ἐστιν ἐν τῇ ψυχῇ etc.

The opening lines of this chapter are rather obscure from

compression. The argument may be fully stated as follows :—There are two main objects of specifically human activity, doing what is good (in the broadest sense of 'good') and knowing what is true. In the attainment of these objects three parts of the soul are directly concerned as efficient causes, sensation (αἴσθησις) desire (ὄρεξις) reason (νοῦς). It will be allowed that ὄρεξις is not an efficient cause in knowing what is true, while αἴσθησις (either immediate or remaining in the form of φαντασία) and νοῦς are concerned therein, either separately or together. It is less clear, and so deserves to be proved, that αἴσθησις, together of course with ὄρεξις, does not cause the doing of what is good or bad. But the lower animals, which have both αἴσθησις and ὄρεξις, nevertheless have no πρᾶξις; they cannot be said to do what is good or bad. The fact is that it is λογιστικὴ φαντασία, and not αἰσθητικὴ φαντασία—the distinction is made in the 'Psychology'—that combines with ὄρεξις to cause human πρᾶξις, and λογιστικὴ φαντασία—as the 'Psychology' has pointed out—is really a kind of νόησις or operation of νοῦς.

1139 a 21—b 5.

The following re-arrangement of the text of 1139 a 21—b 5 (the only important passage in the 6th book which at all seems to require re-arrangement) is I think new and has some advantages over others —(i.) (as at present) a 17 Τρία δή ἐστιν . . . a 20 πράξεως δὲ μὴ κοινωνεῖν: (ii.) a 31 πράξεως μὲν οὖν ἀρχὴ προαίρεσις . . . a 35 ἄνευ διανοίας καὶ ἤθους οὐκ ἔστιν: (iii.) b 4 διὸ ἢ ὀρεκτικὸς νοῦς . . . b 5 καὶ ἡ τοιαύτη ἀρχὴ ἄνθρωπος: here would appropriately follow the foot-note b 6 οὐκ ἔστι δὲ προαιρετὸν οὐδὲν γεγονός . . . b 11 ἀγένητα ποιεῖν ἄσσ' ἂν ᾖ πεπραγμένα: (iv.) a 21 ἔστι δ' ὅπερ ἐν διανοίᾳ κατάφασις καὶ ἀπόφασις . . . a 31 τῇ ὀρέξει τῇ ὀρθῇ: (v.) a 35 διάνοια δ' αὐτὴ οὐθὲν κινεῖ . . . b 4 ἡ δ' ὄρεξις τούτου: (vi.) the last two lines, b 12—13, of course keep their place. The advantages of this arrangement are as follows: 1. All the passages dealing with προαίρεσις are brought together and arranged in their natural order. 2. The discussion of θεωρητικὴ διάνοια is properly separated from that of πρακτική, which is only mentioned again to make the nature of θεωρητική plainer by contrast, no new fact about πρακτική being mentioned. 3. a 35 seq. carries on the contrast smoothly from the end of the sentence a 30 τῇ ὀρέξει τῇ ὀρθῇ: and then, in the light of the now sufficient discussion of both πρακτική and θεωρητική, ποιητική is properly discussed and put in its place. 4. The transition from a 20 πράξεως δὲ μὴ κοινωνεῖν to a 31 πράξεως μὲν οὖν ἀρχὴ προαίρεσις is clear and natural, while the present continuation at a 21 is highly obscure. 5. The meaning of ἀρχή, ὅθεν ἡ κίνησις, is given earlier, and so close to a 18—20 that it serves to explain the use of ἀρχή there too. 6. It would be absurd, after the *assumption* of the truth ἡ προαίρεσις ὄρεξις βουλευτική in a 23, to write later on b 4 διὸ ἢ ὀρεκτικὸς νοῦς ἡ προαίρεσις ἢ ὄρεξις διανοητική, the statement being the grand conclusion of the whole argument: but on the other hand *from* the conclusion b 4 διὸ ἢ ὀρεκτικὸς νοῦς κτλ. (a conclusion that follows naturally enough from a 31—35) the remark a 23 ἡ δὲ προαίρεσις ὄρεξις βουλευτική follows quite well as a recapitulation of an already proved statement. With regard to such a re-arrangement as the above I would say what Professor Stewart says of his own re-arrangement of another passage in this book, 1140 b 3—30: it 'is offered, not as a reconstruction of the text as it may have originally stood, but as an attempt to make the meaning of the passage, as we now have it, clearer.'

1139 a 23.

δεῖ διὰ ταῦτα μὲν τόν τε λόγον ἀληθῆ εἶναι καὶ τὴν ὄρεξιν ὀρθήν, εἴπερ ἡ προαίρεσις σπουδαία, καὶ τὰ αὐτὰ τὸν μὲν φάναι τὴν δὲ διώκειν.

No editor has pointed out, I think, that the above sentence expresses two different requirements, and not the same requirement in two different forms. Professor Stewart (see his note on 1139 a 24) says 'ὄρεξις is ὀρθή when it seeks (δίωξις) what λόγος or διάνοια affirms (κατάφασις) to be good, and shuns (φυγή) what it denies (ἀπόφασις) to be good.' But the harmony of reason with appetite is not the same thing as the goodness of either. It is true of vicious προαίρεσις, where the λόγος is false and the ὄρεξις morally bad, that ὄρεξις seeks and shuns respectively what λόγος affirms and denies. What is wanted is not merely the harmony of reason and appetite—not merely that both should have the same object—but the harmony of right reason with good appetite, so that both are rightly active with regard to the same object. Now the rightness of reason depends on the truth of its affirmations and negations, and not at all on the character of the appetite, and the goodness of appetite depends on the goodness of its pursuits and avoidances, and not at all on the character of the reason. For *every* προαίρεσις, good or bad, it is necessary that the reason and the appetite should be concerned with the same object: otherwise there is merely an opinion, right or wrong, about one thing, and a desire, right or wrong, about another, and no προαίρεσις can occur. For *good* προαίρεσις it is necessary that both reason and desire should be good in themselves, and if they are good, and refer to the same object, it must follow in the nature of things that both feel attraction (κατάφασις and ὄρεξις) or both repulsion (ἀπόφασις and φυγή). It has been shown that this harmony of attraction with attraction and repulsion with repulsion also exists in vicious προαίρεσις, where both reason and appetite are bad in themselves. Two other kinds of bad προαίρεσις, are possible, where this harmony does not exist: when the reason is bad and the appetite good, and when the reason is good and the appetite bad: then there exist the two states considered in the last two chapters of this book, the baneful development of natural moral virtue, which is nameless, and the baneful development of natural intellectual virtue, which is πανουργία. The two requirements stated in this passage are, then, (1) that reason and appetite should combine to form purpose by being directed to the same object, (2) that their relation to the object should be good in each case: and my point is that these two things required are causally independent of each other.

1139 a 34—35.

If obvious and complete inappropriateness and logical unsoundness is warrant enough for bracketing a passage[1], the words εὐπραξία. γὰρ καὶ τὸ ἐναντίον ἐν πράξει ἄνευ διανοίας καὶ ἤθους οὐκ ἐστιν ought to be bracketed. For these words add nothing to the argument of the previous sentence. Moreover they appear to try to prove one statement by another that is logically posterior to it. For the meaning of πρᾶξις depends on that of προαίρεσις, and not vice versa: 1139 a 31 πράξεως ἀρχὴ προαίρεσις: πρᾶξις is action done as the result of προαίρεσις, or by a being capable of προαίρεσις. Also the meaning of εὐπραξία obviously depends on that of πρᾶξις: for εὐπραξία is πρᾶξις of a certain kind. Hence the meaning of εὐπραξία depends ultimately on that of προαίρεσις. Further, the statement 1139 a 33 διὸ οὔτ' ἄνευ νοῦ καὶ διανοίας οὔτ' ἄνευ ἠθικῆς ἐστιν ἕξεως ἡ προαίρεσις, which εὐπραξία γὰρ κτλ. is supposed to prove, follows directly from the previous words a 32 προαιρέσεως δὲ ὄρεξις (sc. ἀρχή ἐστιν) καὶ λόγος ὁ ἕνεκά τινος. So

---

[1] And by common consent this has been held to be the case with the awkward words 1143 b 9—11 διὸ καὶ ἀρχὴ καὶ τέλος νοῦς· ἐκ τούτων γὰρ αἱ ἀποδείξεις καὶ περὶ τούτων.

if the words εὐπραξία γὰρ κτλ. are to be kept, they must present the absurdity of a statement, hitherto unproved, about a derived notion, brought forward to support a statement, already proved, about the notion from which the former is derived. Neither can this ob-jectionable passage be better placed elsewhere.

1139 b 2.

οὐ τέλος ἁπλῶς, ἀλλὰ πρός τι καὶ τινός, τὸ ποιητόν, ἀλλὰ τὸ πρακτόν. This passage contains several difficulties. (*a*) Does τὸ ποιητόν mean 'the thing produced' or 'the process of production'? (*b*) What does τινός mean? (*c*) Is τέλος to be understood with πρός τι and τινός, or not? (*d*) Should πρός be understood again with τινός?

The two latter difficulties are of course purely grammatical, but they make the interpretation of the passage more difficult. Probably the answer in each case is in the negative : with regard to the last it must be noticed that πρός with the genitive is a rare construction in Aristotle.

The answer to (*b*) depends on the answer to (*a*): Professor Burnet's answer to (*a*) is 'the process of production,' disagreeing therein with everyone else's view, it seems. My reasons for thinking Professor Burnet wrong are as follows—

1. In ordinary language ποιητός would naturally be an epithet of the thing made and not of the action of making it. The word does not occur elsewhere in Aristotelian writings, except at 1140 a 1 which throws no light on the question, and at Politics 1275 a 6 (in quite a different sense) where ποιητοὶ πολῖται means 'factitious' or 'adopted citizens.' There is therefore no Aristotelian authority for the special meaning Professor Burnet would give to τὸ ποιητόν, and so far no inducement to depart from the ordinary meaning. Professor Burnet's remark that 'we may say either ποιεῖν ποίησιν or ποιεῖν ποίημα' does not show that τὸ ποιητόν can 'correspond to the internal accusative.'

2. Since the process of production is not an end in any sense at all, it would be absurd to say that it was not an absolute end (οὐ τέλος ἁπλῶς). Only that can be said to be οὐ τέλος ἁπλῶς which is *an* end but is also a means to the absolute end. The thing produced by ποίησις is such; for it is not *the* end but is a means to εὐπραξία (1139 b 3); and at the same time it is *an* end, for the ἔργον is related to the ποίησις as end to means—see Περὶ Οὐρανοῦ 306 a 16 τέλος δὲ

τῆς μὲν ποιητικῆς ἐπιστήμης τὸ ἔργον, Ethics 1094 a 4 τῶν τελῶν τὰ μέν εἰσιν ἐνέργειαι τὰ δὲ παρ' αὐτὰς ἔργα τινά.

3. Grammatically, Professor Burnet's rendering of τὸ ποιητὸν τινός (ἐστι) is easy, 'the process of production is the production of something': easy, that is, granted that τὸ ποιητόν can be equivalent to ἡ ποίησις. But the sense is not forcible. It is equally possible to say of πρᾶξις that 'the process of doing is the doing of something.'

The meaning of 'the thing produced' being given to τὸ ποιητόν, τινός is best taken as neuter, and as meaning 'belonging to' or 'connected with something else,' and thus as almost a synonym of πρός τι. Both τινός and τι must in this case refer to the absolute end εὐπραξία.

1139 b 5—11.

οὐκ ἔστι δὲ προαιρετὸν οὐδὲν γεγονός κτλ.

No editor appears to find any real explanation of the occurrence of this passage at the end of chapter ii. Ramsauer thinks it is out of place, and wishes to read it in book III along with the rest of the description of προαίρεσις. Grant takes it to be an addition made with pride by Eudemus to the statement of Aristotle on the subject. Professor Stewart admits that the statement might have been dispensed with, but sees no reason to bracket it. Professor Burnet calls it 'a detached fragment, loosely appended as usual to the end of a section. It appears to be part of a proof that Practical Thought deals with τὸ ἐσόμενον.'

The passage really is appropriate enough to the reconsideration of προαίρεσις in the light of the new distinction between ἐνδεχόμενα and μὴ ἐνδεχόμενα ἄλλως ἔχειν. For it might be objected, and prima facie quite plausibly objected, that events which have in the past been brought about by the human will belong to the class of ἐνδεχόμενα and not to the class of μὴ ἐνδεχόμενα: and since ἐνδεχόμενα are the subjects of προαίρεσις, it would follow that events in the past brought about by the human will, such as the capture of Troy, are the subjects of προαίρεσις. The difficulty is of course a purely formal one ; but formal difficulties had great terrors for the Greek mind, which could not ride rough-shod over them by the help of common sense, but insisted on due formal explanation. It was therefore necessary to explain that past events are not contingent now, though they may have been contingent once. The historical imagination, projecting itself into the past and imagining the time before Troy fell, rightly thinks of the fall as an ἐνδεχόμενον. But the historical imagination is not the ordinary channel for the contemplation of the contingent, and from the practical point of view, that of the mind *qua* deliberative, the fall of Troy is not ἐνδεχόμενον but μὴ ἐνδεχόμενον.

1139 b 15.

ἔστω δὴ οἷς ἀληθεύει ἡ ψυχὴ τῷ καταφάναι ἢ ἀποφάναι...
τέχνη ἐπιστήμη φρόνησις σοφία νοῦς· ὑπολήψει γὰρ καὶ δόξῃ
ἐνδέχεται διαψεύδεσθαι.

Professor Stewart says 'Νοῦς is infallible as the immediate perception of ἀδιαίρετα or ἁπλᾶ,' implying that the perception of ἀδιαίρετα or ἁπλᾶ, *i.e.* of simple concepts as distinguished from propositions, is the whole function of νοῦς. He is obliged to suppose therefore that the words τῷ καταφάναι ἢ ἀποφάναι are only loosely applied to νοῦς, since they imply the making of propositions, which νοῦς does not make. I can find no evidence that other editors disagree with this view.

Now Professor Stewart admits that νοῦς here means what it means in chapter vi, where it is said εἶναι τῶν ἀρχῶν τῆς ἐπιστήμης. But deductive science cannot start from simple concepts: it must start from propositions. Chapter vi therefore shows that νοῦς makes propositions. This does not prevent its also perceiving simple concepts, according to the doctrine of Metaphysics 1051 b 24: though it is probable that the author is not thinking of νοῦς in that sense anywhere in this book—which need cause no surprise, since, as it is, he uses the word in at least four different senses in this book. Professor Stewart himself admits that the doctrine that the principles of knowledge are reached by νοῦς is not inconsistent, in the author's view or in the view of the writer of Posterior Analytics 100 b 3 *seq.*, with the doctrine that the same principles are reached by induction (ἐπαγωγή). Clearly induction cannot be concerned entirely with ἀδιαίρετα.

But in what sense then is νοῦς infallible? In just the sense in which the other four virtues are infallible and ὑπόληψις and δόξα fallible. It is a matter of names. In so far as a man is deceived, his ἕξις διανοητική is not truly any of the five virtues mentioned, but only in so far as he is right. ὑπόληψις and δόξα are fallible in the sense that they are either good or bad states—the *names* are not confined to virtues but may be applied to vices. They are not distinct from the five virtues as things mutually exclusive are distinct; for all five virtues are ὑπολήψεις of a certain kind, see 1140 b 13 where φρόνησις is, it is implied, a ὑπόληψις, b 31 where ἐπιστήμη is called a ὑπόληψις, 1142 b 33 where φρόνησις is called a ὑπόληψις; and δόξα is at least a part of φρόνησις, which is twice called the virtue τοῦ δοξαστικοῦ μέρους. This infallibility then, which has caused the editors so much trouble, is a notion brought in, rather clumsily perhaps, to distinguish between the names of virtues and the names of states that may be good or bad.

1139 b 23 ἀίδιον ἄρα· τὰ γὰρ ἐξ ἀνάγκης ὄντα ἁπλῶς πάντα ἀίδια, τὰ δ' ἀίδια ἀγένητα καὶ ἄφθαρτα. There ought to be a period, and not a comma, after πάντα ἀίδια. For τὰ δ' ἀίδια ἀγένητα καὶ ἄφθαρτα is a new fact, and not part of the argument whose conclusion is ἀίδιον ἄρα. Fully stated the passage would consist of two distinct syllogisms, thus—

  (a) τὰ ἐξ ἀνάγκης ἁπλῶς πάντα ἀίδιά ἐστιν,
      ἀλλὰ τὸ ἐπιστητὸν ἐξ ἀνάγκης ἁπλῶς ἐστιν,
      ∴ τὸ ἐπιστητὸν ἀίδιόν ἐστιν.

  (b) τὰ ἀίδια ἀγένητα καὶ ἄφθαρτά ἐστιν,
      ἀλλὰ τὸ ἐπιστητὸν ἀίδιόν ἐστιν,
      ∴ τὸ ἐπιστητὸν ἀγένητον καὶ ἄφθαρτόν ἐστιν.

The comma would be the right stop if instead of ἀίδιον ἄρα had been written ἀγένητον καὶ ἄφθαρτον ἄρα.

1139 b 28.

  ἡ μὲν δὴ ἐπαγωγὴ ἀρχή ἐστι καὶ τοῦ καθόλου.

Professor Burnet translates ἀρχή by 'starting-point,' and says it is identical with the προυπάρχουσα γνῶσις of Posterior Analytics 71 a 2 (see his note). He says truly 'it is just as proper to call τὰ καθ' ἕκαστα the 'starting-point' of our knowledge of τὰ καθόλου as to call τὰ καθόλου the 'starting-point' of demonstration.' But just as τὰ καθόλου are distinct from the process συλλογισμός, so τὰ καθ' ἕκαστα are distinct from the process ἐπαγωγή. While therefore it would be correct to say that τὰ καθ' ἕκαστα are the starting-point of ἐπαγωγή, or even of the knowledge of τὰ καθόλου to which ἐπαγωγή leads, it seems impossible to speak of ἐπαγωγή itself as ἀρχὴ τοῦ καθόλου, except in whatever sense συλλογισμός may be called ἀρχὴ τοῦ συμπεράσματος, and this sense cannot be that of 'starting-point'—the syllogism cannot be called the starting-point of the conclusion. ἐπαγωγή is not, any more than συλλογισμός, προυπάρχουσα γνῶσις.

And there seems to be no satisfactory sense of ἀρχή in which ἐπαγωγή can be said to be ἀρχὴ τοῦ καθόλου.

To read ἀρχῆς with L^b removes the difficulty. Professor Burnet's objection to this reading, that it brings in an irrelevant truth instead of the required proof of the statement ἐκ προγινωσκομένων πᾶσα διδασκαλία (1139 b 26), does not hold: for no such proof is required. The point is the difference between συλλογισμός and ἐπαγωγή, and the consequent difference between ἐπιστήμη and the intellectual ἀρετή that is afterwards called νοῦς. Now the difference between συλλογισμός and ἐπαγωγή lies in their relations to τὰ καθόλου, those universals which are the τέλος of ἐπαγωγή but the ἀρχή (in the sense of starting-point) of συλλογισμός. The words ἡ ἐπαγωγὴ ἀρχῆς ἐστιν καὶ τοῦ καθόλου naturally mean τέλος τῆς ἐπαγωγῆς ἐστιν ἡ ἀρχὴ (sc. τῆς ἀποδείξεως), τοῦτο δ' ἐστὶ τὸ καθόλου.

1140 a 3.

ἡ μετὰ λόγου ἕξις πρακτικὴ ἕτερόν ἐστι τῆς μετὰ λόγου ποιητικῆς ἕξεως. διὸ οὐδὲ περιέχεται ὑπ' ἀλλήλων· οὔτε γὰρ ἡ πρᾶξις ποίησις οὔτε ἡ ποίησις πρᾶξίς ἐστιν.

It has not been noticed how obscure the sequence of the argument is here. If the first sentence stood alone, ἕτερον might be taken to mean either (1) 'not exactly the same' in the sense in which a European is ἕτερος from an Englishman—i.e. as genus from species, or (2) 'not at all the same' in the sense in which a Frenchman is ἕτερος from an Englishman—i.e. as species from species. The second sentence is added to show that it is the latter meaning of ἕτερον that is intended: ποίησις and πρᾶξις are mutually exclusive terms. But the fact οὐδὲ περιέχεται ὑπ' ἀλλήλων does not follow from the first sentence. The proof of it is given in what follows, οὔτε γὰρ ἡ πρᾶξις ποίησις οὔτε ἡ ποίησις πρᾶξίς ἐστιν, which clearly shows the trend of the argument and the sense in which ἕτερον was used. It is therefore hard to explain διό. Professor Burnet neglects οὐδέ in his translation 'therefore neither is contained in the other': but it is οὐδέ that makes διό difficult, 'they are not even included either of them by the other': not only are they not identical, but they are not even related as whole and part. Probably διό may be translated 'so different, indeed, that...' But it is rather that the context forces this meaning out of the word than that it could naturally mean this: however, it is just possible to take it to mean 'on account of the great difference that there actually is between ποίησις and πρᾶξις᾽ rather than 'on account of the fact just stated, that the ποιητικὴ ἕξις is different from the πρακτικὴ ἕξις.'

Is the doctrine of 1140 a 5 οὐδὲ περιέχεται ὑπ᾽ ἀλλήλων inconsistent with the doctrine of 1139 b 1 αὕτη γὰρ καὶ τῆς ποιητικῆς ἄρχει?

Ramsauer and Stewart say Yes: Grant and Burnet neglect the point. If 1140 a 5 is inconsistent with 1139 b 1, it must also be inconsistent with the whole of the latter part of this book, in which σοφία and the πρακτικὴ ἀρετὴ φρόνησις are in some sense or other admittedly asserted to cover the whole field of intellectual goodness, leaving no room for a ποιητικὴ ἀρετή distinct from either. But there is no inconsistency. ποίησις can quite well be simply a means to πρᾶξις, as 1139 b 1 asserts, and at the same time be a completely distinct thing from πρᾶξις, as 1140 a 5 asserts. No more subtle distinction is intended in 1140 a 5 than lies in the fact that in ποίησις an external object is produced while in πρᾶξις it is not. Ramsauer has no reason to say that περιέχειν in 1140 a 5 means the same thing as ἄρχειν in 1139 b 1. Περιέχειν in 1140 a 5 has a logical meaning, 'include,' as the genus includes the species: ἄρχειν in 1139 b 1 means 'is superior to' as the end is superior to the means.

1140 a 6.

ἐπεὶ δ᾽ ἡ οἰκοδομικὴ......10 ποιητική.

The argument of this sentence is hardly more than a categorical statement, the statement that the word τέχνη is in fact always used to mean ἕξις μετὰ λόγου ἀληθοῦς ποιητική. Take any sample, Aristotle says in effect, of a τέχνη, say building. Building, or the builder's art, is admittedly a τέχνη. It must also be admitted to correspond exactly to the description ἕξις μετὰ λόγου ἀληθοῦς ποιητική. But it does not follow from these two facts that the word τέχνη and the phrase ἕξις μετὰ λόγου ἀληθοῦς ποιητική are even in any way connected in meaning. So Aristotle appeals to his hearers or readers to take any instance they like of a τέχνη, and say whether that thing is not also a ἕξις μετὰ λόγου ἀληθοῦς ποιητική; and conversely to take any instance they like of a ἕξις μετὰ λόγου ἀληθοῦς ποιητική, and say whether that thing is not also called τέχνη. He does not make the induction for them, beyond suggesting a single instance to begin with. He assumes that anyone who chooses can make the induction, and that it will yield the required result. The only further step is from the statement that the word τέχνη and the description ἕξις μετὰ λόγου ἀληθοῦς ποιητική can always both be applied to anything to which either can be applied, to the statement that the two are identical, *i.e.* that ἕξις μετὰ λόγου ἀληθοῦς ποιητική is the definition of τέχνη. The inference is of course not unavoidable, but Aristotle regards it as at least sufficiently probable and plausible not to need further discussion.

1140 a 16.

ἐπεὶ δὲ ποίησις καὶ πρᾶξις ἕτερον, ἀνάγκη τὴν τέχνην ποιήσεως ἀλλ᾿ οὐ πράξεως εἶναι.

At first sight this sentence seems a pure repetition of what has been said. But the point has not been definitely made before. It has been shown that ποίησις and πρᾶξις are different, and that τέχνη is concerned with ποίησις : but the conclusion, that τέχνη is not concerned with πρᾶξις, has not been stated. But it is worth stating : for the language of lines 10 to 16 does not clearly distinguish τέχνη from the virtue concerned with πρᾶξις, but only from ἐπιστήμη and from unpractical θεωρία τῶν ἐνδεχομένων : moreover, the loose uses of the word τέχνη include its application to rhetoric and other practical systems. The sentence would indeed read better after the end of line 10 : but it is quite intelligible where it is.

1140 a 20.

ἡ μὲν οὖν τέχνη, ὥσπερ εἴρηται, ἕξις τις μετὰ λόγου ἀληθοῦς ποιητική ἐστιν, ἡ δ᾿ ἀτεχνία τοὐναντίον μετὰ λόγου ψευδοῦς ποιητικὴ ἕξις.

In this book τέχνη is used in two senses, one good, the other in itself neither good nor bad. These two senses are conveyed by the phrases (*a*) ἕξις μετὰ λόγου ποιητική (*b*) ἕξις μετὰ λόγου ἀληθοῦς ποιητική. The former sense occurs in two other places in this book, where the above definition has been forgotten : 1140 b 22 τέχνης μὲν ἔστιν ἀρετή, φρονήσεως δ᾿ οὐκ ἔστιν, and 1141 a 12 σημαίνοντες τὴν σοφίαν ὅτι ἀρετὴ τέχνης ἐστίν. In these two places τέχνη is perhaps not really thought of as a ἕξις at all, but as an activity or process or body of rules or something that is not a quality or fixed condition of the mind of the τεχνίτης. If it is thought of as a ἕξις, the words τέχνης ἔστιν ἀρετή cannot mean that τέχνη can *have* an ἀρετή so much as that τέχνη can *be* an ἀρετή. In any case these two passages are inconsistent with the above definition of 1140 a 20, where τέχνη is clearly said to be a virtue, and has its vice ἀτεχνία opposed to it. Τέχνη in this sense can no more have an ἀρετή than φρόνησις can. It would have been an excellent thing if the word εὐτεχνία—which occurs in Hippocrates and Lucian but not in Aristotle—had been in common use enough to have displaced τέχνη here. How far the author clearly distinguished in his own mind his double use of τέχνη is doubtful; but as he does not generally mention intellectual vices, probably he had the neutral sense of τέχνη in his mind at 1140 a 20, and mentioned ἀτεχνία on purpose to show that it is not the neutral but the good sense that is there intended.

1140 b 3.

> (οὐκ ἂν εἴη ἡ φρόνησις) τέχνη...ὅτι ἄλλο τὸ γένος πράξεως καὶ ποιήσεως.

This argument is so badly expressed that what is to be proved appears as the reason for what is to prove it. The point is not that φρόνησις is different from τέχνη because it is concerned with πρᾶξις and not with ποίησις, but that it is concerned with πρᾶξις and not with ποίησις because it is different from τέχνη. That φρόνησις is different from τέχνη according to the belief that underlies popular usage has been said already: 1140 a 29 τοὺς περί τι φρονίμους λέγομεν, ὅταν πρὸς τέλος τι σπουδαῖον εὖ λογίσωνται, ὧν μή ἐστι τέχνη. Since it is simply the usage of the word φρόνησις that Aristotle is here trying to fix, he accepts the popular usage with the belief that underlies it. So it is known already that φρόνησις is different from τέχνη. On the other hand, nothing has so far been said to show that πρᾶξις (as opposed to ποίησις) is the peculiar sphere of φρόνησις. That the φρόνιμος is the βουλευτικός certainly does not show this; for βούλευσις is said to be concerned with the arts in particular, see 1112 b 3—7 βουλευόμεθα...μᾶλλον...περὶ τὰς τέχνας ἢ τὰς ἐπιστήμας· μᾶλλον γὰρ περὶ ταύτας διστάζομεν. It is true that the immediately preceding distinction of φρόνησις from ἐπιστήμη, made on the ground that ἐνδέχεται τὸ πρακτὸν ἄλλως ἔχειν, implies that πρᾶξις is the sphere of φρόνησις, but the assumption is there made for the first time, and without any warrant from the previous argument.

1140 b 4.

λείπεται ἄρα αὐτὴν εἶναι ἕξιν ἀληθῆ μετὰ λόγου πρακτικὴν περὶ τὰ ἀνθρώπῳ ἀγαθὰ καὶ κακά. τῆς μὲν γὰρ ποιήσεως ἕτερον τὸ τέλος, τῆς δὲ πράξεως οὐκ ἂν εἴη· ἔστι γὰρ αὐτὴ ἡ εὐπραξία τέλος.

The transposition of these two sentences proposed by Rassow (Forschungen, page 30) seems to me so certain that I have introduced it into the text. For (a) τῆς μὲν γὰρ κτλ. is a simple recapitulation of a well-known distinction, and is introduced here to explain the statement ἄλλο τὸ γένος πράξεως καὶ ποιήσεως: it does not, as the received order makes it appear to do, in any way justify the conclusion λείπεται ἄρα κτλ. (b) The words of the definition περὶ τὰ ἀνθρώπῳ ἀγαθὰ καὶ κακά lead immediately up to 1140 b 7 διὰ τοῦτο Περικλέα καὶ τοὺς τοιούτους φρονίμους οἰόμεθα εἶναι, ὅτι τὰ αὐτοῖς ἀγαθὰ καὶ τὰ τοῖς ἀνθρώποις δύνανται θεωρεῖν. This connection of thought is most awkwardly broken by the intervening sentence.

1140 b 10.

εἶναι δὲ τοιούτους ἡγούμεθα τοὺς οἰκονομικοὺς καὶ τοὺς πολιτικούς.

Professor Burnet strangely holds that the οἰκονομικοὶ and πολιτικοὶ are instances of the φρόνιμοι κατὰ μέρος. Surely not. Τὸ εὖ ζῆν ὅλως, the great final τέλος, is the end that the οἰκονομικοί and πολιτικοί, as such, have in view—their end is not any particular τέλος such as health and victory. The φρόνησις of the politician, or rather statesman, is 'architectonic' above all other forms of φρόνησις, and the φρόνησις of the householder is more architectonic than that of the individualist (ἡ περὶ αὐτὸν καὶ ἕνα): and yet none of these three forms of φρόνησις are κατὰ μέρος, for they all have as their end τὸ εὖ ζῆν ὅλως, whether for a country or a family or an individual. It is in no κατὰ μέρος sense that in the Politics φρόνησις is called the peculiar virtue of the ruler: 1277 b 25 ἡ δὲ φρόνησις ἄρχοντος ἴδιος ἀρετή.

1140 b 11.

For the relation of σωφροσύνη to φρόνησις, as set forth in vi v, compared with the relation of ἠθικὴ ἀρετή to φρόνησις, as set forth in vi xii—xiii, see Introduction, pages 51–53.

1140 b 24.

δῆλον οὖν ὅτι ἀρετή τις ἐστὶ καὶ οὐ τέχνη.

As Ramsauer says, the conclusion here stated is at first sight very unsatisfactory. For φρόνησις is not a moral ἀρετή, and the preceding words ὥσπερ καὶ περὶ τὰς ἀρετάς appear to make the words ἀρετή τις ἐστὶν (sc. ἡ φρόνησις) mean that it *is* a moral ἀρετή. Also τέχνη *is* an ἀρετή, and the sentence seems to imply that it is not.

I think it is possible to translate 'It is plain then that φρόνησις is an ἀρετή which is not τέχνη': no τις being understood with τέχνη. This allows ἀρετή τις to be taken as referring to διανοητικὴ ἀρετή, which is certainly rather abrupt after the use of τὰς ἀρετάς just before in the sense of τὰς ἠθικὰς ἀρετάς, but is evidently the sense required. ἀρετή τις ἐστί will then be quite unemphatic, and οὐ τέχνη will be the point of the sentence.

A meaning can be given to 1140 b 22 τέχνης μὲν ἔστιν ἀρετὴ φρονήσεως δ' οὐκ ἔστιν that is in accordance with this view. Τέχνη is used, not in the necessarily good sense of 1140 a 20, but in the neutral sense of 1141 a 12, in which it includes the ποιητικὴ ἀρετή called τέχνη in 1140 a 20 and the ποιητικὴ κακία called ἀτεχνία in the same passage. Τέχνης ἔστιν ἀρετή means that τέχνη may be an ἀρετή or may not, φρονήσεως οὐκ ἔστιν ἀρετή means that φρόνησις must always *be* an ἀρετή. This is, so far as it goes, a quite definite ground of distinction between τέχνη and φρόνησις, though it only shows that the two terms are not co-extensive in meaning, and does not even show that φρόνησις is not the same as the ἀρετὴ τέχνης, *i.e.* not the same as τέχνη in the sense given to the word in 1140 a 20. The latter truth is shown in the following sentence 1140 b 22 καὶ ἐν μὲν τέχνῃ ὁ ἑκὼν ἁμαρτάνων αἱρετώτερος, περὶ δὲ φρόνησιν ἧττον, ὥσπερ καὶ περὶ τὰς ἀρετάς: this shows that τέχνη and φρόνησις are totally distinct, and not only as genus is distinct from species.

The whole argument seems to aim at establishing the distinctness of τέχνη from φρόνησις independently of the view that τέχνη is only ποιητική. The reason for so doing is no doubt that τέχνη has for some people a wider meaning than that of ποιητικὴ ἕξις. Aristotle himself commonly calls rhetoric a τέχνη: and the sophists who taught the ἀρετῆς τέχνη would certainly have denied that τέχνη was concerned with ποίησις only.

1140 b 29.

ἀλλὰ μὴν οὐδ' ἕξις μετὰ λόγου μόνον· σημεῖον δ' ὅτι λήθη μὲν τῆς τοιαύτης ἕξεως ἐστιν, φρονήσεως δ' οὐκ ἔστιν.

Professor Burnet holds that 'the point is that the ἐνέργεια of φρόνησις is more continuous than that of other ἕξεις μετὰ λόγου (ἐπιστήμη and τέχνη) just because it is πρακτική.' He quotes the passage 1100 b 17 that describes the highest activities κατ' ἀρετήν as not subject to λήθη because (for the μακάριοι) they are the most continuous. But these highest activities are not πρακτικαί but θεωρητικαί, as book x shows: and it is the θεωρητικαὶ ἐνέργειαι that are the most continuous, θεωρεῖν γὰρ δυνάμεθα συνεχῶς μᾶλλον ἢ πράττειν ὁτιοῦν (1177 a 21). Though complete continuity of any high activity is impossible for man, yet θεωρία, which is μετὰ λόγου only, is more continuous than πρᾶξις, which is *not* μετὰ λόγου only. The difficulty is then that whereas from 1177 a 21 and 1100 b 17 it appears that the theoretic activities are less subject to λήθη than any others, from this passage 1140 b 29 it appears that the practical excellence φρόνησις is not subject to λήθη, whereas the theoretic excellences are.

The solution I offer is that λήθη means two different things in the first two contexts and in the third. What 1177 a 21 and 1100 b 17 mean is that the theoretic activities are less destructible than any others, no matter what their destruction may be called: a fact that follows well enough from the statement that the theoretic activities are the most continuous. But what 1140 b 28 means is that, whether φρόνησις is or is not more destructible than those excellences which are purely intellectual (μετὰ λόγου μόνον), the destruction of it is not λήθη or forgetfulness: a fact that is perfectly plain, as may be learnt by simple observation of the usage of the word λήθη in ordinary speech. There is no reason to suppose that Aristotle would not allow the purely intellectual element of φρόνησις (what he afterwards calls δεινότης) to be subject to λήθη.

1140 b 31.

ἡ ἐπιστήμη περὶ τῶν καθόλου ἐστὶν ὑπόληψις.

Professor Stewart says 'It is awkward to begin a chapter, intended to present the distinction between ἐπιστήμη and νοῦς, with words ascribing to the former a characteristic (τὸ περὶ τῶν καθόλου ὑπόληψιν εἶναι) which it shares with the latter.' The question turns on the meaning of περὶ τῶν καθόλου. This cannot mean 'having universals as its ἀρχή or starting-point,' which would be ἐκ τῶν καθόλου. Stewart therefore supposes it must mean 'having universals as its τέλος.' If this were so, the awkwardness that Stewart complains of would really exist: for νοῦς like ἐπιστήμη has universals as its τέλος. But the word can mean 'concerned with universals' in a general sense, including the two notions of 'having universals as its ἀρχή' and 'having universals as its τέλος.' Now ἐπιστήμη has universals as its ἀρχή, but νοῦς has particulars as its ἀρχή. Therefore ἐπιστήμη is, while νοῦς is not, 'concerned with universals' in the above general inclusive sense. On this showing the awkwardness that Stewart complains of does not exist: for the characteristic τὸ περὶ τῶν καθόλου ὑπόληψιν εἶναι is not shared by ἐπιστήμη with νοῦς. Instead of awkwardness the phrase περὶ τῶν καθόλου ἐστὶν ὑπόληψις shows great pertinence: for it does not (pace Professor Burnet) distinguish φρόνησις from ἐπιστήμη, but begins the distinction of ἐπιστήμη from νοῦς that is the subject of this vith chapter.

1141 a 20.

> ἄτοπον γὰρ εἴ τις τὴν πολιτικὴν ἢ τὴν φρόνησιν σπουδαιοτάτην οἴεται εἶναι.

Why does the author mention πολιτική here before explaining its relation to φρόνησις, when the mention of φρόνησις alone would have answered the purpose of the argument equally well? Because at the beginning of book I πολιτική has been described as the master science: 1094 a 26 τῆς κυριωτάτης καὶ μάλιστα ἀρχιτεκτονικῆς· τοιαύτη δ' ἡ πολιτικὴ φαίνεται ... ὁρῶμεν δὲ καὶ τὰς ἐντιμοτάτας τῶν δυνάμεων ὑπὸ ταύτην οὔσας .. τὸ ταύτης τέλος περιέχοι ἂν τὰ τῶν ἄλλων. All of this has raised a presumption that πολιτική is σπουδαιοτάτη, and this idea it is important to remove. The argument is indeed less clear and cogent than if the relation of φρόνησις to πολιτική had been settled already, but the nature of each and their general similarity are already understood well enough for the purpose in hand.

1141 a 20.

> ἄτοπον γὰρ ... b 2 ὁ κόσμος συνέστηκεν.

In this passage a 22 εἰ δὴ ... 33 πάντων τῶν ὄντων is so markedly parenthetical that parenthesis brackets ought to be printed in the text: otherwise the argument is confusing. The parenthetical passage merely aims at proving φρόνησις or πολιτική to be different from σοφία, and makes no mention of their comparative excellence. But the main argument, begun in a 20—22 and resumed abruptly in a 33—b 2, assumes that φρόνησις or πολιτική is different from σοφία, and aims at proving σοφία the better.

1141 a 33.

> εἰ δ' ὅτι βέλτιστον ἄνθρωπος τῶν ἄλλων ζῴων, οὐδὲν διαφέρει κτλ.

The statement made by way of objection to the theory that φρόνησις or πολιτική is not σπουδαιοτάτη is, Aristotle says, not relevant. He implies that it is true; and he thinks so. But it does not follow that man is, because βέλτιστον τῶν ἄλλων ζῴων, therefore τὸ ἄριστον τῶν ἐν τῷ κόσμῳ, and in point of fact he is not this latter.

The view here taken, that the knowledge of the nobler of two things is always ipso facto itself nobler than the knowledge of the less noble, is plainly at the bottom of Aristotle's final conclusion about the summum bonum. It was an axiom of his thought that the excellence of a state of mind varies directly, other things remaining constant, as the excellence of its object. This is a conclusion that it was natural for him to draw from his metaphysical doctrine of the formal identity of the knowing mind and the thing known. But the view, or something like it, pervaded all Greek thought. In art the most beautiful handling of base material was not held to produce a perfectly beautiful whole. It was on this ground among others that the tragedies of Euripides were condemned.

1141 b 2—3.

> ἐκ δὴ τῶν εἰρημένων δῆλον ὅτι ἡ σοφία ἐστὶ καὶ ἐπιστήμη καὶ νοῦς τῶν τιμιωτάτων τῇ φύσει.

Stewart, Ramsauer and Susemihl are surely not right in wishing to bracket these words. For (a) repeated definitions are common: see those of τέχνη, 1140 a 10 and 20, and those of φρόνησις, 1140 b 5 and 20: also the repetition of 1144 a 7—9 at 1145 a 5—6. (b) There is a special reason for the repetition here, for τῶν τιμιωτάτων has now been justified, which had not been done when the former statement of the definition was made at 1141 a 18. (c) The words διὸ 'Αναξαγόραν κτλ. do not (though Stewart seems to think they do) depend immediately on the passage ending b 2 συνέστηκεν. The fact that σοφία is superior to φρόνησις because the stars are nobler beings than men hardly leads up to the statement that we call Anaxagoras and Thales σοφοί because they know fine things that are of no use to them personally and practically. The latter statement follows much better from the definition of σοφία, which must therefore stand.

1141 b 20 κοῦφα καὶ must surely be bracketed in spite of Professor Burnet's defence of the words. It is hard to take the words ὅτι τὰ κοῦφα εὔπεπτα κρέα καὶ ὑγιεινά to mean 'that light meat is digestible, and since digestible meat is wholesome therefore light meat is wholesome.' It is much more natural to take εὔπεπτα and ὑγιεινά as synonyms, so that εὔπεπτα καὶ might even be omitted without destroying the reasoning. So also if κοῦφα καὶ is read in line 20 it is hard to take ὅτι τὰ ὀρνίθεια κοῦφα καὶ ὑγιεινά to mean 'that poultry is light meat, and since light meat is wholesome therefore poultry is wholesome.' Leaving out κοῦφα καὶ we obtain a quite simple and clear argument: otherwise it is needlessly and confusingly complicated. Rassow's emendation for κοῦφα καὶ—κρέα καὶ (Forschungen page 96)—is unlikely, if for no other reason, because of the καί, which would spoil the sense by throwing emphasis on ὑγιεινά instead of on ὀρνίθεια. Κρέα without καί would be free from objection, and may have been the original reading.

1141 b 22.

εἴη δ' ἄν τις καὶ ἐνταῦθα ἀρχιτεκτονική. καὶ ἐνταῦθα clearly means 'in the sphere of φρόνησις too.' But there is some doubt as to the reference of καί. Burnet interprets 'in this case as well as in that of diet.' Stewart seems to take ἐνταῦθα to mean 'as regards the καθ' ἕκαστα of φρόνησις.' Ramsauer says of this sentence that the words in their present place 'ita sunt obscura ut inania videantur.' It is simpler to take καί to refer to σοφία, which is architectonic in the theoretic sphere, κεφαλὴν ἔχουσα. The sentence is not a mere saving clause, added as a tail-piece to § 7, but definitely introduces the discussion of πολιτική and its sub-divisions that follows. The architectonic form of φρόνησις is, as Burnet says, πολιτική: particularly that division of πολιτική called νομοθετική, but also, as compared with other forms of φρόνησις, πολιτική as a whole.

1141 b 26.

αὕτη δὲ (sc. ἡ ὡς τὰ καθ' ἕκαστα φρόνησις περὶ πόλιν, or πολιτική in the narrow sense) πρακτικὴ καὶ βουλευτική.

All φρόνησις is to some extent πρακτική and βουλευτική, as was laid down at the beginning of the discussion of φρόνησις, 1140 a 30 and b 5. But it is nevertheless true that πολιτική (in the narrowest sense) is both πρακτική and βουλευτική in a sense in which νομοθεσία is neither. For πολιτική has to do with particulars, but νομοθεσία only with universals, and since πρᾶξις is always particular (one cannot have action that is not particular action) πολιτική is πρακτική in a sense in which νομοθεσία is not. Again, βούλευσις may occur about general principles, but it is strictly speaking about particular actions only, and not about what the general nature of actions should be; therefore πολιτική is also βουλευτική in a sense in which νομοθεσία is not. Νομοθεσία is nevertheless both πρακτική and βουλευτική as compared with the purely theoretic σοφία.

1141 b 27.

τὸ γὰρ ψήφισμα πρακτὸν ὡς τὸ ἔσχατον.

There is disagreement among commentators as to what ἔσχατον means. Grant thinks it means the minor term in the syllogism: Professor Stewart, the last step in deliberation: Professor Burnet agrees with Stewart, but says that the ψήφισμα is the minor premiss of the political syllogism and the νόμος the major. Now it is not the minor term or minor premiss but the conclusion of the practical syllogism that is the statement of the πρακτόν or thing to be done, the last step in deliberation and the first in action. The νόμος is the major premiss: the statement of the particular circumstances is the minor premiss: the ψήφισμα is the conclusion. Professor Stewart therefore is right, Grant wrong, and Burnet inconsistent. But I can see no reason for thinking that τὸ ἔσχατον here means anything more than 'the particular' (τὸ καθ' ἔκαστον): particulars are so-called (as Stewart points out) because they are the ultimate units in which the process of analysis ends, but the process of analysis is not always thought of whenever the word ἔσχατον is used in the meaning of 'particular.'

1141 b 34.

ἔχει διαφορὰν πολλήν. What does διαφορά mean here?

Two meanings are excluded. (a) 'Superiority' is not an Aristotelian meaning of διαφορά: so that we cannot translate 'it has great advantages over the other species of φρόνησις or γνῶσις.' (b) The use of the singular prevents our translating with Welldon 'it has many varieties,' which moreover gives no satisfactory sense. There remain two other possible meanings: (c) 'controversy'—'the subject admits of considerable controversy': (d) 'difference'—'this kind of φρόνησις or γνῶσις is very different from the other kinds.'

Aristotelian usage supports both (*c*) and (*d*). But except in two or three instances διαφορά in the sense of 'controversy' is used of persons, and of quarrels as distinguished from simple differences of opinion: thus it is coupled with στάσις in the Politics. The exceptions are

Ethics 1094 b 15 τὰ δὲ καλὰ καὶ τὰ δίκαια, περὶ ὧν ἡ πολιτικὴ σκοπεῖται, πολλὴν ἔχει διαφορὰν καὶ πλάνην, ὥστε δοκεῖν νόμῳ μόνον εἶναι, φύσει δὲ μή.

Politics 1299 a 4 ἔχει. γὰρ τοῦτο τὸ μόριον τῆς πολιτείας πολλὰς διαφοράς, πόσαι τε ἀρχαὶ καὶ κύριαι τίνων, κτλ.

Politics 1303 b 14 ἔοικε πᾶσα διαφορὰ ποιεῖν διάστασιν

—though in the last instance διαφορά may mean 'quarrel.' On the other hand there are countless instances of διαφορά='difference,' whether in the technical logical sense or more generally. Combined as here with ἔχειν it occurs as follows

Analytics 32 a 15 περὶ μὲν οὖν τοῦ ἀναγκαίου, πῶς γίνεται καὶ τίνα διαφορὰν ἔχει πρὸς τὸ ὑπάρχον, εἴρηται.

Topics 103 a 14 δόξειε δ᾽ ἂν τὸ ἀπὸ τῆς αὐτῆς κρήνης ὕδωρ ταὐτὸν λεγόμενον ἔχειν τινὰ διαφορὰν παρὰ τοὺς εἰρημένους τρόπους.

Meteorology 360 b 14 ἐὰν μή τι διαφορὰν ἔχωσιν ἴδιον.

Hist. Anim. 524 a 20 ἔχουσι δὲ διαφορὰν οἵ τε πολύποδες καὶ τὰ εἰρημένα τῶν μαλακίων.

Politics 1269 a 24 εἰ κινητέοι οἱ νόμοι...; ταῦτα γὰρ ἔχει μεγάλην διαφοράν (possibly an instance of the meaning 'controversy').

Of these two meanings the former is supported by the absence of the article and the use of πολλήν instead of μεγάλην: the latter by the occurrence of εἶδος in the preceding sentence (which Professor Stewart points out)—this suggests that εἶδος and διαφορά are used in the technical sense of 'species' and 'differentia.' I think the latter view is right, but yet that neither εἶδος nor διαφορά is used with strict logical exactness: thus εἶδος is not distinguished from γένος, and διαφορὰν ἔχει means not so much 'its differentia is considerable' as 'it is a very different sort of thing': a looseness that explains the absence of the article and the use of πολλήν instead of μεγάλην. The argument that follows is that people in general have refused community of name to the various forms of φρόνησις simply because these forms are so very different.

1142 a 9.

καίτοι ἴσως οὐκ ἔστι τὸ αὑτοῦ εὖ ἄνευ οἰκονομίας οὐδ᾽ ἄνευ πολιτείας.

It might appear that this is a statement of altruistic doctrine; but it is not. It is not a denial of the view that enlightened self-seeking is the best spirit in which a man can go about seeking good. What it does say is that the self-seeking which takes the form of isolation of interests and life is not enlightened self-seeking. This is quite an adequate argument in this place. The popular view stated a few lines before is not attacking altruism, which it certainly could not even conceive as a rule of life : it is attacking the view that the individual gains most good for himself by devoting himself to the public service and to family life : a view that Aristotle, on the other hand, maintains, not perhaps without some confused perception of the higher altruism, but certainly without any clear statement of it here.

1142 a 10.

ἔτι δὲ τὰ αὑτοῦ πῶς δεῖ διοικεῖν ἄδηλον καὶ σκεπτέον.

There are two main views to be taken of the meaning of σκεπτέον. It may refer to the investigation

(a) of the author and his readers (so Stewart, Burnet, and perhaps Ramsauer) :

(b) of the would-be φρόνιμος (so Heliodorus, Eustratius, Grant, Welldon, Peters).

Of (a) Stewart remarks that 'it would be more in accordance with Aristotelian usage than (b),' but he can give no reference to any subsequent discussion of the question τὰ αὑτοῦ πῶς δεῖ διοικεῖν, and Burnet's reference to the end of Book x does not convince even himself. The question is certainly not discussed any further in this book, and Aristotelian usage would demand some word like ὕστερον if the discussion referred to were to be delayed for some time. Also the introductory words ἔτι δέ do not suit this meaning well.

There remains (b). This admits again of two lines of argument. (A) Heliodorus and Eustratius agree that the argument is that the σκέψις of the would-be φρόνιμος implies ἐμπειρία, and ἐμπειρία implies κοινωνία ἢ οἰκονομικὴ ἢ πολιτική, so that the knowledge of τὸ αὑτοῦ καὶ ἑνὸς ἀγαθόν is in practice unattainable unless a man takes part in social life and activities. (B) Grant's argument is : If φρόνησις were pure selfishness, it would be such a simple matter that boys would grasp it at once. But boys do not grasp it at once (1142 a 13): plainly therefore other than selfish considerations enter into it.

Both of these views make ἔτι δὲ...σκεπτέον a second proof of the position ὅτι οὐκ ἐστὶν ἡ φρόνησις μάλιστα ἡ περὶ αὐτὸν καὶ ἕνα. Both connect ἔτι δὲ...σκεπτέον with what follows by taking τοῦ εἰρημένου to refer to ἔτι δὲ...σκεπτέον and not to 1141 b 14 οὐδ' ἐστὶν ἡ φρόνησις τῶν καθόλου μόνον ἀλλὰ δεῖ καὶ τὰ καθ' ἕκαστα γνωρίζειν. Both are open to material objections. (A) ἐμπειρία is in the following passage said to be due not to any sort of κοινωνία but to πλῆθος χρόνου: and at the beginning of the Metaphysics it is said to be gradually produced from the accumulations of memory. (B) The view that φρόνησις is pure selfishness does not imply that the knowledge of how to attain purely selfish ends is easy to acquire.

I think that ἔτι δὲ...σκεπτέον is not a second reason, parallel with καίτοι ἴσως...πολιτείας, for considering pure selfishness an unintelligent state of mind: but that it simply introduces some further facts about φρόνησις, in order to make the survey of the subject as complete as possible—this general rather than particular relevancy marks all the rest of chapter viii. In this view σημεῖον δ' ἐστὶ τοῦ εἰρημένου, κτλ., is closely connected with ἔτι δὲ...σκεπτέον, to which τοῦ εἰρημένου refers. But ἄδηλον καὶ σκεπτέον does not in this view imply that social life is therefore necessary, but only that time is necessary for experience to grow. Also τὰ αὐτοῦ is not contrasted with τὰ τῶν ἄλλων, but τὰ αὐτοῦ πῶς δεῖ διοικεῖν is simply the general expression for the knowledge given by all φρόνησις. It may be thought an objection to this view that it makes Aristotle use τὰ αὐτοῦ in the general sense of 'the good for man' immediately after using it in the special sense of 'one's own individual good.' But it must be remembered that the function of φρόνησις was originally defined as τὸ καλῶς βουλεύσασθαι περὶ τὰ αὐτῷ ἀγαθὰ καὶ συμφέροντα: so that the general sense is at least quite natural in itself.

If there has been any mis-arranging of the text of this chapter by ancient editors, which many modern commentators suppose has happened, the occurrence of the two phrases τὸ αὐτοῦ and τὰ αὐτοῦ has probably caused the two sentences containing them to be wrongly placed next each other.

1142 a 20.

ἔτι ἡ ἁμαρτία ἢ περὶ τὸ καθόλου ἐν τῷ βουλεύσασθαι ἢ περὶ τὸ καθ' ἕκαστον· ἢ γὰρ ὅτι πάντα τὰ βαρύσταθμα ὕδατα φαῦλα ἢ ὅτι τοδὶ βαρύσταθμον.

What is the connection of this passage with the rest?

I cannot think (with Eustratius Heliodorus and Stewart) that it is meant as a further proof of the statement 1142 a 9 οὐκ ἔστι τὸ αὑτοῦ εὖ ἄνευ οἰκονομίας οὐδ' ἄνευ πολιτείας. Stewart says 'The universal, πάντα τὰ βαρύσταθμα ὕδατα φαῦλα, is parallel to the knowledge of the social good: the particular, τοδὶ βαρύσταθμον, to the knowledge of one's own good.' But to be really parallel the propositions ought to be πάντα τὰ βαρύσταθμα (or τοδὶ τὸ βαρύσταθμον) πᾶσιν ἀνθρώποις φαῦλα, and πάντα τὰ βαρύσταθμα (or τοδὶ τὸ βαρύσταθμον) ἐμοὶ φαῦλα. In the form in which they occur here the universal and the particular offer only the most shadowy resemblance to the knowledge of the general good and one's own good respectively.

It is much more likely that this section is meant as a proof of 1142 a 10 τὰ αὑτοῦ πῶς δεῖ διοικεῖν ἄδηλον καὶ σκεπτέον. In that case the emphasis will be on περὶ τὸ καθ' ἕκαστον rather than on περὶ τὸ καθόλου. Translate: 'Error in deliberation may occur not only about general principles but also about particular facts.' The medical illustration fits this meaning well enough. It is important to notice that the illustration is not an example of the working of φρόνησις in the strict sense, any more than was the example about poultry as digestible food in 1141 b 18—21: they are both examples of φρόνησις κατὰ μέρος.

It is quite possible that this section is not directly connected with the preceding argument at all, but is only meant to make still clearer the nature of φρόνησις. There is some emphasis on ἁμαρτία. Neither the general nor the particular judgments involved in an act of φρόνησις are in any way infallible, and the possibility of two distinct kinds of error in ethical judgments is a clear sign of the complex nature of φρόνησις.

1142 a 24.

τοῦ γὰρ ἐσχάτου ἐστίν, ὥσπερ εἴρηται.

τοῦ ἐσχάτου is here equivalent to τοῦ καθ' ἕκαστον, as Ramsauer and Stewart agree. Burnet, however, is wrong in supposing, as he plainly does, that ἔσχατον here means 'last in order of analysis.' For it must have the same meaning here as in line 26, and in line 26 it must mean the particular judgment that forms the minor premiss of the practical syllogism. Therefore in this line 24 also τοῦ ἐσχάτου refers to the minor premiss and not to the conclusion. But it is the conclusion and not the minor premiss that comes last in the order of deliberative analysis. Therefore ἔσχατον does not here mean 'last in order of analysis,' but simply 'particular': though it is no doubt true that ἔσχατον gets the meaning of 'particular,' which it has here, from its other meaning of 'last in order of analysis,' which it actually has for instance in 1141 b 28.

τὸ γὰρ πρακτὸν τοιοῦτον is to be explained as follows. It means 'an action is always particular.' It is the conclusion, and not the minor premiss, that states the πρακτόν. The conclusion is therefore a particular proposition. Now the major premiss is of course a universal proposition: and a particular conclusion cannot be drawn from two universal premisses: therefore the minor premiss is a particular proposition. This shows that the statement τοῦ γὰρ ἐσχάτου ἐστίν, explained as I explain it above, is not only consistent with the statement τὸ γὰρ πρακτὸν τοιοῦτον, but is explained by it, as the γάρ shows it should be. It is true the explanation is less direct than if τοῦ ἐσχάτου could refer to the conclusion instead of to the minor premiss: but it is not less sound and plain: and I have already shown why τοῦ ἐσχάτου must refer to the minor premiss and not to the conclusion.

ὥσπερ εἴρηται refers to 1141 b 15 δεῖ καὶ τὰ καθ' ἔκαστα γνωρίζειν, where φρόνησις is spoken of, and not to 1141 b 27 τὸ γὰρ ψήφισμα πρακτὸν ὡς τὸ ἔσχατον, where it is not φρόνησις that is spoken of, but the particular form of φρόνησις that is called πολιτική in the narrow sense. I note this fact because I have already argued that at 1141 b 27 ἔσχατον means 'last in order of analysis,' and the ψήφισμα refers to the conclusion and not to the minor premiss: and it is well to observe that, since that passage is not referred to by the words ὥσπερ εἴρηται, it cannot support Professor Burnet's view of the meaning of 1142 a 24.

1142 a 25.

ἀντικεῖται μὲν δὴ τῷ νῷ... 30 ἐκείνης δ' ἄλλο εἶδος.

These lines are probably the hardest to explain in the whole book. They are quite full of equivocal terms, and the reading is uncertain in one important point at least. I have followed Bywater in reading ἢ in line 30, but not in bracketing ἐν τοῖς μαθηματικοῖς.

ἀντικεῖται is a word of vague meaning. It is best translated by 'corresponds': not by 'is opposed,' for the relation said to exist between φρόνησις and νοῦς is a likeness and not a difference. The likeness consists in the apprehending by each of its proper facts directly, without syllogistic reasoning (λόγος) of any kind.

νοῦς has, undoubtedly, exactly the same meaning as in chapters vi and vii.

ὅρων may not itself mean 'propositions.' But if this passage— ὁ νοῦς τῶν ὅρων, ὧν οὐκ ἔστι λόγος—is compared with chapter vi, and especially with 1141 a 7 λείπεται νοῦν εἶναι τῶν ἀρχῶν, it is evident that νοῦς is said to be concerned with the ὅροι (even if they are 'terms' and not 'propositions') as combining them into propositions, such namely as become the ἀρχαί or premisses of scientific syllogisms. Aristotle is not here thinking simply of isolated concepts of which there is no λόγος because they involve no proposition of any kind. He is thinking of the 'axioms,' undemonstrable propositions made by induction from particular facts that are apprehended by sense-perception.

The minor premiss in the practical syllogism is apprehended by some kind of αἴσθησις: whereas no kind of αἴσθησις apprehends the conclusion. Therefore τοῦ ἐσχάτου must refer to the minor premiss and not to the conclusion. It may seem an objection to this view that the ὅροι ὧν οὐκ ἔστι λόγος, as has been admitted, compose the conclusions or final results at which νοῦς aims and arrives. Ought not therefore τὸ ἔσχατον, in the antithesis, to mean the conclusions or final results at which φρόνησις aims and arrives? Not necessarily: the antithesis need not be carried out in this detail. In any case the inductive work of νοῦς is quite different from the syllogistic work of φρόνησις. There is no reason why part of the work of φρόνησις should not be said to correspond to the whole of the work of νοῦς in virtue of the common characteristic, direct apprehension as opposed to syllogistic reasoning: and this is in fact all that constitutes the antithesis.

στήσεται γὰρ κἀκεῖ. Mathematics are one branch of σοφία, and νοῦς therefore is concerned with them. It thus makes no practical difference whether κἀκεῖ refers to (a) φρόνησις as distinguished from mathematics—or vice versa, or to (b) νοῦς generally as distinguished from φρόνησις—or vice versa.

Two lines of explanation of ὅτι τὸ ἐν τοῖς μαθηματικοῖς ἔσχατον τρίγωνον have been suggested. (a) In analysing a geometrical figure such as a polygon, by joining its angular points we can divide it into various figures which have a smaller number of sides than it has itself. But no rectilinear figure can have less than three sides, and therefore the analysis of the figure can be carried no further than its division into triangles.   It cannot be proved, but must be directly perceived, that the triangle *is* the simplest possible rectilinear figure, and so the last in order (ἔσχατον) that analysis into simpler figures can produce.   So in a problem of conduct we eventually reach simple facts that contain no general principle to be analysed into simpler facts, but can only be apprehended as true in themselves. In both the geometrical and the ethical processes, analysis stops at a certain point.   (*b*) In working out a geometrical problem with a diagram it is necessary that the senses should perceive the nature of the figures that are drawn, for example, on the blackboard before them.   If for instance a triangle is the subject of the problem, it must be seen that the figure in the diagram *is* a triangle before anything can be shown about it ; and if sense-perception does not convince the observer that the figure in the diagram *is* a triangle, no proof of the fact can be given.   The same is true, of course, of a diagram mentally conceived. So too in a problem of conduct, no deliberation can help the apprehension of the particular concrete facts that go to make up the circumstances under which conduct is to take place.   These concrete facts must be apprehended by sense-perception.

Of these two explanations the latter seems to me the better, for the following reason.   The predicate in ὅτι τὸ ἔσχατον τρίγωνον is not ἔσχατον but τρίγωνον : the thing perceived by the αἴσθησις in question is not ultimateness but triangularity.   According to the former explanation, however, it is ultimateness that is perceived.   It is far more natural to suppose (as Professor Stewart does) that ἔσχατον simply means 'the particular figure in the diagram,' so that any other word such as κύκλος might be substituted for τρίγωνον without changing the essence of the argument.   This result Professor Stewart unfortunately goes on to spoil in his note : for he confuses the minor premiss of the practical syllogism with the conclusion.   He says that the φρόνιμος (meaning the φρόνιμος as such) directly perceives things as good or bad in the same way as the geometer perceives things to be triangular or circular.   He thereby adds goodness and badness to the qualities, such as size, number, motion, shape, that can be perceived by the κοινῇ αἴσθησις.   He thus does away at once with the whole principle of the practical syllogism, for he ascribes to direct perception what is as a matter of fact the conclusion of reasoning. This is the result of taking τοῦ ἐσχάτου in line 26 to refer to the conclusion of the practical syllogism and not to the minor premiss. He is led in his next paragraph to entertain the notion that τοῦ ἐσχάτου may have some reference to 'the last step in ζήτησις,' since that is the conclusion of the practical syllogism and not the minor premiss. But this is to lose the whole point of the analogy of φρόνησις with νοῦς, which is that certain facts are reached by both directly, without any kind of reasoning : whereas 'the last step in ζήτησις,' the conclusion of the practical syllogism, is the result of reasoning.

I hold then that ὅτι τὸ ἔσχατον τρίγωνον means 'that the particular figure in the diagram is a triangle,' and that statements of this sort are regarded as forming minor premisses of practical syllogisms. But why, it may be asked, if this be the case, should not ἡ τῶν ἰδίων αἴσθησις apprehend τὸ ἔσχατον? Consider for instance such a practical syllogism as

> It is wrong to give people nasty food :
> But this food is nasty :
> Therefore I ought not to give you this food.

Here the minor premiss 'This food is nasty' is a proposition that may, it would seem, depend directly upon the sense of smell and that only, or upon the sense of taste and that only: so that ἡ τῶν ἰδίων αἴσθησις does here, it seems, apprehend the minor premiss. The best way out of the difficulty is this. All that the ἴδιαι αἰσθήσεις entitle a man to do is to say 'I have a sensation of nastiness' or the like : they do not entitle him to go on to make a judgment about the cause of the sensation. But the minor premiss of the practical syllogism must be a judgment about the cause of the sensation, as in the example above, 'This food is nasty.' Such a judgment involves κοινὴ αἴσθησις. This view is justified by the mathematical parallel οἷα αἰσθανόμεθα κτλ. For, as Professor Stewart points out, σχῆμα is a 'common sensible'; and it is the perception of σχῆμα that leads to the judgment ὅτι τὸ ἔσχατον τρίγωνον.

Finally there is the sentence ἀλλ' αὕτη μᾶλλον αἴσθησις ἢ φρόνησις, ἐκείνης δ' ἄλλο εἶδος. αὕτη I take to refer to the common sensation faculty that apprehends particulars and supplies minor premisses, not only in mathematics but also in the sphere of φρόνησις. ἐκείνης, I agree with Professor Stewart, means τῆς τῶν ἰδίων αἰσθήσεως : the δέ is concessive. ἐκείνης ἄλλο εἶδος means not 'another species belonging to that genus' (*i.e.* to αἴσθησις), but 'a species different from that species' (*i.e.* from αἴσθησις τῶν ἰδίων) : the γένος is αἴσθησις, the two εἴδη here distinguished are αἴσθησις τῶν ἰδίων and κοινὴ αἴσθησις. Professor Stewart is surely wrong in saying that the distinction in αὕτη μᾶλλον αἴσθησις ἢ φρόνησις is between the sense operative in mathematical ζήτησις and the sense operative in ethical ζήτησις. The distinction is between φρόνησις itself, which states the whole syllogism and draws the conclusion, and the αἴσθησις that enables φρόνησις to state the minor premiss: an αἴσθησις precisely the same in kind as that operative in mathematics, but different (as that operative in mathematics is different) from ἡ τῶν ἰδίων αἴσθησις, and also different from φρόνησις itself. It would be absurd to say of the αἴσθησις operative in mathematics that it was μᾶλλον αἴσθησις ἢ φρόνησις, for it is clearly in no possible way φρόνησις at all. But the αἴσθησις operative in ethical ζήτησις has a prima facie claim (*qua* so operative) to be called φρόνησις: and Aristotle thinks that there is a danger of this claim's being wrongly regarded as valid owing to his having said ἡ φρόνησις τοῦ ἐσχάτου ἐστίν. It is therefore worth his while to point out that the αἴσθησις in φρόνησις is not the φρόνησις itself, though perhaps in practice it cannot be completely distinguished from φρόνησις except as part from whole. It is in fact this αἴσθησις that is called νοῦς in 1143 b 5, νοῦς πρακτικός as distinguished from νοῦς ὁ κατὰ τὰς ἀποδείξεις or θεωρητικός (1143 b 1): though νοῦς πρακτικός includes more than this αἴσθησις.

1142 b 16.

διὸ ἡ βουλὴ ζητητέα πρῶτον.

No ζήτησις occurs in the text. But the words need not therefore be thought an interpolation with Ramsauer, nor need it be supposed with Burnet that the lecturer trusts to memory to fill in the usual facts about βούλευσις. 'Since the notion of εὐβουλία is a complex one, the notion of ὀρθότης together with the notion of βουλή, the two ingredient notions must be understood first. Now the notion of ὀρθότης here clearly depends on the notion of βουλή. But it is already known from previous discussion what the notion of βουλή is. Bearing this in mind, we may at once go on to determine the meaning of ὀρθότης.'

1142 b 18.

ὁ γὰρ ἀκρατὴς καὶ ὁ φαῦλος ὃ προτίθεται ἰδεῖν ἐκ τοῦ λογισμοῦ τεύξεται.

Surely ἰδεῖν may be taken in the sense of λαβεῖν, μαθεῖν, εὑρεῖν, and will thus give a quite satisfactory meaning? (See Bonitz, Index s.v. 520 b 20—33.) I have translated 'will reach through his calculation the conclusion which it lies before him to discover.' Dr Jackson's quotation from Plato (sophist 221 A) ὅπερ ἄρτι προὐθέμεθα δεῖν ἐξευρεῖν is not an exact parallel to προτίθεται δεῖν here, if δεῖν be read for ἰδεῖν, since here there is in that case nothing to correspond to ἐξευρεῖν: besides which the meaning 'which is put forward as being necessary' is less forcible here than 'which it lies before him to discover.'

1143 a 10.

ταὐτὸν γὰρ σύνεσις καὶ εὐσυνεσία καὶ συνετοὶ καὶ εὐσύνετοι.

All that this means is, The word σύνεσις used just now (line 9) means just the same as the word εὐσυνεσία—the adjectives have also identical meanings—and so no separate discussion of εὐσυνεσία is needed, but whatever statements are made about σύνεσις apply equally to εὐσυνεσία. The sentence is a mere footnote, and the γάρ does not connect it with the previous sentence, with which it has indeed no special connection. The identity here stated is practically illustrated by line 16—17 ἡ σύνεσις καθ᾽ ἣν εὐσύνετοι, where the adjective of one pair corresponds to the noun of the other. The great attention paid to the prefix εὖ in discussing εὐβουλία probably suggests the explanation here. The compound forms are far rarer than the simple ones, but are useful as emphasizing the virtuous nature of σύνεσις.

1143 a 12.

ὥσπερ τὸ μανθάνειν λέγεται συνιέναι, ὅταν χρῆται τῇ ἐπιστήμῃ, οὕτως ἐν τῷ χρῆσθαι τῇ δόξῃ ἐπὶ τὸ κρίνειν περὶ τούτων περὶ ὧν ἡ φρόνησίς ἐστιν, ἄλλου λέγοντος, καὶ κρίνειν καλῶς.

This passage has I believe been generally misunderstood. Ramsauer expands it as follows: ὥσπερ γὰρ τὸ μανθάνειν λέγεται συνιέναι ὅταν χρῆταί τις τῇ ἐπιστήμῃ ἐπὶ τὸ κρίνειν περὶ ὧν ἡ ἐπιστήμη ἐστὶν ἄλλου λέγοντος, οὕτω καὶ τὸ μανθάνειν λέγεται συνιέναι ἐν τῷ χρῆσθαι τῇ δόξῃ ἐπὶ τὸ κρίνειν περὶ ὧν ἡ φρόνησίς ἐστιν ἄλλου λέγοντος. I propose the following instead: ὥσπερ ὅταν χρῆται τῇ ἐπιστήμῃ περὶ ὧν ἡ σοφία ἐστίν, ἄλλου λέγοντος, τὸ μανθάνειν καλῶς λέγεται συνιέναι· οὕτως ἐν τῷ χρῆσθαι τῇ δόξῃ περὶ ὧν ἡ φρόνησίς ἐστιν ἄλλου λέγοντος τὸ κρίνειν καλῶς λέγεται συνιέναι.

The following points have hitherto been overlooked : (*a*) μανθάνειν is appropriate only to the use of ἐπιστήμη and not to the use of δόξα. This is proved by line 16 ἐντεῦθεν ἐλήλυθε τοὔνομα ἡ σύνεσις, καθ' ἣν εὐσύνετοι, ἐκ τῆς ἐν τῷ μανθάνειν· λέγομεν γὰρ τὸ μανθάνειν συνιέναι πολλάκις. That is, the use of σύνεσις to mean 'practical intelligence' has come from its use to mean 'scientific intelligence.' If μανθάνειν is understood (as Ramsauer would have it) in the δόξα part of the antithesis, surely ἐντεῦθεν ἐλήλυθε κτλ. becomes unintelligible. (*b*) τὸ κρίνειν in the second part of the antithesis is opposed to τὸ μανθάνειν in the first. The formal expression is loose, but quite natural to a writer who is careless of formal precision as long as he thinks the sense clear : I have avoided the looseness by a slight paraphrase in my expansion. (*c*) ἐπιστήμη and δόξα are here used in the sense not of ' the contents of knowledge' and 'the contents of opinion' but of 'the faculty of knowledge' and 'the faculty of opinion': χρῆται τῇ ἐπιστήμῃ = χρῆται τῷ ἐπιστημονικῷ and not χρῆται τῷ ἐπιστητῷ, χρῆσθαι τῇ δόξῃ = χρῆσθαι τῷ δοξαστικῷ and not χρῆσθαι τῷ δοξαστῷ. Coraes and Stewart think otherwise—see Stewart's notes. (*d*) The emphasis is not on χρῆται and χρῆσθαι but on ἐπιστήμῃ and δόξῃ, in spite of the order. The usual Greek rule of putting emphatic words at the beginning of a sentence or phrase is not regularly observed by Aristotle as it is by Plato. To take an instance close at hand, in 1142 b 16 ἀλλ' ὀρθότης τίς ἐστιν ἡ εὐβουλία βουλῆς the context shows the emphasis to be not on ὀρθότης but on βουλῆς—Plato would have written ἀλλὰ βουλῆς ὀρθότης τίς ἐστιν ἡ εὐβουλία or the like. (*e*) The two meanings of μανθάνειν that the editors quote may be borne in mind here : but whereas one of these two meanings of μανθάνειν admits συνιέναι as a synonym of μανθάνειν, while the other does not, the point is that συνιέναι can also be used in a sense in which it is not a synonym of μανθάνειν.—The passage may be paraphrased as follows : 'Learning is often called "understanding," when a man uses his faculty of scientific knowledge (which is the faculty always used in "learning") to grasp what another teaches him about necessary truth : and when a man uses his faculty of discriminating judgment to grasp what another teaches him about practical contingent truth, that exercise of the judgment is by analogy called understanding, if it is of the right kind. The name understanding, in this latter sense, has been diverted from its use as the name of excellence in "learning" necessary truth from another's teaching, as may be seen from the fact that we still (perhaps somewhat improperly now the later use is established) often give the name of "understanding" to this excellence in "learning" necessary truth.'

1143 a 19.

Ἡ δὲ καλουμένη γνώμη, καθ' ἣν συγγνώμονας καὶ ἔχειν φαμὲν γνώμην, ἡ τοῦ ἐπιεικοῦς ἐστι κρίσις ὀρθή.

This section is a remarkable instance of confusion caused by the view that etymological connection between words must carry with it kinship of meaning. γνώμη is taken as the common element in συγγνώμη and γνώμην ἔχειν, which in ordinary language represent two completely different notions; the meaning of γνώμη is arbitrarily fixed as about half-way between the meanings of συγγνώμη and γνώμη in γνώμην ἔχειν: a vague attempt is made to reconcile the two meanings, and συγγνώμη is forced, by mere unproved assertion, into being a synonym of γνώμη. As a matter of fact συγγνώμη represents the notions of 'forgiveness,' 'making allowances,' 'fair kindness,' and the like: the moral element in it, as in ἐπιείκεια, is essential. γνώμη on the other hand has properly no moral significance. γνώμην ἔχειν can mean two things: (a) 'to have an opinion' whether a true or a false one; (b) 'to have a true opinion,' 'to be right' intellectually, 'avoir raison.' The latter meaning, where γνώμη=ὀρθὴ or ἀληθὴς γνώμη, is chosen here to the exclusion of the former. Professor Burnet would, I believe, find it hard to justify his statement that in actual speech γνώμη had a sense corresponding to that of our 'feeling.' Stewart's paraphrase (*Notes* ii. 89) shows well how the author attempts to unify the two different notions of συγγνώμη and γνώμη: but no hint is given by him or any one else of what I believe to be the true explanation, that the whole attempt is the result of etymological confusion.

1143 a 32.

ἔστι δὲ τῶν καθ' ἔκαστα καὶ τῶν ἐσχάτων ἅπαντα τὰ πρακτά· καὶ γὰρ τὸν φρόνιμον δεῖ γινώσκειν αὐτά, καὶ ἡ σύνεσις καὶ ἡ γνώμη περὶ τὰ πρακτά, ταῦτα δ' ἔσχατα.

As the argument stands it is absurd on the face of it, for ταῦτα δ' ἔσχατα assumes the very point to be proved. Some improvement may be effected by bracketing τὰ πρακτά after ἅπαντα in line 33, as Ramsauer does. ἅπαντα will then mean 'all the subject-matter of these ἕξεις': and the argument will be:—φρόνησις is concerned with ἔσχατα (this was stated 1141 b 15, 1142 a 24): also σύνεσις and γνώμη are concerned with πρακτά, and πρακτά are ἔσχατα (1142 a 25 τὸ γὰρ πρακτὸν τοιοῦτον, sc. ἔσχατον), and therefore σύνεσις and γνώμη also are concerned with ἔσχατα. The chief objection to this view is that αὐτά after δεῖ γινώσκειν in line 34 will have to refer not to ἅπαντα but to τῶν καθ᾽ ἕκαστα καὶ τῶν ἐσχάτων, and this the structure of the sentence is distinctly against. The sense is not much mended by the alternative course of putting a colon or a full stop after γινώσκειν αὐτά. This makes τὸν φρόνιμον δεῖ γινώσκειν αὐτά the only reason given in support of the statement that all πρακτά are ἔσχατα. But it is obviously a very bad reason.

1143 b 21.

ἡ μὲν φρόνησίς ἐστιν ἡ περὶ τὰ δίκαια καὶ καλὰ καὶ ἀγαθὰ
ἀνθρώπῳ, ταῦτα δ᾽ ἐστὶν ἃ τοῦ ἀγαθοῦ ἐστὶν ἀνδρὸς πράττειν.

Grant points out that we are told here for the first time that φρόνησις takes cognizance of the δίκαιον and the καλόν: before, it was only said to be concerned with the ἀγαθὸν καὶ συμφέρον. It is easier to see why the fresh statement is introduced here than to allow that Aristotle is justified in introducing it without proving it. The object is to bring together the two different meanings of ἀγαθός contained in 1143 b 22 ἀγαθὰ ἀνθρώπῳ, and b 23 τοῦ ἀγαθοῦ ἀνδρός. Formally, indeed, the argument would stand if the words δίκαια καὶ καλὰ καὶ were left out: for it is obvious that τοῦ ἀγαθοῦ ἀνδρός ἐστι τὸ τὰ ἀγαθὰ ἀνθρώπῳ πράττειν, provided that ἀγαθός means the same thing each time it is used. But as a matter of fact τὰ ἀγαθὰ ἀνθρώπῳ suggests self-interest as opposed to moral goodness, while ὁ ἀγαθὸς ἀνήρ suggests moral goodness as opposed to self-interest. The notions of δίκαιος and καλός are therefore contained in the words ὁ ἀγαθὸς ἀνήρ, but not in the words τὰ ἀγαθὰ ἀνθρώπῳ. It ought to be *proved* that according to the true view of life self-interest and moral goodness coincide so that ἀγαθός really does mean the same thing in each phrase. Aristotle appears to shirk this proof, and simply to assume its conclusion by making δίκαια and καλά synonyms of ἀγαθὰ ἀνθρώπῳ. The assumption is to a certain extent prepared for by the taking of the φρόνιμος as the fixer of the mean in all kinds of moral virtue (ὡς ἂν ὁ φρόνιμος ὁρίσειεν). It will readily be admitted that, whether τὰ δίκαια καὶ καλά are the same as τὰ ἀγαθὰ ἀνθρώπῳ or not, φρόνησις is concerned with them, even if with other things as well. The question for discussion is, How far, *qua* concerned with τὰ δίκαια καὶ καλά, the possession of φρόνησις is any help to the performance of δίκαιαι καὶ καλαὶ πράξεις. The ἀπορία is produced by the objector's contention that it is no help at all.

The words at 1144 a 11 τῶν δικαίων καὶ καλῶν further emphasize the illicit identification at 1143 b 22 of δίκαιον καὶ καλὸν with συμφέρον, and confine the following discussion to that kind of πρᾶξις which is distinctly connected with moral virtue. Other kinds of human ἀγαθά, it may be supposed, are meant to be apprehended by φρόνησιϛ κατὰ μέρος of some sort, ὑγίεια, for example, by ἰατρική. φρόνησις ὅλως· which apprehends ποῖα ἀγαθὰ ἀνθρώπῳ πρὸς τὸ εὖ ζῆν ὅλως, is limited to conduct that is liable to be influenced by pleasure or pain.

1143 b 30.

οὐδὲ τοῖς μὴ ἔχουσιν.

It has not been noticed that strong support is given to the reading ἔχουσιν here, as against the οὖσιν of Argyropylus, by 1144 b 5 καὶ γὰρ δίκαιοι καὶ σωφρονικοὶ καὶ ἀνδρεῖοι καὶ τἄλλα ἔχομεν εὐθὺς ἐκ γενετῆς.

1144 a 9.

τοῦ δὲ τετάρτου μορίου τῆς ψυχῆς οὐκ ἔστιν ἀρετὴ τοιαύτη, τοῦ θρεπτικοῦ· οὐδὲν γὰρ ἐπ᾽ αὐτῷ πράττειν ἢ μὴ πράττειν.

This passage must not be supposed to have too wide a reference. ὑγίεια, the ἀρετὴ τοῦ θρεπτικοῦ, is a part of ἡ ὅλη ἀρετή, and as such is what I have called a 'component' means to the end εὐδαιμονία : this is stated above, 1144 a 3—6. It is when the ἔργον of man comes to be considered, the specifically human activity, that consideration of τὸ θρεπτικόν and its ἀρετή ὑγίεια becomes out of place. τοιαύτη means οἵα ἀποτελεῖσθαι τὸ ἔργον. Health becomes degraded, from this point of view, to the position of a mere external means or prerequisite to happiness, on a level with friends and riches and so on. The fact is, Aristotle thinks, worth pointing out after the statement of 1144 a 3—6, which would otherwise be likely to mislead.

1144 a 27.

διὸ καὶ τοὺς φρονίμους δεινοὺς καὶ πανούργους φαμὲν εἶναι.

Much the best sense will be got by transposing δεινοὺς and φρονίμους. The use of the first person in φαμέν surely points to an opinion with which the writer does not wholly disagree : but the view that the φρόνιμος may be called πανοῦργος (which is the view conveyed by the text as it stands) is the direct negation of the distinction just made, which it cannot therefore be introduced to illustrate. To understand, or to supply in the text, τούς before πανούργους is hard if not impossible : and in any case the best sense is got by making δεινούς subject rather than φρονίμους καὶ πανούργους: 'we say that clever persons are 'prudent' or 'rascally' as the case may be' rather than 'we say that prudent persons are 'clever,' and also that rascally persons are 'clever'.' Rassow's defence of the text will hardly stand: it amounts to showing that φρόνιμος has sometimes a slightly bad meaning, and πανοῦργος sometimes a slightly good one. But this is irrelevant in face of the distinction just laid down, ἂν μὲν οὖν ὁ σκοπὸς ᾖ καλὸς, ἐπαινετή ἐστιν (sc. ἡ δεινότης), ἐὰν δὲ φαῦλος, πανουργία: which distinction, as the word διό shows, is regarded as the reason for the usage of words stated in the following sentence.

1144 b 13.

ἡ δ' ἕξις ὁμοία οὖσα τότ' ἔσται κυρίως ἀρετή.

Burnet says "ὁμοία οὖσα, i.e. τῷ ὄψιν ἢ νοῦν λαβόντι." This seems to mean "like the person who acquires sight or reason," which is surely impossible. ὁμοία οὖσα means "like what it was before." The moral quality remains in itself unchanged ; by combination with φρόνησις it produces a better whole, and therefore has a new name given to it; but in itself it no more changes than bodily strength changes in a man when he recovers or acquires the power of sight.

1144 b 32.

ἀλλὰ καὶ ὁ λόγος ταύτῃ λύοιτ' ἄν, ᾧ διαλεχθείη τις ἂν ὅτι χωρίζονται ἀλλήλων αἱ ἀρεταί.

With what object should anyone advance the statement that the various moral virtues are independent of each other?

1. It cannot be an objection to the theory just laid down of the relation of ἠθικὴ ἀρετή and φρόνησις, for that theory is itself the means of refuting this statement, as the word ταύτῃ shows.

2. I do not think Professor Stewart's view can be right, that the object is 'to make a casuistical interpretation of duty possible, by showing that there may be a conflict of duties in any given case': for the uneven development of virtuous tendencies does not make conflict between them more likely—the more developed virtues there are present, the greater the possibility of conflict between them.

3. It is possible that the statement is an objection to the way in

which, in this and in the previous chapters, ἠθική ἀρετή has been spoken of as a connected whole.

4. It seems most likely to me that the statement is a mere observation about what seems to be a curious fact demanding explanation : the answer consists not in explaining the statement as a fact, but in challenging its truth.

The independence of the virtues is simply what is noticed in line 34. οὐ γὰρ ὁ αὐτὸς εὐφυέστατος πρὸς ἁπάσας, ὥστε τὴν μὲν ἤδη τὴν δὲ οὔπω εἰληφὼς ἔσται. The different virtuous tendencies are not possessed by all people in the same proportion : and for this reason, it is argued, a man may have acquired one virtue, and yet not have acquired another. The answer is that in so far as any person is in a state of uneven moral development he has not acquired any true virtue at all. True virtue can only be produced in the man who possesses practical wisdom, and on the other hand in such a man it cannot but be produced. Practical wisdom shows what goes to make up the life of happiness, and leaves no virtue out of account : the great complex μεσότης that is ἡ ὅλη ἀρετή is necessarily compounded of all particular μεσότητες. Nor does this view regard only the unattainable ideal of goodness. φρόνησις and the various moral virtues may be present only in what may be called a quantitatively small amount, but if the equilibrium is maintained, there are present true φρόνησις and true moral virtue so far as they go. But a man may have certain virtuous tendencies that are very strong indeed, and yet he may be without real virtue altogether. In so far as a man has practical wisdom to tell him what the means to the end are, component means as well as external, his virtuous tendencies will develop with that even balance which will best lead to the attainment of the end—the great final end εὐδαιμονία or Happiness.

ENGLISH INDEX

G.   14

GREEK INDEX

CAMBRIDGE: PRINTED BY JOHN CLAY, M.A. AT THE UNIVERSITY PRESS.

CPSIA information can be obtained
at www.ICGtesting.com
Printed in the USA
BVOW09s1701160418
513501BV00028B/1675/P